PROVIDING ADEQUATE RETIREMENT INCOME

THE UNIVERSITY PRESS OF NEW ENGLAND

Sponsoring Institutions

Brandeis University

Clark University

Dartmouth College

University of New Hampshire

University of Rhode Island

University of Vermont

PROVIDING ADEQUATE RETIREMENT INCOME

Pension Reform in the United States and Abroad

BY

JAMES SCHULZ · GUY CARRIN · HANS KRUPP

MANFRED PESCHKE · ELLIOTT SCLAR

J. VAN STEENBERGE

Published for

BRANDEIS UNIVERSITY PRESS

by

THE UNIVERSITY PRESS OF NEW ENGLAND

Hanover, New Hampshire

1974

CONTENTS

TABLES

FIGURES

THE AUTHORS

JAMES H. SCHULZ, Ph.D. Yale University, is Associate Professor of Welfare Economics, Florence Heller Graduate School for Advanced Studies in Social Welfare, Brandeis University. His earlier study, *The Economic Status of the Retired Aged in 1980: Simulation Projections*, dramatized the continuing economic plight of the elderly and drew wide attention from Congressional committees, government policymakers, and academics in the field of income maintenance. He has written extensively on the economics of aging, social security, private pension plans, and retirement issues.

GUY CARRIN, M.A. University of New Hampshire, is Research Associate, Center for Operations Research and Econometrics, Katholieke Universiteit Te Leuven. He has recently assisted in the construction of an econometric model for the European Economic Community and published a number of articles in the fields of econometrics and social security. He has held a Canada Council Scholarship for doctoral studies at the University of Toronto and is currently completing his advanced studies at the University of Leuven. His thesis, now in preparation, is "The Welfare Economics of Social Security."

HANS-JUERGEN KRUPP, Dipl.-Wirtsch. Ing., Dr. rer. pol., and Privatdozent, Technical University of Darmstadt, is Vice-President and Professor of Social Policy, Johann Wolfgang Goethe-University, Frankfurt am Main. His research activities have been in the areas of social policy, income distribution, and socioeconomic simulation systems. He is currently a member of the Sozialpolitische Forschergruppe Frankfurt/Main/Mannheim, which is developing a sociopolitical decision and indicator system for the Federal Republic of Germany. In addition to many published papers, he is the author of *Theory of Personal Income Distribution: General Principles and Simulations Oriented to a Distribution Policy*.

MANFRED PESCHKE, M.A. University of New Hampshire, is Director of Research and Planning, New Hampshire State Council on Aging. He has worked many years for private industry, universities, and government agencies in the field of computer utilization and information retrieval. He is currently a doctoral candidate at Brandeis University, writing his thesis on the pension plans of state and local governments.

ELLIOTT SCLAR, Ph.D. Tufts University, is Assistant Professor of Urban Political Economy, Florence Heller Graduate School for Advanced Studies in Social Welfare, Brandeis University. His principal research interests are in the areas of urbanization and public finance. A present interest involves exploring the relationship between urban spatial patterns and the delivery of social services. He has authored several journal articles in the area of urban development and public finance and has co-authored the book *Access for All: Transportation and Urban Growth.*

JOSSE VAN STEENBERGE, LL.D. and a "special degree" in Social Law, Katholieke Universiteit Te Leuven, is a professor at the University of Antwerp, where he teaches courses in Social Security and Labor Law. His research activities and publications have been in the areas of workmen's compensation, family allowances, and social security development as it relates to economic integration within the European Economic Community.

PREFACE

In 1961 when, as a graduate student at Yale, I first became interested in the economic problems of the aged, very little was known about the extent and exact nature of these problems. Writings by Corson and McConnell, Steiner and Dorfman, Margaret Gordon, and Eveline Burns, and, of course, personal observation, indicated that large numbers of the aged in the United States were experiencing severe economic problems, but their nature and extent were poorly understood at that time.

Two very important developments occurred in the early 1960's, however, which changed this situation dramatically. The Social Security Administration compiled and published statistics from the first national, in-depth, comprehensive survey of the economic status of the elderly ("The 1963 Survey of the Aged"). At the same time, Mollie Orshansky, Lenore Bixby (then Lenore Epstein), Lamale and Stotz, and James Morgan led the search for measures of income adequacy, contributing insight into the meaning of the extensive body of new data becoming available from the Social Security surveys and other sources.

In a little more than a decade our knowledge has grown by leaps and bounds. The economic problems of the aged have been thoroughly documented, and public and private institutions have responded—many would say dramatically. Whereas a decade ago one could accurately generalize that almost all the aged (especially the retired) were poverty stricken, today the answer is much more complex. Major changes in social security and private pensions have solved the retirement-income problems of a significant minority of today's aged, and the incidence of poverty among the others has dropped sharply. At the same time, for many, major economic problems remain.

We have reached a critical period in deciding where we go from here. The old and previously satisfactory answer (for both private and public pensions) that we need expanded programs with better benefits is no longer satisfactory. As I argue later in the book, some workers no longer need more pension benefits; yet others face the threat of economic deprivation in retirement even greater than that experienced by earlier generations of retirees.

This book—which focuses on the social-security old-age pension programs in the United States and a number of other countries —attempts to place pension developments at home and abroad within an analytical framework that we hope will clarify some of the important decisions that must be made in the near future.

When important pension reforms in Europe first came to my attention three years ago, I was surprised to discover the paucity of studies that would help those interested in social security reform in this country to assess the significance of foreign developments. The project reported upon in the present book was in large part motivated by this discovery.

The number and selection of countries chosen were influenced by a number of factors, including my subjective judgment (before thorough study) of the innovative importance of pension reforms in various countries, financial limitations, and the availability of collaborators.

I was indeed fortunate to be joined in the study by an outstanding group of colleagues with a common interest in various pension issues. Because they were willing to focus their efforts on a common set of questions about pensions abroad, the resulting "country study" chapters of this book have a common focus, and far more analytical consistency than is usually the case. The principal responsibility and credit for the various chapters are as follows: 1, 2, and 3, Schulz; 4, Krupp; 5, Carrin and Van Steenberge; 6, Sclar; 7, Schulz and Peschke (with the assistance of Krupp, Carrin, and Sclar); and 8, Schulz.

The interviews for this project were conducted jointly by me and the person primarily responsible for each country. Interviews took place in the fall of 1972 in Sweden, Germany, and Belgium and in the spring of 1973 in Canada and Belgium.

We are grateful for the many people in the various countries who took the time to be interviewed (sometimes numerous times and for many hours): Professor Achinger, General Director (retired) Rolf Broberg, Mr. G. De Broeck, Mr. J. Clark, Mr. Lars Dahlstrom, Dr. Paul Fisher, Professor J. Gaebler, Mr. J. Van Geel, Mr. E. S. Hanes, Dr. Hartmut Hensen, Dr. Heubeck, Mr. Ingemar Holmquist, Mr. Sven Hyden, Mr. Andre Laurent, Dr. R. Masyn, Professor H. Meinhold, Minister John E. Osborne, Honorable P. de Paepe, Judge Carl Axel Petre, Mr. Jacques Jean Ribas, Mr. L. Vergauwen, Dr. Otto Wayland, and Dr. Detlev Zöllner.

We also wish to express our appreciation for the advice and suggestions received from a number of persons who read all or part of the manuscript: Ms. Lenore E. Bixby, General Director (retired) Rolf Broberg, Professor Robert Consael, Dr. Paul Fisher, Mr. Max Horlick, Mr. Sven Hyden, Dr. Ida Merriam, Mr. William Mitchell, Dr. Gunnar Myrdal, Dr. Velma Rust, Professor G. Spitaels, and Dr. Detlev Zöllner.

Permission to reproduce parts of earlier articles has been given by *The Journal of Human Resources* and the *Annals of Economic and Social Measurement*. Financial support for some of the simulation analysis was provided under contract with the Office of Research and Statistics, U.S. Social Security Administration.

Finally, my personal appreciation and gratitude to Dr. Ida Merriam, for her inciteful and challenging comments and suggestions for improving the book's content; my wife, Dr. Ann Schulz, for her encouragement and understanding; my father-in-law, Dr. Clark Tibbitts, for stimulating my initial interests in the field of gerontology; Ms. Katherine Brooks and Ms. Margaret Stubbs for their secretarial assistance; and Dr. Robert Morris and the Levinson Gerontological Policy Institute for providing some of the financial support for the project.

J.H.S.

Waltham, Massachusetts
March 1974

PROVIDING ADEQUATE RETIREMENT INCOME

Chapter 1

THE UNITED STATES AND OTHER COUNTRIES

In a report by a "task force" studying the economic problems of growing old, the basic retirement preparation problem is succinctly stated.

> Every American—whether poor or rich, black or white, uneducated or college-trained—faces a common aging problem: How can he provide and plan for a retirement period of indeterminate length and uncertain needs? How can he allocate earnings during his working lifetime so that he not only meets current obligations . . . but has something left over for his own old age? (U.S. Senate Special Committee on Aging, 1969)

This basic economic problem must be faced by all persons before the retirement period. Today older workers are increasingly likely to find themselves automatically retired at a certain age from their regular job and left with no viable alternative work opportunities. At the same time, over the years that follow their departure from the labor force they are faced with the prospect of expenditure needs which do not decrease as significantly as many would like to believe. In the retirement period there are usually rising health expenditures, increased leisure activities, and increased need for supportive services. And finally there is a continuing desire or need for all the other goods and services at levels not greatly diminished from preretirement consumption levels.

The aged are faced also with rising levels of prices, an economic phenomenon that is almost certain to occur throughout every retirement period. Moreover, the retired quickly become well aware of any rise in the living standards of nonretired families as these younger families share in the general, long-run economic growth of the country. Such increases no doubt generate a desire among many if not most of the aged to "keep up."

All these factors when viewed together indicate that there are strong economic pressures on persons when they retire which make their perceived economic "needs" in retirement not much different from those just prior to retirement. Whether an individual's financial resources in retirement will be adequate to meet this situation depends not only on what sort of life style he wants in retirement but, more importantly, on the economic preparations that have been made before retirement and that make the desired life style possible.

To provide for old age, an individual is faced with the option of (a) either saving during his working years and/or (b) supporting the development of private and/or public institutions that either assist him in saving or that provide for and facilitate the transfer of income from the working population to those retired. Basically, therefore, to improve his retirement living, these options necessitate higher private pensions and/or insurance, higher taxes to support public pension programs, or higher personal savings.

Figure I summarizes the various sources of retirement income which an individual in the United States can build up or utilize in meeting his economic needs in retirement. The sources can be divided into private versus public means and further subdivided, in the case of private sources, by whether the source is controlled solely by the individual's saving/financial investment behavior or by whether the source emanates from individuals or institutions outside the core family.

Juanita Kreps (1970) has summarized the economic problem of retirement preparation as follows:

> There are no simple solutions to the dilemma of today's worker. He could easily consume all his earnings, leaving no claims (either public or private) for future retirement needs. Social policy cannot hope to satisfy all his present and future needs, for they far outstrip his lifetime earnings. All social policy can do is provide a mechanism that allocates aggregate output in some democratically agreed-to optimal fashion, the optimum allocation in this case having a lifetime as well as a temporary dimension. And just as there are differences of view as to how evenly income should be distributed at any point in time, so, too, men vary in the rates at which they discount the future— that is, in how highly they prize present over future consumption.

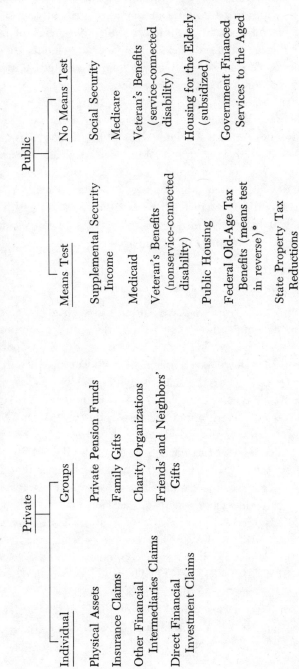

FIGURE I

Current Options for Retirement Income

Private

Individual

Physical Assets

Insurance Claims

Other Financial
Intermediaries Claims

Direct Financial
Investment Claims

Groups

Private Pension Funds

Family Gifts

Charity Organizations

Friends' and Neighbors'
Gifts

Public

Means Test

Supplemental Security
Income

Medicaid

Veteran's Benefits
(nonservice-connected
disability)

Public Housing

Federal Old-Age Tax
Benefits (means test
in reverse) *

State Property Tax
Reductions

No Means Test

Social Security

Medicare

Veteran's Benefits
(service-connected
disability)

Housing for the Elderly
(subsidized)

Government Financed
Services to the Aged

*Federal tax benefits can be utilized only by persons with taxable income high enough to require that they pay taxes, hence take advantage of special tax provisions.

In recent decades, as the United States and other countries have reacted to widespread poverty among the aged, increased reliance has been placed upon institutional or collective means of providing economic resources for old age. Collective arrangements are not new, however; people since earliest times have attempted to mitigate or eliminate economic insecurity by banding together in groups—families, tribes, associations, guilds—to share income and goods. What is new is the increased importance of industrial and government action in this area. As Kenneth Boulding (1958) has observed: "It is when the 'sharing group' becomes too small to ensure that there will always be enough producers in it to support the unproductive that devices for . . . insurance . . . become necessary. When the 'sharing group' is small there is always a danger that sheer accident will bring the proportion of earners to non-earners to a level at which the group cannot function."

THE UNITED STATES

Around the world we have fallen into such a habit of talking about the economically impoverished, destitute, forgotten, disadvantaged aged that we are apt to miss or ignore the important improvements that have taken place over recent decades in income provision for old age. In the chapters which follow we examine major reforms that have occurred in four foreign countries, but significant progress has not been limited to these countries. Major changes in income provision for the elderly have occurred in almost every industrialized country of the world, including the United States.

During the postwar period significant changes in retirement security took place in the United States. Social security coverage has now been extended (along with higher benefits) to all but a very small minority of the regular work force. In 1950, 21 percent of the population aged 65 and over was receiving social security benefits. By 1970 the percentage had risen to 85.5 percent and is expected to continue to rise (see Figure II). There are two major reasons for this increase. First, the number of aged workers (and their spouses) who retired in the 1930's before becoming eligible for social security in covered industries is declining and is becoming a smaller proportion of the total aged population. The second major reason is the

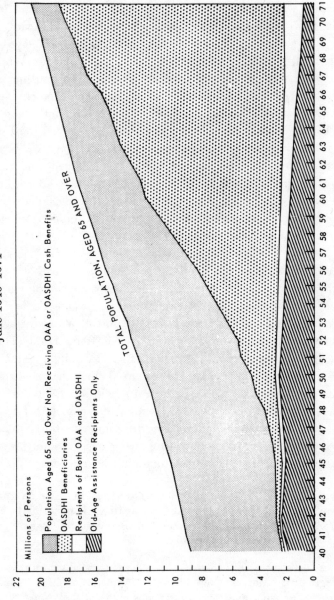

FIGURE II

Population Aged 65 and Over and Social Security Programs for the Aged
June 1940–1971

Source: United States Department of Health, Education, and Welfare (1973).

series of social security amendments that went into effect in 1950, 1954, 1956, and 1965. These revisions extended social security coverage to regularly employed farm and household employees; self-employed persons; state and local government workers and those employed by nonprofit organizations, by special arrangement; farm operators; most self-employed professional people (including physicians); and members of the Armed Forces. All gainfully employed workers are now covered by social security except (a) some government employees with other retirement coverage, (b) farm and domestic workers who are not regularly employed, and (c) self-employed persons who have very low incomes. In addition to this extended coverage, social security provisions were changed by these amendments to liberalize work requirements, creditable earnings, and the general benefit structure.[1]

During the first two and a half decades of the United States Social Security system's operation, the major changes were aimed at the expansion of coverage described in the preceding paragraph. Benefit increases in the first twenty-five years (see Table 1) were infrequent and usually were aimed at protecting the real value of benefits from the inflation occurring over the period. Thus the benefit increases in 1950, 1952, 1958, and 1965 roughly equaled the rise in the price level which had occurred since the last benefit increase; only the 13 percent increase in 1954 represented a real increase in benefits—prices having risen only 0.5 percent between 1952 and 1954. A study by the Social Security Administration published in 1968, for example, reported the following major findings regarding benefit increases up to and including the 1967 increase:

1. OASDHI retirement benefits have been increased to the point where they have regained for the time being [1968] the purchasing power of the amount received by all workers at the time they came on the rolls.

---

1. A summary of the current United States social security system and its legislative history are reproduced in Appendix A at the end of the book. See also the most current editions of *Social Security Programs in the United States* and (for a much more technical description) the *Social Security Handbook,* both of which are published regularly by the Social Security Administration.

TABLE 1

Percentage Increases in Social Security Benefits and
Consumer Prices, 1939–1972

Effective Date	Across-the-Board Increases	Average Increases for All Beneficiaries	Increases in CPI between the Effective Dates[a]
9/50	77.0	81.3	75.5
9/52	12.5 [b]	14.1 [c]	9.3
9/54	13.0	13.3	0.5
1/59	7.0 [d]	7.7	7.9
1/65	7.0 [e]	7.7	7.9
2/68	13.0	14.2	9.3
1/70	15.0	15.6	10.8
1/71	10.0	10.4	5.2
9/72	20.0	20.7	5.9
3/74	7.0	— [f]	—
6/74	4.0	— [f]	—

[a] 1957–59 + 100%.
[b] Greater of 12.5% or $5.00.
[c] 15.2% for old-age beneficiaries.
[d] Guarantee of 7% or $3.00.
[e] Guarantee of 7% or $4.00.
Source: Social Security Administration as prepared by Congressional Research Service and distributed by Special Senate Committee on Aging.

2. Liberalizations of the retirement benefits by the 1967 amendments still do not match the strides made by the American worker in achieving higher wage levels and hence a higher standard of living, though they helped to close the gap.

3. Unless statutory benefit increases more than just match upward price movements from the time of one benefit increase to the next, inflation will continue to adversely affect retirees' purchasing power, because the value of their fixed benefits deteriorates as prices rise steadily between the passage of amendments to the law.   (Price, 1968)

Thus the succession of increases which occurred in 1968, 1969, 1971, and 1972 were unprecedented and, for the first time, increased real old-age pension benefits significantly. In this period individual benefits rose by nearly 60 percent.

The Improving Economic Situation of the Aged

Over this thirty-two year period of social security development, the economic status of the aged has improved slowly but steadily.[2] Now for the first time in America's history we find not insignificant numbers of the elderly retiring on incomes above poverty and prospects for the overwhelming majority to do so in the future. For example, in 1967—*before the major OASDHI increases took place*— 57 percent of aged social security beneficiary couples had total incomes exceeding $3000 and 17 percent (admittedly a very small percentage) of aged nonmarried beneficiaries had incomes exceeding $2500 (Bixby, 1970).

Thompson (1973) has reorganized the 1971 Current Population Survey data so that the "survey unit" definition conforms to the one used in the "1968 Social Security Survey of the Aged." Table 2

TABLE 2

Percentage Change in U.S. Aged Median Income, 1967–1971

Age	Married Couples	All Nonmarried Persons	Nonmarried Men	Nonmarried Women
62–64	42	32	17	36
65 and older	46	50	48	52
65–72	43	50	34	51
73 and older	58	53	59	58

Source: Thompson (1973).

shows the percentage change in median income of aged units occurring over the 1967–1971 period. The increases range from 17 percent for nonmarried men age 62–64 to 59 percent for nonmarried men age 73 and older. In general, median incomes have risen for all groups. These increases must be adjusted downward, however:

> Because prices also rose during this period, increases in real income have been lower than the increase in money incomes reported here. The Consumer Price Index rose by 21.3 percent from 1967 to 1971. This means that the increase in real income

---

2. The original Social Security Act of 1935 specified that payments would begin in 1942. Amendments in 1939 changed the beginning date of payments to 1940.

was about 20 percent for couples aged 65 or over instead of the apparent 46 percent; and for the nonmarried, the improvement for those 65 and older was 23 percent in real terms as opposed to 50 percent in cash terms, based on median incomes.

(Thompson, 1973)

More recent data for spring 1972 (which, however, still do not take into account the large increases in social security effective in 1973)[3] show that 80 percent of aged families had incomes of more than $3000 and that 40 percent of unrelated individuals had more than $2500 (see Table 3); median money income for families with

TABLE 3

Total Money Income in 1972 for Aged [a]
Families and Unrelated Individuals
(percentages)

Income	Families	Unrelated Individuals
Under $1000	1.2	7.2
$ 1000–1499	1.3	13.1
1500–1999	2.8	17.0
2000–2499	4.4	15.9
2500–2999	5.6	11.3
3000–3499	6.2	7.2
3500–3999	6.3	5.4
4000–4999	12.2	7.1
5000–5999	10.3	4.0
6000–6999	7.9	2.9
7000–7999	6.9	1.9
8000–8999	5.3	1.8
9000–9999	4.8	1.1
10,000–11,999	6.3	1.4
12,000–14,999	6.1	1.2
15,000–24,999	8.9	0.8
25,000–49,999	2.9	0.4
50,000 and over	0.6	0.1
Total percentage	100	100

[a] Head aged 65 or over.
Source: United States Bureau of the Census (1973a).

---

3. The 1972 social security amendments increased the *average* benefit for retired workers to $161.47 per month—a monthly increase of close to $28.

FIGURE III
Proportion of Aged Persons and Families Below the Poverty Level

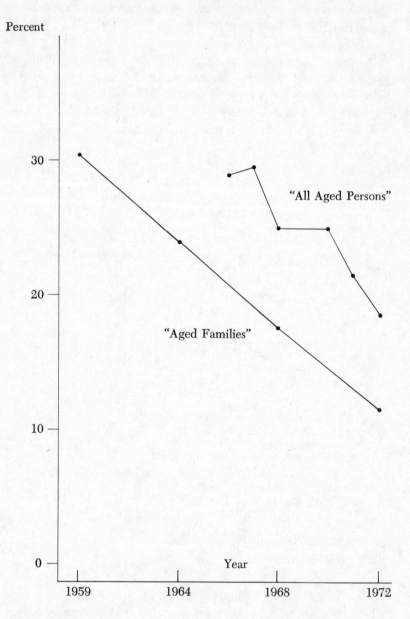

Sources: United States Bureau of the Census (1969, 1972b, and 1973b).

the head age 65 or more was $5453 in 1971 and $2199 for unrelated individuals. Figure III shows the declining trend of poverty among aged families over the 1959–72 period, which reached a low of 11.6 percent in 1972.

It is important to put these improvements in perspective by looking at poverty rates between age groups and among various groups of the aged themselves. Table 4 highlights some of these differences.

TABLE 4

Families with 1972 Income below the "Low-Income Level" [a]

Age of Head	All Races		White		Black	
	Thousands	*Percent*	*Thousands*	*Percent*	*Thousands*	*Percent*
Under 25	684	16.3	453	12.6	228	41.2
25–44	2153	9.5	1348	6.8	742	30.7
45–64	1360	6.8	961	5.3	375	22.2
65 and over	878	11.6	678	9.8	184	30.5

[a] Low-Income Level is the level that separates "poor" from "non-poor" families using the poverty index adopted by the Federal Interagency Committees in 1969.
Source: United States Bureau of Census (1973b).

In contrast to 11.6 percent of aged families with incomes below the poverty level, only 6.8 percent of the families with the head age 45–64 had incomes below. And, in the same year, 30.5 percent of Black aged families had poverty-level incomes.[4]

A major limitation of the 1971 and 1972 statistics discussed above is that they are for all the aged—the retired, the semiretired, and those still working. The "total income" picture for the aged, which includes earnings, tends to hide the lower-income situation of those substantially or fully retired. Unfortunately, published data that make this distinction are rare. Table 5 presents data from the "1968 Social Security Survey of the Aged," which contrasts the in-

4. For additional data and further discussion of the incidence of poverty among various groups of the elderly, see Chen (1971). And see Murray (1972) for recent data on the asset holdings of the aged.

TABLE 5

Income Size by OASDHI Beneficiary Status, 1967
(percentages)

Total Money Income	All Units		Married Couples	
	Beneficiaries	Nonbene-ficiaries	Beneficiaries	Nonbene-ficiaries
Less than $1000	17	30	3	5
1000–1499	20	20	7	4
1500–1999	16	8	12	6
2000–2499	12	8	13	6
2500–2999	8	3	11	4
3000–3499	6	3	11	6
3400–3999	5	2	9	4
4000–4999	6	6	12	11
5000–7499	6	8	14	19
7500–9999	2	7	5	20
10,000–14,999	1	2	3	7
15,000 or more	1	2	1	7
Percent	100	100	100	100
Median income	$1904	$1490	$3199	$5218

Source: Bixby (1970).

come distribution for aged units based on whether units were receiving cash benefits under the OASDHI program at the end of 1967:

> The differing contribution of employment income and retirement benefits in determining the level of total income is emphasized by the fact that the median income of all non-beneficiary couples as a group was almost two-thirds above that of beneficiary couples . . . The income of beneficiary, couples would have been further below that of non-beneficiary couples but for the receipt of other types of income. About 40 percent of them had some earnings, and about 30 percent a second pension . . .
> (Bixby, 1970)

Thus the economic status of the aged is certainly improving but not for all the aged. In an important study examining the replacement rates for public and private pension systems over the past twenty years, Henle has summarized the current situations as follows:

Public and private retirement systems in the United States have matured to the point that taken together they can provide a married couple a level of living close to what they had before retirement. However, most retirees do not find themselves in a position to take advantage of this possibility, either because they are not covered by a private industry pension plan or are forced to apply for public (social security) benefits before they are 65, thus reducing their annuity under the Old Age, Survivors, Disability and Health Insurance system.   (Henle, 1972)

This improvement in the economic status of the elderly in the United States is the result of a number of diverse factors operating over three decades. The most important of these factors are:

1. The continued general economic growth of the United States economy and a sharing in the results of this growth by most segments of the working population.

2. The expansion of private pension coverage and substantial liberalization of many of the benefits paid.

3. The blanketing-in of new groups under social security and the continued increase in old-age pensions to keep pace with the cost of living.

4. Most recently, a significant rise in the real value of old-age benefits under OASDHI.

Though significant improvement has occurred—at least from the standpoint of keeping people out of poverty—few experts and certainly few of the elderly themselves would argue that we have developed completely satisfactory institutional mechanisms for ensuring adequate retirement income above the poverty line. There is no denying that many of the old problems remain and, as indicated above, that large numbers of the aged remain impoverished.[5] And, most important, the relative economic situation of the aged—as compared to the living standard of the working population and their own preretirement standard—still needs to be improved.

---

5. For example, in 1971 there were about 1½ million families with incomes below $3000 and about 3½ million with incomes below $5000. In addition there were another 3½ million unrelated individuals with income below $2500.

The Problem of Relative Poverty

There seems to be a growing acceptance in the United States that incomes should be raised as soon as possible to an agreed-upon poverty level for all Americans not adequately sharing in the nation's economic abundance. As we continue to discuss taking this giant step in providing minimum economic security to all Americans, a new look at our economic goals for the retired aged seems timely. Hopefully, it will not be too long before there will be a satisfactory welfare program to ensure that *all the aged have a minimum level of income* which will be adequate to provide for their most basic needs. The new "supplemental security program" (summarized below, Chapter 8) is the most recent major legislation toward this end. But minimum income provision is only a first step. Over the years we have developed elaborate pension systems to provide additional income in old age.

In evaluating these pension systems, it is important to keep in mind the basic economic question of how much income is to be allocated by persons in their younger years, either individually or in groups, for retirement preparation purposes. For example, we have accepted in the design of the current United States Social Security system the concept that the current generation of workers provides the funds via payroll taxes to provide current retirees with pensions, in return for a promise of similar pension support from future workers. At the same time, we have no consensus on what that level of support should be. Thus the first "income-needs issue" discussed by delegates to the 1971 White House Conference on Aging was: "The long-range goal for older people is that they should have income in accordance with the American standard of living. What should be regarded as an adequate income for older couples and older non-related individuals?"

As indicated above, the most popular method of evaluating the economic status of the aged (and other groups) is to look at the aged population at a given moment in time and compare their actual incomes to some standard level. The two most widely used measures for aged families are the United States Social Security Administration's "poverty" and "low income" indexes and the United States Bureau of Labor Statistics' "Budget for a Retired Couple." These measures have been useful for setting levels of income above which minimum income adequacy is indicated. But the levels established by these indexes are somewhat arbitrary. In the case of the BLS budgets, the designated levels are above a minimal level and seek to provide something called a "modest but adequate" living standard. Alternatively, the Social Security index is based on an emergency food budget (in 1966 providing for a 75-cent-a-day expenditure per person in an average four-person family) and the assumption that these food costs constitute one third of total required living expenditures.

Mollie Orshansky, one of the original developers of the Social Security index has called attention in Congressional testimony to the potential obsolescence of it:

> The index, of course, as time goes on, suffers the same limitations we all do, namely advancing age. Arrived at late in 1964 in the light of then readily available data, data already in the main 9 years old at that point, the income criteria have not been updated in a real sense, that is, to take account of the greater degree of a consumption potential that prosperity has made possible for the majority of American families.
>
> (Orshansky, 1971)

More generally, Derek Bok (1967) has succinctly summarized the major limitations of such absolute budget standards as follows:

> Experience in other countries has revealed how difficult it is to determine the expenditures that are appropriate for any group of people. Moreover, it is not enough simply to establish a single retirement budget. Separate determinations would have to be made for each of many income classes reaching retirement age, since a budget suitable for a day laborer would hardly seem adequate to a highly paid technician. Furthermore, the standard budget is probably too static a conception for the task at hand. While it may be possible to define the minimum living expenses which should be guaranteed here and now to the poorest of the aged, it is much more difficult to determine what standard of living will be considered adequate many years hence when present generations of workers begin to retire. Yet under our contributory system this question is important. We must concern ourselves with future benefit levels if employees are to have an adequate notion of the pensions they can count on in retirement and if they are to make contributions bearing some reasonable relation to the benefits they will eventually receive. In view of these problems, any effort to establish an

adequate social security policy should aim at defining the proportion of prior wages which each worker can count on receiving when he retires.

In addition to the aged who have always lived in poverty and the aged who find themselves for the first time in poverty because of inadequate pensions, there are and will be many retired aged families above the poverty level, whose earnings during their work life allowed them a comfortable living standard but whose retirement incomes have dropped far below their preretirement levels. Their income problem grows out of the cessation of earnings of one or more family members and the failure of their savings and/or private and public pensions to replace a sufficiently large proportion of these earnings.

Measuring Adequacy by Earnings Replacement

The importance of the pension-earnings ratio in influencing the decisions of workers to retire is indicated by a recent study of retiring United States automobile workers. Reporting on the study's findings, Richard Barfield (1970) states:

> . . . for the great majority of the sample [943 auto workers] only one factor—the retirement/preretirement income ratio— was found influential [in explaining early retirement]; the analysis technique divided workers into five groups in which the ratio ranged from less than 0.20 to more than 0.79 . . . the explanatory power of this single factor was really quite enormous, with the average propensity to retire score rising smoothly and swiftly across the five groups.

Unfortunately there is a great paucity of data available which directly measure the earnings replacement levels of public and private pensions being received by those who have retired in the past and those who are currently retiring. The findings of two different surveys provide useful information on this question based on individuals' perceptions of living standard reduction (see Table 6). A fifth to a third of the respondents in these two surveys felt that their 1966 retirement standard of living was below their preretirement standard.

Barfield and Morgan (1969) have also reported on the subjective evaluation of income differences expressed as the ratio of retirement to preretirement income. They found that 60 percent of re-

TABLE 6

Distribution of Retirees' Perception of Change from
Preretirement to Retirement Living Standard, 1966

Perceived Change	Percentage	
	Barfield	*Greene*
Better	5.0	7.6
Same	53.0	70.8
Worse	32.0	21.1
No response	10.0	.5
Total	100.0	100.0

Sources: Barfield and Morgan (1969) and Greene, Pyron, Manion, and
Winklevoss (1969).

tirees interviewed reported a ratio of less than one half and that 34
percent reported a ratio of one fourth or less (see Table 7).

Under OASDHI, social security pension benefits are related to
prior earnings up to a specified earnings ceiling. Computation of
these benefits, therefore, is affected not only by changes in the
benefit formula but also by changes in the creditable-earnings ceiling and the period of average earnings upon which benefits are
based. An estimate (Horlich, 1970) of the replacement rate or pension-earnings ratio provided by the United States social security
system has been made by the Social Security Administration's

TABLE 7

Retirees' Perception of Retirement to
Preretirement Income Ratio, 1966

Ratio	Percentage of Retirees
Less than 1/4	8
1/4	26
1/2	26
3/4	4
1	14
Greater than 1	4
No response	18
Total	100

Source: Barfield and Morgan (1969).

Office of Research and Statistics. The replacement of earnings in the year before retirement by a social security retirement pension *for a single male full-time industrial worker with average earnings in manufacturing* retiring at age 65 in 1968 was 29 percent. The replacement rate for a similar worker who had a wife who was at least aged 65 and receiving a spouse benefit was 44 percent.[6]

The above rates are based upon preretirement earnings defined as earnings in the year before retirement. If the measure of preretirement earnings is defined to be average earnings during the 1950–68 period and excluding (in accordance with current calculation procedures) the five years, 1950–55, of lowest earnings, the replacement rate for a single male worker rises from 29 to 38 percent. Such replacement rates differ significantly from the 60 to 75 replacement rates necessary to maintain living standards if other financial resources are not available.[7]

Finally, Kolodrubetz (1973b) reports on the amount of earnings replacement provided by private pensions received by persons retiring between July 1969 and June 1970. Persons surveyed were asked to report the monthly pension amount (if any) related to earnings on their *longest* job. Two thirds of the men receiving private pensions received amounts replacing 10–39 percent of earnings. Few had private pensions that replaced more than 50 percent.

Why Low Replacement?

Both private and public pension systems in the United States have badly satisfied the relative-adequacy standard (i.e., adequate earnings replacement) for persons with incomes above the lowest income levels because of three major factors:

1. United States pension programs (especially social security) have been deliberately constructed to favor low wage earners.

2. Social security and private pension systems do a poor job of dealing with general increases in the level of prices which occur before and after retirement.

3. United States pension systems do not provide any formal mechanism for taking account of changing productivity (eco-

---

6. See also Ceccarelli and Skolnik (1973).

7. The derivation of this 60–75 percent estimate is discussed below, Chapter 2.

nomic growth) and the resulting improved general living standards which result.

Regarding the first factor, the United States social security system has (a) a minimum old-age benefit, (b) a benefit formula weighted in favor of low earners, and (c) up until 1972 a creditable earnings ceiling which did not adjust automatically. These features operated to help achieve the Congressional objective of providing "socially adequate" incomes to the low-income aged. But they also operated, as a consequence, to keep down the replacement levels for persons above these low-income levels.

One cannot easily generalize about private pension systems because of the large number of independent systems and the wide diversity of provisions. However, collectively bargained plans currently tend to provide uniform benefits that vary by length of service but not earnings—thus placing low-paid workers in an advantageous position (Heidbreder et al., 1966).[8] Minimum benefit provisions in private plans with earnings-related formulas also tend to favor the below-average wage earner.

Regarding the second factor (adjustment for price increases), up to 1972 United States social security benefits paid in retirement were adjusted frequently by Congress to keep pace with price level increases—though sometimes after a considerable time lag between the price change and the benefit increase. And beginning in 1972, benefits are adjusted by an automatic index mechanism. At the time the initial social security benefit is calculated for a retiring employee, however, the benefit is based upon average earnings which include the worker's earlier earnings that were paid at a time when the price level was much lower. *Thus benefits calculated at the time of retirement are based upon earnings unadjusted for subsequent price increases.*[9]

---

8. The other group that generally receives generous private pensions relative to preretirement earnings is high-paid executives.

9. The effect of not adjusting earnings is compounded by the taxable earnings limit. If total wages were covered, one could, in theory, completely compensate for the failure to revalue by designing a benefit formula that provided a higher percentage replacement. Beginning in 1975, the taxable earnings limit will be adjusted automatically. This will not completely eliminate its depressing effect but will serve to mitigate its impact somewhat.

In the case of private pensions, only a handful of plans currently have a provision for adjusting pensions *during* retirement for price level changes. Many plans in recent years have adjusted periodically the benefit formula used to calculate benefits at the time of retirement—raising benefits often more than necessary for compensating for price level changes. While no systematic analysis by government or private researchers has been made to quantify and generalize the extent to which such adjustments are occurring, one would not expect to find a very complete adjustment being made by private pension systems using various ad hoc procedures. And certainly we know that many private pension plans, unfortunately, do little or no adjusting at and/or during retirement.

Finally, with regard to the third factor—productivity or economic growth adjustment—the practice of present pension systems is clear. Both the social security system and private pensions have done very little to adjust pension levels *in retirement* to reflect the general improvement in living standards over time.[10]

The current lack of dynamic adjustment mechanisms in United States pension systems promises the continuation of a fundamental retirement problem. Even if aged poverty—as defined, for example, by the SSA poverty index—were to be eliminated, there would still remain the problem of *relative* income adequacy. Past public discussions regarding aged income adequacy (and the adequacy of private and public pension programs) have been dominated by a search for ways of improving the poverty or near-poverty incomes of the aged. We think that it is time to give much more attention to the question of the desirability of creating pension systems that will not only provide adequate minimum old-age incomes but also *provide the elderly with pensions that permit them to maintain or more closely approach their preretirement living standard in retirement* and, perhaps, even improve upon it.

Whether individuals in fact wish to maintain or improve their standard of living in retirement is, of course, still an open question. Many people apparently prefer to gamble on having very low income for a retirement period of unpredictable length if, as a result, they

10. The minor exception to this statement is the small number of private pension plans with variable annuity provisions.

can live better before retirement. And even for those who do desire to maintain living standards in retirement, there still remains the question whether this should be primarily a matter of personal choice (and, hence, personal savings) or whether the matter should be handled through the public and/or private pension systems.

As the action in numerous other nations indicates, the United States may want to act collectively to provide an opportunity for persons to maintain prior living standards in and throughout retirement. Up to now the advantages and disadvantages of such an approach have not been carefully studied in the United States. And in stark contrast to the extended and vigorous debates that have occurred in Europe, there has been no public discussion in the United States with regard to ways of maintaining living standards in retirement.

OTHER COUNTRIES

Addressing the question of achieving relative income adequacy, many European countries have adopted public pension systems that have as their primary goal the achievement of "adequate" earnings replacement and/or the maintenance of prior living standards. These countries have made major changes in their pension programs—significantly increasing social security pension levels and introducing various dynamic mechanisms.

This movement toward "dynamic pensions" has occurred as part of a general movement in industrialized countries away from the flat rate or weighted benefit formulas that characterized many of the early social security systems. Early old-age pension systems evolved in large part as a reaction to the economic instability that characterized the industrialization process and the widespread economic destitution then existing among the elderly—together with the continuing breakdown of traditional means of providing economic security, especially through family ties. The early systems, therefore, tended to emphasize getting some minimal income into the hands of the current elderly ("social equity"), while maintaining the dignity of the recipients. As a consequence, income-redistribution systems using flat-rate or weighted benefit formulas (weighing low earnings more heavily)—both with "minimum pension" floors—were instituted in most countries.

Various developments in these countries quickly made this type of social security pension system unsatisfactory. As summarized by Paul Fisher (1971):

> . . . shifts in the composition of the labor force, the rise in the income level, the extension of social security coverage to the self-employed and other factors substantially increased the proportion of middle and high earnings among the covered population in the affluent societies. These higher earnings find a ready expression in income-related benefits. It would seem that economic progress made by the great masses of insured requires more than an egalitarian payment, increasingly less related to a subsistence minimum, and seeks a pension which maintains for the pensioner a significant part of the preretirement income and the same status in the social hierarchy which he held when he was economically active.

Currently, flat-rate systems are the exclusive form of public pensions in only Australia, Finland, Ireland, Israel, the Netherlands, and New Zealand.[11] Among the industrialized countries in Western Europe and the Americas, only the United States retains the weighted formula, it having been most recently abandoned in Italy (1968) and Switzerland (1969).[12]

A number of countries, (e.g., Sweden, Canada, and Great Britain) have retained a flat pension benefit, supplementing it with an earnings-related pension program. Such double-decker systems provide higher replacement for workers with low wages while permitting major increases in benefits for middle and high wage earners.

The current trend is to establish social security-old-age pension systems that explicitly recognize that the adequacy of pension income in retirement must be measured in terms of the amount of preretirement income it replaces. The trend has been toward establishing replacement levels between 60 and 80 percent of variously defined

---

11. The so-called developing countries are excluded from this summary.

12. Weighted formulas are still used in certain Eastern European countries.

measures of preretirement earnings. Also, the trend has been away from defining replacement standards based on lifetime earnings. Instead, most systems now base benefits on earnings during the later part of the work history, the period just prior to retirement. Finally, there has been a tendency for contribution/earnings ceilings to be increased significantly.[13]

In 1970 Horlick published an international comparison of replacement rates in certain industrialized countries. Based on this study, Figure IV shows the replacement levels of old-age pension systems for an average worker retiring in 1968, in fifteen different countries. The replacement rates vary from a low of about 20 percent in Ireland to a high of about 64 percent in France.

In assessing foreign social security developments, the reforms in West Germany and Sweden are of special interest. Fundamental pension reform occurred in both countries about fifteen years ago. Along with other social security reforms, both countries introduced automatic and semi-automatic mechanisms to assure (a) that the level of pension benefits paid at retirement represented a high proportion of annual earnings received during the latter years of work experience, and (b) that pensions paid *at* retirement and also *during* retirement are adjusted for various dynamic shifts in the economy.[14]

The current West German social security system was enacted in 1957 and experience with its operation has begun to accumulate. Writing in 1966, Paul Fisher observed:

> There is no doubt that the 1957 reform of the German old-age and disability insurance system, in particular the linking of pensions to wage-level changes, has achieved widespread acceptance by management and labor, the various branches of the government, and public opinion. Even those who would substitute price-level changes for wage-level changes as the basis for the adjustments of old-age benefits consider the principle of the dynamic pension for all practical purposes unassailable at the present time. As long as wages increase at a faster rate than prices, the system meets the wishes of large

---

13. See, for example, the Horlick and Lucas (1971) study of ceilings in five countries.

14. Developments in both countries are described and analyzed in great detail in later chapters.

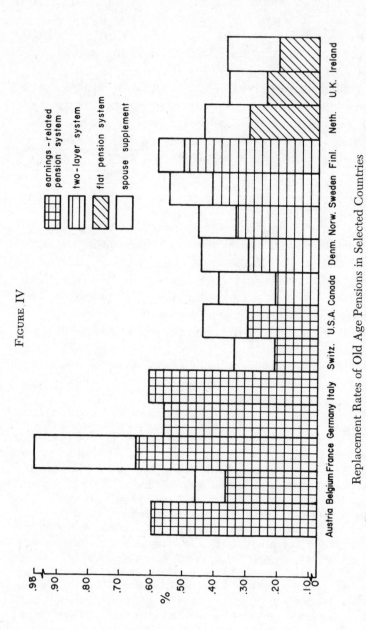

FIGURE IV

Replacement Rates of Old Age Pensions in Selected Countries

(Pension as percent of earnings in manufacturing of a male worker in 1968) *

Note: Retirement at the end of 1968; Ireland at the end of 1967. Assumed working period—40 years; for the Netherlands only—49 years.

* Average earnings.

masses of employees. As long as Germany's economic growth continues at a satisfactory rate, the dynamic pension will not lead to serious financial problems . . . Changes in the benefit formula and in the adjustment mechanism offer fairly easy technical ways to achieve flexibility in case of prolonged economic downtrends. The system's very success has aroused international interest. Consequently, it has gained and will continue to gain an increasing number of admirers and imitators in the international marketplace of ideas. It has provided a powerful stimulus to a trend which will have to be taken into account wherever the adjustment of long-range social security benefits to subsequent changes in economic conditions is under discussion.

As indicated by Fisher, West German pensions for retired persons are adjusted (through a semi-automatic mechanism) to keep income throughout the entire retirement period increasing at a rate approximating the rise in average wages of persons still working. Thus pension adjustments not only reflect changes in money wages which are a part of inflationary pressures, but also allow persons, even though they are no longer working, to share in the economic growth occurring over time. Also, at the time of retirement, the German worker's pension is brought in line with current earnings levels by a calculation which relates his earnings to average national earnings for each year throughout his earnings history. This comparison results in a pension being paid which takes account of both real and monetary increases in general earnings levels over his work life. And, most important, it permits a pension to be paid which allows the retired worker to enjoy a living standard directly related to that which is currently being enjoyed by a current worker of equivalent status.[15]

In Sweden a universal pension is paid to everyone without regard to earlier residence, former gainful activity, or payment of contributions. This pension is automatically adjusted at and during retirement for changes in the consumer price level. In addition, a

---

15. "Equivalent status" refers to a worker with current earnings that bear the same relationship to national average earnings as does the average of the ratios of the worker's yearly earnings to national average earnings (over the work period). See Chapter 4, below, for a more detailed explanation.

supplementary pension covers all employed persons (and the self-employed who do not elect to contract out).

The Swedish supplementary pension is earnings-related. An adjustment mechanism exists to base pension entitlement at retirement on the relative position of the insured person's earnings as they relate to a specified *base amount*—which is adjusted upward by the price index each year. This ratio is expressed in "pension points," determined by dividing the pension income by the base amount in force at the beginning of each year. When the pension at retirement is calculated, a person's average pension points for the fifteen "best years" is multiplied by the current base amount. The resulting sum is thus based on the person's average pensionable income during the best years of his working career, adjusted to current purchasing power. From this adjusted pension base the actual pension is calculated, using a formula that gives a long-term worker a total pension (universal pension plus supplemental pension) of about two thirds his preretirement average earnings.

The German and Swedish social security systems are examples of two different ways of implementing the principle of "maintaining living standards in retirement." Other countries have adopted somewhat similar systems but with additional variants. Later chapters will look more closely at the German and Swedish pension programs and will also discuss pension developments in Belgium and Canada— analyzing various implications of their features for aged retirement security.

The Challenge

In recent years institutional pension mechanisms (both public and private) in the United States have come under heavy criticism. Much of the criticism has centered around the adequacy of benefits realized and the extent to which the pension systems are fulfilling the needs of "social adequacy" at the expense of individual equity and public policy efficiency.

For example, in a well-reasoned review of the social security system Pechman, Aaron, and Taussig (1968) have argued as follows:

> The basic dilemma in considering reform of the social security system is that the United States has attempted to solve two

problems with one instrument—how to prevent destitution among the aged poor and how to assure to people, having adequate incomes before retirement, benefits that are related to their previous standard of living. The earnings replacement function calls for benefit payments without an income test. Basic income support, on the other hand, can be carried out most efficiently if payments are confined to households with low income.

Two separate systems are needed to accomplish the two functions at the lowest cost. The earnings replacement function should continue to be performed by a social security system. Social security would become strictly wage-related, with the replacement rate roughly the same at all earnings levels between subsistence and the median earnings level. The income support function should be transferred to a negative income tax system or to a comprehensively reformed system of public assistance. With a good negative income tax, dependents' allowances would be unnecessary under social security. The payroll tax might be retained, but it should be used only as a withholding mechanism for the individual income tax.

It is time that a broad review of our retirement income maintenance system be undertaken and serious thought given to the requirements of providing adequate retirement incomes for *the future aged*. A study by Schulz (1968) of the economic status of the retired aged in 1980 showed that given past trends in the improvement of United States old-age pension benefits, poverty among the aged would not be eliminated and their relative economic status would remain very poor. Present trends indicate that we must be prepared to deal with the economic implications for the aged of (a) ever-increasing living standards in the working years, (b) retirement at earlier ages, (c) longer life, and (d) consequent changing retirement life-style expectations.

To a large extent pension benefit levels in the past and the increases in these levels have been stimulated not so much with the purposeful intent of tapping a greater part of the nation's rising national product for old people but rather as a secondary result of attempts to deal with the severe and potentially explosive hardship problems facing many old people. In consequence, these past efforts have been aimed primarily at raising the economic status of the aged to some minimum standard or subsistence level in the face of rising prices. There now remains the task of developing a set of private and public pension policies and programs which focus on an *adequate* income for the aged, not simply on raising them above some arbitrary low measure of poverty.

What has been proposed by some, however, is to develop mechanisms that allow the retired aged to share in the growing productivity and output of the nation—to share in some of the harvested fruits. What this no doubt requires is finding orderly and equitable ways to make possible a substantial transfer of income from the working to the retired population—in order to improve the latter's relative economic status. Happily, as the United States begins this search it can profit from the experience of those who began before it. Just as many of the industrial giants of today (e.g., Germany, Japan, and Russia) benefited from the technological research and development work carried out by Great Britain and the United States, this country can learn from, imitate, and hopefully improve upon the development of pension programs taking place in other parts of the world.

The national dialogue and debate over such a change of focus with regard to developing better retirement-income programs is just beginning in the United States. It is hoped that the information and analysis provided in this book regarding the pension developments in a number of other foreign countries will provide useful insights concerning alternative pension mechanisms which might be used in responding to the challenge of providing adequate income in the retirement years.

Chapter 2

DYNAMIC PENSION SYSTEMS

IN recent years there have been numerous calls for research to evaluate and build upon the social security experiences of various foreign countries in the old-age income maintenance area. As early as 1963, Margaret Gordon wrote that "a promising method of inquiry that has been almost totally neglected is comparative analysis of the impact of various types of welfare programs, including old-age insurance programs, on the economy in various countries."

More recently, the Social Security Advisory Committee on Research commented as follows:

> A good deal of light could be shed on the issues involved through analysis of the rather wide variety of relationships among income-maintenance systems that have been developed in other industrial countries. There, income-conditioned pensions and payments not related to income, such as universal old-age pensions and family allowances, exist in varying combinations with social insurance and public assistance systems . . .
> (U.S. Social Security Administration, 1968)

Finally, the stimulus for broadening the scope of the study reported in the present book, so as to cover more than one country was provided in part by two recent cross-national studies in the field of social gerontology. Ethel Shanas et al. in *Old People in Three Industrial Societies* (1968) and Havighurst et al. in *Adjustment to Retirement—A Cross-National Study* (1970) demonstrate through their findings the value and potentialities of policy studies using comparative analysis.

Concurrent with these calls for research and an increase in comparative research, another important development has occurred. As described in the previous chapter, there have been developed and implemented in a number of industrialized countries a variety of highly innovative social security systems. These new systems have been in large part motivated by dissatisfaction with the existing programs of old-age income maintenance in each country and have attempted to overcome many of the existing problems.

Given the continuing interest in the United States in evaluating and improving our own system, knowledge about the experiences other countries have had with different systems is a necessary part of the information required to formulate public policy in this area; most of the changes, for example, proposed for the United States system (e.g., a two-tiered system of benefits, automatic pension adjustment mechanisms, and higher earnings replacement) have already been implemented abroad.

There have been some articles and books in English on the social security systems of various countries. In general these studies have concentrated on describing the laws guiding past and present systems and highlighting the major historical developments and issues surrounding these evolving systems. There is little analysis in the English literature of the systems themselves or of their development. Nor do we know how these new systems are working—the extent to which they are meeting objectives, their effects on private pension systems, and the satisfaction or dissatisfaction with them.

Important exceptions to this lack of analysis of foreign systems are the works of Gordon, Aaron, Taira and Kilby, Kreps, Rimlinger, Heclo, and the several members of the research staff of the United States Social Security Administration. Gordon (1963) studied eighteen industrial countries and found a significant correlation between the date of establishment of an old-age pension program for a sizable segment of the population and the level of average benefits measured as a percentage of national per capita income. Aaron (1967) also studied industrialized countries and found age of programs a major factor determining the size and adequacy of social security outlays, and similar findings are reported by Taira and Kilby (1964) and Pryor (1968). Kreps (1968) makes international comparisons of labor force activity and variations in leisure-time patterns. A comparative analysis of the *historical* development of the social security systems in Germany, Russia, Great Britain, and the United States has been recently published by Rimlinger (1971); Heclo (1971) compares the political history of the social security programs in Great Britain and Sweden. Finally, there have been a number of important (but limited) studies by members of the Office of Research and Statistics of the Social Security Administration which have looked at particular aspects of a number of foreign pension systems (Horlick, 1970; Horlick and Lewis, 1970; Fisher, 1970; Horlick and Lucas, 1971; Horlick and Skolnik, 1971).

ECONOMIC PREPARATIONS FOR RETIREMENT— INDIVIDUAL OR COLLECTIVE?

In most countries with highly developed social security systems (including the United States), at least five broad concerns have dominated recent discussions with regard to developing satisfactory public systems of old-age income maintenance. First, there is the question of the appropriate public-private pension mix and the effect of developing public pension systems on personal and private institutional income-provision for old age. Second, there has been increasing interest in how to provide, for middle-income groups, public pension benefits which (with or without other income sources) would permit retired families to maintain a standard of living in old age similar to that achieved during the later years of the workers' earnings period. Third, there is the question of the desirability of automatic public pension adjustments and the search for suitable adjustment mechanisms. Fourth, there is the problem of how to ensure adequate incomes for the aged poor while maintaining the integrity of income-maintenance programs for all income groups (i.e., maintaining a program that is equitable, financially viable, and without major economic disincentives). Finally, there is the question of the best way to finance a public income-maintenance program for the aged. This book focuses primarily on the first three questions: the private/public pension mix, pension adequacy for middle-income groups, and dynamic adjustment mechanisms.

With regard to the question of pension adequacy, we noted in Chapter 1 that there has been a shift in thinking away from accepting as the sole role of public pensions the prevention of poverty by providing minimum levels of benefits—the so-called *floor of protection*. The assumption that individuals can effectively and efficiently handle the major part of their retirement-income planning is increasingly questioned and open to serious doubt, given historical experience and the nature of the problem. Even assuming a new individual awareness of the need for retirement preparation, a look at the uncertainties the individual has to deal with reveals the magnitude of the problem:[1]

1. He doesn't know with certainty his time of death (or the time of death of his spouse). Hence he must assume the worst and presumably save for age 100 (or more) or decide to go on public assistance (or perhaps seek help from relatives) at a certain age. Thus arises one reason for public and/or private retirement insurance. By pooling this risk, the cost of protection from uncertainty is decreased.

2. He doesn't know with certainty what his future income stream will be. He must protect himself from such hazards as ill health, cyclical economic fluctuations, and job obsolescence. Again, a case for public and/or private insurance arises (unemployment, disability, and medical insurance).

3. He doesn't know what his retirement needs will be. He cannot predict, for example, his state of health throughout the retirement period. Not only does his health have a direct influence on medical costs, but it also affects retirement mobility—influencing recreation and transportation expenditures.

4. He doesn't know when he will retire. Although the individual has some control over this, increasingly the decision is becoming institutionalized with (a) the growth of mandatory retirement rules, (b) the growth of early retirement options (often accompanied by management and/or union retirement pressures), and (c) the continued existence of age discrimination practices in hiring (see Schulz, 1971).

5. He cannot easily predict the future rate of inflation, which, if it occurs, will depreciate the value of those retirement assets that do not adjust fully for this happening and reduce the buying power of income from those assets. In addition, he cannot easily predict the rate of economic growth—which is likely to affect his economic position relative to the working population.

---

1. See chapter 4 in Pechman, et al. (1968) for an excellent discussion of this question.

As stated in Chapter 1, providing adequate funds for expenditures in the retirement period requires that individuals utilize one or a combination of two basic options: either they can save (individually or collectively) during the nonretirement years or they can become a part of an institutional arrangement that assures the required amount of retirement income transfer from the then working population. Of course, the present practice in the United States is a combination of these two basic alternatives. In either case, providing for retirement requires that disposable income in the working years be lower than it would be otherwise.

Required Rates of Saving to Provide Adequate Income

Assume that public and private pension systems did not exist and therefore that an individual must provide for his own retirement. What rate of saving would be necessary to provide adequate funds for the retirement period?

The amount of saving required to meet retirement needs is dependent upon the following major variables:

1. The standard of adequacy: the yearly amounts of "necessary" and "discretionary" retirement expenditures.

2. Price level changes.

3. Productivity increases.

4. The number of years in retirement (which is dependent on the age at retirement and also at death).

5. Earnings levels and years in the labor force.

6. The yield on savings.

The amount of financial resources needed in retirement depends upon the standard of adequacy used. While any of a large number of adequacy standards could be chosen, let us use the standard that is receiving increased acceptance by developed and relatively prosperous countries: relating retirement needs to the individual's preretirement standard of living. If the retired person's living standard is to be related in some way to a standard of living experienced before he retired, sources of retirement funds must enable him to replace a certain proportion of the income lost when works stops.

Having determined an appropriate rate of earnings replacement, the individual must also be concerned about the possible deterioration of his economic situation during retirement. Any inflation which occurs after the individual stops working will result in a deterioration of buying power for retirement savings unless these savings are held in a form that appreciates at the same rate. Given existing financial institution arrangements, however, individuals often will not hold funds in the form of such adjusting securities; this results from the lack of such asset forms that are both available and appealing to the financially unsophisticated investors.

The practical implication of such an institutional situation is that most individuals must save more during their working years to ensure that sufficient funds will be available in retirement to maintain their desired living standard in the face of anticipated increases in the price level.

In addition to the problem of inflation, still another important economic consideration arises. Ida Merriam and many others have pointed this out in discussing the adequacy of pension system benefits: "the difficult question posed by technological change and rising national income is not that of determining the benefit amounts of different individuals at the time they retire, but rather that of reaching a consensus as to what happens to their benefits over the subsequent 10, 15, or 20 years" (Merriam, 1966).

When an economy is growing, a gradual worsening of the aged person's relative economic position to that of the wage earner occurs under any income-maintenance scheme that does not adjust the level of retirement payments as general economic growth occurs in the economy. For example, the higher the annual rate of growth, the more rapidly real earnings tend to rise, hence the faster the decline in fixed incomes relative to average earnings.

Thus the two effects—inflation and productivity increases—must be kept in mind if economic arrangements for retirement are to provide the aged with resources that will permit them to maintain living standards into and during retirement.

Let us suppose, for example, that an individual wishes to have sufficient funds in retirement to permit expenditures throughout retirement at a rate equal to a certain percentage of the average of earnings he received during the last five years prior to retirement.

In addition let us assume that in line with the above discussion the individual wishes to take into account not only prices but also productivity adjustments in his planning. What rate of saving (i.e., what percentage of earnings before taxes) must the individual maintain over his working lifetime to achieve the desired level of retirement economic security?

We have listed above the key factors determining the answer to this question. In order to provide a determinate answer, let us assume that the individual lives the average life expectancy of a person reaching age 65.[2] Of course, as indicated above, for an individual himself to make such an assumption, he must be resigned to calling upon relatives or friends for substantial financial help if he lives long or, alternatively, must be resigned to relying on public charity (with the stigma and level of living so provided).

The rate of required saving, of course, will vary with changes in the level of retirement living specified and with the following other special variables:

1. The replacement rate
2. The number of working years
3. The number of years of preretirement earnings averaged
4. Price and/or productivity adjustments

With regard to the first variable, it is generally agreed that expenses in retirement will be somewhat lower than before retirement, hence that 100 percent earnings replacement is not necessary. To equate living standards in retirement with the standard in the middle years therefore requires a rate of earnings replacement less than 100 percent. Various estimates of the difference have been made by different researchers and are discussed below.

Table 8 gives sixty-four required savings rates for a worker aged 65 retiring at the end of 1969 after 40 years of work with final year earnings of $5980 (which approximates average earnings of United States private nonagricultural workers in that particular year).[3] In

---

2. In the analysis that follows, no account is taken of the possibilities that the worker may be married and that the spouse may live longer.

3. The economic model and assumptions used to calculate the required savings rates are described in Schulz and Carrin (1972).

TABLE 8

Required Savings Rates
(percentages)

Adjustment Assumption	No Adjustment				Price Adjustment Only				Productivity Adjustment Only				Both Price and Productivity Adjustment			
Measure of preretirement earnings	Replacement Rate															
	1	.8	.65	.5	1	.8	.65	.5	1	.8	.65	.5	1	.8	.65	.5
Average lifetime earnings of the worker	18.3	14.7	11.9	9.1	19.4	15	12.6	9.7	19.6	15.6	12.7	9.8	22.1	17.6	14.3	11.0
Average income of the last 10 working years	27.6	22.1	17.9	13.8	29.2	23	19.0	14.6	29.5	23.6	19.2	14.7	33.3	26.6	21.6	16.6
Average of the last 5 working years	29.8	23.8	19.4	14.9	31.5	25.2	20.5	15.7	31.8	25.4	20.7	15.9	35.9	28.7	23.3	17.9
Last working year's income	31.7	25.4	20.6	15.8	33.5	26	21.8	16.7	33.8	27.1	22.0	16.9	38.1	30.5	24.8	19.0

Source: Schulz and Carrin (1972).

calculating these savings rates various combinations of assumptions were used. First, four different earnings replacement rates are used: 100, 80, 65, and 50 percent. Second, estimates are made using four different measures of the worker's preretirement standard of living:

1. An average of his *lifetime* earnings
2. An average of the *last ten years* of earnings
3. An average of the *last five years* of earnings
4. The *last year* of earnings

Finally, four different assumptions with respect to price and productivity adjustments during retirement are introduced:

1. No adjustment for price and productivity changes
2. Adjustment for price only
3. Adjustment for productivity only
4. Adjustment for both price and productivity changes

The range of "required" savings rates varies from a low of 9.1 percent to 38.1 percent. *This wide range clearly indicates that what general standard of living is decided upon by the individual or society can make a significant difference in the magnitude of the task in preparing financially for retirement.* Moving from 50 percent replacement to 100 percent replacement, for example, requires that the lifetime savings rate also be doubled.

From all of the various savings rates presented in Table 8, we can identify a few of particular interest. These are presented in Table 9. The first pair of rates are the rates required if one wished to maintain in retirement a living standard equivalent to that experienced during the middle years of life. In a sense, this measure can be viewed as the individual's average standard of living with lower levels being experienced during the early years of work and higher levels in the later years. This standard "rests on an assumption that most individuals will have as great a desire for better living standards in their family years as they will during their retirement. Thus, it is considered undesirable to require employees to set aside substantial amounts of their earnings in earlier years to finance higher standards of living in their old age" (Bok, 1967).

According to the equivalent income scale developed by the

TABLE 9

Required Savings Rates

Alternative Living Standard Measures	Rates	
	No Adjustment	Price and Productivity Adjustments
(I) Same as the middle years of average lifetime earnings	9.1%	11.0
(II) AAUP standard	15.8	19.0
(III) Same as just before retirement or highest earnings	19.4	23.3

United States Bureau of Labor Statistics (1968) for families of different size and age (on the basis of the relation between food expenditures and income), an elderly couple generally requires 51 percent as much income for goods and services as a husband-wife family living on the same standard (head aged 35–54 and two children 6–15 years old). The first pair of rates (9.1, 11.0) in Table 9, therefore, are based on 50 percent replacement and average lifetime earnings.

An alternative standard upon which to base retirement needs has been adopted by the American Association of University Professors. The Association voted in 1969 to recommend "that a person's benefits [be] equivalent in purchasing power to approximately two thirds of the yearly *disposable* income realized from his salary after taxes and other mandatory deductions during the last few years of full-time employment" (AAUP, 1969, emphasis added). The effect of this formulation of a retirement standard is to base replacement on the final years of work instead of the middle years, with about the same rate of replacement (i.e., 50 percent).[4] The result is a retirement living standard that more closely approximates accustomed living standards in the later years (than does Standard I) but still results in a decrease in living standard compared to the

---

4. If one translates the disposable income into income before taxes (as is the case with our calculations), two thirds is roughly equivalent to 50 percent of "before tax income," given present tax levels.

years just prior to retirement. Using this second standard, the required savings rates would be 15.8 and 19.0 percent.

Whereas the Bureau of Labor Statistics equivalence scales show a difference of nearly 50 percent in expenditure needs when comparing a middle-aged four-person family with an aged couple, the difference between childless couples aged 55–64 and couples aged 65 or more is much less: only a 13.5 percent difference in goods and services needs.

We can use these estimated differences to help establish another retirement living standard—the one referred to frequently above. This standard would *maintain the same living standard in retirement as existed just prior to retirement.* To estimate the required savings rate, one can use the same earnings base as was used for the AAUP standard (last five years), or alternatively the last-year measure can be used. To maintain the same living standard, however, the 50 percent replacement rate used in the AAUP standard is too low. In addition to the 13.5 percent expenditure difference, one must also take into account the reduced income-tax burden in retirement due to the current federal income tax law's special provisions for persons aged 65 and over. Also, presumably the individual upon reaching retirement can discontinue saving for retirement, an obligation that reduces his disposable income in the working years. Taking all three factors into account, the appropriate replacement is 60–65 percent.[5] Table 9, therefore, shows the required savings rate (using 65 percent replacement) to be about 19 and 23 percent respectively.

As indicated in Chapter 1, a variant of this standard is currently used as a basis for the social security system in West Germany. The goal there is to allow the retired individual a living standard roughly equivalent to that which is being enjoyed by a current worker of equivalent status. A German worker who on average had received earnings that were, say, 1½ times mean national earnings would receive a pension at retirement that was 1½ times the earnings of a current worker whose earnings were 1½ times average national earnings—reduced by a formula percentage reflecting (a) reduced expenditure needs in retirement and (b) the number of years worked.

---

5. This figure is based on a 12–14 percent expenditure reduction, a 19–21 percent reduction when saving is discontinued, and a 4–6 percent tax saving.

Given the fact that earnings over one's work life tend to increase for many workers at a rate greater than national mean earnings, the resulting German pension (hence the required savings rates) would usually be lower than a pension based on earnings just prior to retirement.

The savings rates calculated for the various standards described above assume a constant rate of saving over all the working years. An individual might desire, however, to save at a lower rate in the earlier years when earnings are relatively low compared to anticipated earnings later in his career.[6] In such cases disposable income in the years prior to retirement (5 and 10 years in the calculations made) would be lower than in the constant-savings rate cases. Consequently, the amount of funds, hence the savings rate, required to maintain a similar standard of living in retirement would be lower.

In addition, the question of child-rearing expenses arises. A family with children has a lower standard of living than a family without children but with a similar income. Once a couple's children are self-supporting, the couple's standard of living may rise as a result of reduced expenditures of this sort.[7]

Introduction of Social Security and Private Pensions

The analysis of the preceding section assumed that the individual saved for retirement without the help of either public or private pension plans. We know, however, that public and private pension plans exist and are growing; we have evidence, also, that

---

6. For example, Goldstein's (1965) analysis of data from the Bureau of Labor Statistics "Survey of Consumer Expenditures—1960" shows that average savings rates (as measured by net changes in assets and liabilities) were negative or very low for households with the head less than age 45. The data indicated that the rate of savings rises with age, reaching a peak for the 55–64 age group. Also, Thurow's (1969) analysis of the same data indicates a desire by families to substantially redistribute lifetime income toward the younger and very late years "by borrowing from the years between 35 and 75."

7. Whether this occurs in part depends on whether the family has incurred previous debts arising, for example, from educational or unusual medical expenses. Paying off these debts might prevent any significant increase in living standards in the preretirement years.

these plans influence the saving decisions of individuals.[8] Thus, in the case of public pensions, the magnitude of the individual's job in preparing for retirement by saving is partly reduced because of benefits rights acquired through his payments to the social security system.

Another set of required savings rates can be computed which takes into account social security old-age pensions. In the past few years United States social security pensions have been increased a great deal, the biggest increase occurring in 1972. Table 10 con-

TABLE 10

Alternative Required Savings Rates

Living standard measure	Without Social Security		With Social Security			
			1969 FORMULA		1972 FORMULA	
	No Adjustment	*Price Adjustment*	*No Adjustment*	*Price Adjustment*	*No Adjustment*	*Price Adjustment*
Same as the middle years (of average lifetime earnings)	9.1%	9.7	.4	.4	−5.1	−5.0
AAUP standard	15.8	16.7	7.2	7.6	1.7	1.8
Same as just before retirement (or highest earnings)	19.4	20.5	10.7	11.3	5.2	5.5

trasts the required savings rates for three cases: the rates required without social security, required rates given social security pensions based on the 1969 formula, and, finally, the rate of saving required as a result of pensions based on the 1972 social security formula.

---

8. Katona (1965) finds pension coverage associated with *higher* discretionary saving in a 1962–63 national survey. Because there is no national sample, less reliable but supportive evidence is given by Phillip Cagan (1965).

Table 10 shows the very large drop in required savings rates as a result of introducing and improving public pensions.[9]

At the time that the hypothetical worker retired in 1969, social security benefits were nearly sufficient to meet the middle-years retirement standard without supplemental savings effort. To reach the other two standards, however, the worker had to do considerable saving—between 7 and 8 percent per year.

The required savings rates presented above help explain why the recent generations of older Americans have found themselves in a relatively poor economic condition. Average personal savings rates in the United States have remained relatively constant over the years and have not equaled by far the rates required to provide adequate funds in retirement (see Table 8). Moreover, average rates of saving are an aggregation of the differing rates for many individuals, most of whom saved at rates below the average.[10] The introduction of social security in the late thirties provided the aged with benefits which at best satisfied only a very minimal standard of adequacy. Again, personal savings rates were below the rates required to provide sufficient supplementation to raise the retirement funds to a higher and more acceptable standard of adequacy. Moreover, the introduction of private pension plans, which grew significantly in the 1940's and 50's, did not have a significant impact on these aged, most of whom retired without such coverage.

The situation for many of the current elderly, especially those retiring in recent (and future) years, is much brighter. Table 10 indicates that with the increases in social security benefits occurring between 1969 and 1972, the middle-years standard actually requires negative saving and the AAUP standard requires very little supplementary effort. Only a goal of maintaining living standards into

9. Table 3 also shows the difference between existing social security benefit costs expressed as a percentage of total (not taxable) payroll and the calculated total percentage of payroll costs for benefits using an alternative standard.

10. The "1963 Survey of the Aged," for example, found 29 percent of aged couples and about 53 percent of unmarried aged with total net worth of less than $5000. Married couples with net worth less home equity of less than $1000 were 37 percent of all couples; for unmarrieds it was 52 percent. Five years later the "1968 Survey of the Aged" found 43 percent of couples with net worth minus home equity of less than $1000 and 61 percent for unmarrieds. (Murray, 1972.)

retirement requires a significant personal savings effort of about 5–6 percent.

Moreover, the phenomenal growth of private pension plans which we have witnessed since the late 1940's is beginning to have a significant impact. Even more important is the fact that private-pension eligibility requirements and benefit levels have continued to undergo significant liberalization.

What is the impact of this private pension growth on the adequacy of aged retirement income? For many workers who are covered and who are able to meet the various eligibility requirements, private pensions result in significant improvement of retirement income. Table 11 shows, for example, two different income

TABLE 11

Total Money Income of OASDHI Married Couple Beneficiaries, by Type of Pension Benefit Received and Income Group, 1967 (percentages)

Income	OASDHI Only	OASDHI and Public[a]	Private
$ 2000 or less	29	5	2
2000 to 2999	27	14	17
3000 to 4999	26	49	48
5000 to 9999	14	27	27
10,000 or more	3	6	5
Total	100	100	100

[a] Railroad retirement or a staff retirement system for federal, state, or local government employees.
Source: Bixby (1970), table 10 (adapted).

distribution, one for 1967 social security recipients *also receiving a private pension* and one for those *receiving no private pension*. The difference is dramatic.[11]

11. Although the differences in incomes of the groups is explained in large part by the differences in pension coverage, it has also been shown that most private pensioners have higher preretirement earnings than workers receiving only social security. "Retirees with private pensions tended, therefore, to be concentrated at higher social security benefit levels and [were] more likely to have personal savings" (Bixby and Reno, 1971).

In testimony before the United States Senate Special Committee on Aging, Edwin Shields Hewitt recently argued that "if the historical pattern of 'follow the leader' in pension matters continues, we can expect many more plans to be generating income that will supplement social security at 70 percent [replacement] levels within the next few years . . ." (United States Senate Special Committee on Aging, 1970). For example, the 1970 plans of one pension leader, the auto industry, provided long-term retiring workers with income from their private pension together with social security sufficient to replace about 70 percent of disposable earnings for an unmarried worker and 77 percent for married workers.[12] The results of a study (Kolodrubetz 1972) by the Social Security Administration of the pension plans of 30 well-known companies also indicate the high income replacement rates possible in the future under certain plans already existing.

The day is here (or not far away) for many Americans when financial planning for retirement will no longer be a major problem. Social security together with private pensions will reduce dramatically or eliminate for many Americans the need to save individually for their retirement. We are developing in our country a "pension elite" for whom a major problem of old age will be solved. For them income under normal circumstances will be adequate.

But at the same time the evidence indicates that for many years to come the majority of workers will *not* be among that pension elite. Currently less than half of private industry workers are covered by a private pension plan. Of those covered, many are employed not by the pension leaders but by the followers; thousands of workers at one time covered by pension plans in these companies never qualify for benefits because of a failure to meet stringent eligibility requirements (often due to no fault of their own).

How long it will take the thousands of smaller companies and less enlightened companies with pension plans to solve the retirement-income problem is not known. Moreover, whether it is possible (and desirable from an economic standpoint) to cover workers

---

12. The calculation is for workers earning $4.00 hourly at the time of retirement and relates to that pay rather than to a final average pay during the last five or ten years.

currently not covered by private pension plans is not clear at this time.

On this issue (as well as others enumerated above) there was extensive discussion in various countries abroad as these countries sought to develop aged income-maintenance policies and programs. The United States would be able to learn a great deal from the discussions and experience of these countries if more information were available. And certainly the United States should be constantly evaluating the appropriateness of promising reforms abroad for improving its own programs in this area.

COMPARATIVE ANALYSIS OF SOCIAL SECURITY SYSTEMS

The private and public institutions created to assist and in some cases to force changes in the individual's economic pattern of retirement preparation (Musgrave, 1968) continue to develop. And with the development of these pension institutions and mechanisms has come a new conception of what "adequate pension" should be. Many countries now have public pension systems which not only relate pension benefits to prior earnings but seek to guarantee through these public and private benefits a relatively high level of earnings replacement at retirement. As we have indicated, the trend seems to be toward developing public (and also private) pension systems which will be adequate enough to permit the retired population to at least maintain a level of living which approximates that which they enjoyed during their working years.

As indicated in Chapter 1, social security programs and policies in the United States currently do not achieve this objective. Nor have past discussions and debates about future benefit increases explicitly dealt with the role of earnings replacement in determining the appropriate pension formulas. Thus the 1971 Advisory Council on Social Security observed and recommended:

> While past and proposed legislative actions have approximately achieved the goal of maintenance of purchasing power, the replacement rates have shifted over time and between different levels of average wages. There has been insufficient analyses of public discussion of the role of replacement rate in prescribing the benefit formulas. If policy were formulated in relation to replacement rates, the method of calculating the rate should

be stated precisely. A replacement rate derived from the relationship between the benefit and the average wage over the entire period of an individual's participation in the labor market will differ markedly from a ratio of the benefit to his average wage in the 5 year period immediately preceding retirement. Careful study and serious consideration should be given before establishing a specific policy about replacement rates. However, the policy should be explicit and not implicit as is inherent in the use of the level wage assumption.

(U.S. Social Security Administration, 1971)

The present book reports on a project designed to study this question and to make an in-depth collection and analysis of information concerning retirement-income maintenance programs in four countries—Sweden, West Germany, Belgium, and Canada. The aim was to pose a common set of questions regarding the development of pension programs in these countries and to use a common analytical framework for collecting relevant information needed to answer the questions.

Almost all countries in Western Europe during the past two decades have adopted (or are considering adoption of) major social security reforms. Three countries led the recent wave of reform: Belgium in 1955/1957, West Germany in 1957, and Sweden in 1959. Since these systems have now been in operation for over a decade, it would be valuable to look at how the systems have developed during this period, what transition problems were encountered, whether they are operating as expected, and what effect they have had on the development of alternative income-maintenance mechanisms (insurance, private industrial/occupational pension plans, etc.). For each country the project sought to survey already existing literature and analyses of the operation of these systems and to synthesize their findings. In addition, supplementary evaluations of systems operations were obtained through the interviewing of informed persons in the various countries.

In Sweden and Germany the principal aim of the reform "can best be described as an aim of providing a standard of old-age security for all citizens commensurate with the standard of living which they attained in their mature years of active work" (Uhr, 1966). Also, in both countries pensions dynamically adjust to changes in the economy before and after retirement. For example, "the core of the German pension reform lies in the adiustment of pensions in force to wage-level changes" (Fisher, 1966). It is these two major innovations, maintaining living standards into retirement and dynamic adjustment of pensions at and during retirement, which were given special attention in evaluating the two systems.

In addition to Sweden and Germany, two other countries, Belgium and Canada, were studied. Together with Sweden and Germany, Belgium was one of the first countries to introduce innovative earnings-related pensions; Canada introduced major pension reform more recently and attempted to blend the approaches embodied in the earlier reform efforts of other countries.

Although valuable insights into the various proposed changes in the United States social security system can be obtained by reporting on the development and operation of systems in other countries, we also seek to examine the economic implications in the United States of adopting reforms similar to those in other countries. Simulation analysis is utilized for this purpose.

Two simulation models were developed. The first was a relatively simple model which estimates the earnings replacement rates for hypothetical workers under various pension programs. The other model is much more complex and enables us to study the income-distribution effects of alternate pension reforms on an actual sample of the United States population.

Using the latter model, which simulates the retirement process in the United States, the pension programs existing in Germany and Sweden were programmed for computer analysis. Estimates are made of pension-income distributions, earnings-replacement rates, and program costs. In addition, comparisons are made of the projected results using the proposed alternative adjustment mechanisms and projections based upon the present United States social security system. The results of the simulations using the two different models—together with the country studies—permit a comprehensive evaluation of the various foreign pension programs.

A GENERAL FRAMEWORK FOR ANALYZING PENSION SYSTEMS

In order to present a more meaningful analysis of the old-age pension systems currently existing in the various countries studied, a common framework was developed for describing and evaluating each system. This framework evolves around four major questions that can be asked about any pension system which relates benefits to earnings and which seeks to maintain living standards in retirement, to a greater or lesser degree.[13] These four questions, discussed in detail below, are:

1. The adequacy philosophy: what preretirement standard of living is used and how is it measured?

2. To what extent and how are pension rights adjusted *at* the time of initial *retirement* for changes during the individual's working lifetime in prices and general economic growth?

3. What replacement rate is embodied in the pension formula?

4. To what extent and how are pension benefits adjusted *during* retirement for changes in prices and general economic growth?

The Preretirement Standard

It is common to judge the adequacy of income by relating it to some minimum level of living as embodied in legislated welfare support levels, a poverty index, or family-budget cost estimates. These types of adequacy measures might be labeled "absolute" measures, although they are subject to manipulation upward or downward. One characteristic of all these measures which creates problems in measuring the adequacy of retirement income is that they are designed to be poverty or low-income measures and operationally must set up a number of discrete levels (often small in numbers). As a consequence, these measures reflect very poorly the wide divergence of economic circumstances (i.e., income levels) that characterize the poor and low-income persons prior to retirement and do not deal at all with the question of income adequacy for those above low-income levels. For example, the United States Social Security Administration's poverty index has separate poverty indexes for the farm and nonfarm population and further subdivides by age and sex for unrelated individuals and, for families, by sex of

13. A major question not included among the four is the issue of the appropriate private/public pension mix. Although this was not a major question investigated in the various countries, information regarding the different attitudes in the countries was collected and is presented in the country-study chapters.

head, total number of members, and number of related children under 18 (Orshansky, 1965).

There has been increased interest in judging the adequacy of retirement income by "relative" measures which take into account the many different levels of living of families with incomes above various absolute measures of adequacy.[14] Such a measure of adequacy which takes into account the wide range of individual circumstances is the ratio of retirement income to preretirement income for incomes above the minimum specified by one of the absolute measures. Presumably post- and preretirement income should include all income—from financial assets, rent, etc.[15] Moreover, some economists have argued that the potential to draw down assets should also be estimated and included in the measure (Wisbrod and Hansen, 1968).

Existing pension systems which embody a relative-adequacy standard are not designed to relate total income before and after retirement but rather to relate only income from *earnings* before retirement to *pension* after retirement.[16] This alternative measure is used primarily because of the administrative difficulties of operationalizing the other measure, because of a wide variety of philosophical arguments related to the role of pensions, and most importantly because the financing of pensions has traditionally been based on earnings rather than total income.

Having accepted the concept of measuring pension adequacy by the ratio of pension income to preretirement earnings, there still remains the question of what measure of preretirement earnings is to be used. Expressed another way, if one wishes to construct a pension system that will permit families to maintain their preretirement living standard when they stop working, what period before retirement should be used as the standard—given that the standard of

---

14. One of the earliest and best discussions of relative-income adequacy which has appeared in recent years is Epstein (undated). See also Merriam (1969), pp. 61–65.

15. See, for example, the discussion in Morgan, et al. (1962).

16. Some pension systems, for example in Sweden and Germany, pay benefits at a designated age regardless of the work status of the recipient. In these cases, pension income is related through the mechanisms of the system to earnings prior to the designated age.

living for most individuals changes throughout life? For example, should the pension seek to maintain the most recent standard, the highest standard, the average lifetime standard, or what? In practice, we find all three of these standards used by various pension systems in various countries (see Table 12). Typically, these three

TABLE 12

Measures of Preretirement Earnings for Old Age
Pension Programs in Selected Countries, 1971

"Last Years" Measure

Austria	Last 5 years (or earnings when age 45–50) [a]
Czechoslovakia	Last 5 or 10 years (plus 1% of yearly earnings between ages 26–35)
France	Last 10 years[a]
Hungary	Last 5 years
Poland	Final year (or highest 2 of last 10)
USSR	Final year (or best 5 of last 10)

"Best Years" Measure

Italy	Best 3 of last 5 (in 1976: best 3 of last 10)
Poland	Best 2 of last 10 (or final year)
Sweden	Best 15 years
USSR	Best 5 of last 10 (or final year)
Yugoslavia	Best consecutive 5 of last 10 [a]

"Lifetime Earnings" Measure

Belgium	Average lifetime earnings[a]
Canada	Average lifetime earnings[a]
Federal Republic of Germany	Average ratio of earnings to national average earnings over lifetime[a]
Norway	Average lifetime earnings[a]
Switzerland	Average lifetime earnings
United Kingdom	Average lifetime earnings
United States	Average lifetime earnings (after 1950) minus lowest 5 years

[a] Revalued by an earnings index or some other sort of economic growth adjustment.

preretirement standards have been operationalized in pension systems as follows:

1. By taking an average of the "last *a* years" of earnings, where *a* is a small number, or

2. By taking an average of a specified number of years of "best earnings," or

3. By taking an average of "lifetime earnings" or all earnings after a specified year.

Looking at the first method (the "last years" measure), we can be certain that it reflects by definition the earnings levels and, in most cases, the living standards of persons *just prior* to retirement (i.e., his "most recent" standard)—as long as the number of years measured is small.

For persons whose lifetime-earnings pattern is such that his earnings generally increased over the entire worklife, this measure will also reflect a person's "best earnings." But this is not necessarily true for all workers. There are some workers (especially workers outside the professions and government employment) whose earnings reach a peak many years prior to retirement. The "last years" standard is not, for these workers, equivalent to a "best years" standard. A simple example can illustrate this problem.[17]

Assume that pensions are paid equal to 60 percent of earnings after a certain coverage period and eligibility age are satisfied. Table 13 gives three hypothetical earnings histories and the pension which would be paid using in the one case "average lifetime earnings" and in the other case "final earnings." In all three cases, the pensions are the same if lifetime earnings are used but differ considerably when the final earnings are used.

Some pension systems, in order to avoid this variation in treatment among various earners which results from the "last years" measure, use the average of a worker's "best earnings" for a given period as the measure of his preretirement standard. This measure avoids basing pensions on different standards resulting from different wage patterns or from periods of unemployment or illness. Pensions are based on the highest achieved wages, regardless of when they occurred in the life span.

A problem of a different nature arises, however, with this meas-

---

17. This example is similar to one presented by Detlev Zöllner (1970).

TABLE 13

Hypothetical Pensions Based on
Different Earnings Patterns

Earnings Period	Earnings		
	Worker A	Worker B	Worker C
Period I	100	80	80
Period II	100	120	90
Period III	100	120	110
Period IV	100	80	120
Average lifetime earnings	100	100	100
Pension based on average earnings	60	60	60
Pension based on final earnings	60	48	72

ure. If the number of years of best earnings is small, there is an incentive for workers to plan their workload so that their income is "extra large" in the years to be counted for pension purposes (or enter into formal or informal agreements with employers). Although this opportunity may not be open to all workers, it seems wise to discourage such practices by making fairly large the number of years of best earnings which are averaged. Thus in Sweden, for example, the best fifteen years are averaged.

The larger the number of "best years" averaged, the more the averaged earnings will differ from the "last years" earnings (i.e., most recent earnings). For workers whose earnings are highest just before retirement, this will cause a decline in their living standard from the highest standard they experienced; for workers with peak earnings before the final years, a reduction from the highest living standard (but not necessarily the most recent standard) will result. Of course, it is possible to compensate fully or partially for such reductions by adjusting the pension benefit formula upward by an appropriate amount or by adjusting the best earnings used by an index that takes account of price and economic growth.

The "lifetime earnings" measure avoids basing pensions on atypical years but tends to generate pension benefits that are well below the most recent and/or the best preretirement living standard.

This is most obvious in the case where lifetime earnings are not even adjusted for price changes occurring during the period between the particular year of work and the year of retirement. If each year's earnings are adjusted by a price index, the resulting measure generates a pension that is related to a real standard of living which is an average of the real standards throughout the working period.[18] These lifetime earnings, however, can be adjusted by some sort of growth or productivity index (in addition to a price adjustment) to reduce the discrepancy between pensions based on the "lifetime earnings" measure and the "last" and "best" measures.

Index Adjustments of Pension Rights at Retirement

Repeated reference is made in the preceding section to the possibility of adjusting pension claims for price changes and economic growth. The question of adjustment *at* retirement is discussed in this section, while the question of adjustment *during* retirement is treated in a later section, given the difference in considerations with regard to each.

The question of adjustment arises as a result of the fact that earnings used as a measure of a prior living standard become, in an important sense, distorted as a result of subsequent price level changes and general economic growth. As indicated in the previous section, the "last years" measure automatically avoids this problem by basing pensions on earnings which are, in part, a resultant of the previous growth and price experience. Of course, workers with peak earnings prior to the later years get pensions based on nonpeak earnings which have been adjusted for the two factors.

Pensions based on the other two measures, "best years" and "average lifetime," will result in living standards below prior living standards unless adjustments are made. If, for example, a "best fifteen years" measure is used and these best earnings are adjusted only for price changes (as is done in Sweden), the resulting pension

18. There is another factor operating here. The concept of a living standard is ambiguous. How does one account for the changing expenditure needs over the life span? When a couple, for example, has children to house, clothe, feed, educate, etc., it is difficult to argue that their living standard will or should be the same at a later period when the children are gone, even if their real income is the same in both periods.

will be reflective of the living standard that occurred 7½ years before[19] (or more in cases where best earnings occur in earlier years). The effect is a decline, on retirement, in a worker's economic situation relative to the working population, regardless of his earnings pattern. In the special but common case of workers with regularly and constantly increasing earnings levels, their pensions result in living standards lower both in relation to their own recent level and in relation to workers in general.

Similar problems and questions of adjustment arise when lifetime earnings are used. But here the problem is much more serious because of the longer periods involved. If one adjusts lifetime earning only for price, one gets a pension in retirement which permits a living standard similar to those of middle-life—perhaps two decades earlier.

The Replacement Rate

In a prior section of this chapter we discussed the concept of earnings replacement as related to required savings rates. As we indicated above, the replacement rate embodied in a pension system can be based upon one or more of the following factors:

1. Reduced expenditure needs in retirement associated with any particular living standard.

2. The existence and role of other complementary pension systems—the private/public mix and the collective/individual provision mix.

3. Varying replacement by earnings levels in response to equity or social considerations.

With regard to the first factor, there has been little empirical research. As we indicated above, however, there is general agreement that expenses in retirement will be somewhat lower than before retirement; hence a replacement of 100 percent of earnings is not necessary. According to the scale developed by the United States Bureau of Labor Statistics (BLS) for families of different size and age (on the basis of the relation between food expenditures and income), for example, an elderly couple generally requires 51 percent

---

19. Assuming a regularly and constantly increasing earnings level until retirement.

as much income for goods and services as a couple (head aged 35–54) living at the same standard with two children of ages 6 and 15. However, as we indicated previously, the difference between couples without children aged 55–64 and aged 65 or more is more relevant. In this comparison, the BLS scale estimates only a 13.5 percent difference in goods and service needs. Based on BLS equivalency scales and various assumptions, we estimated above (page 41) that a two-thirds replacement was necessary to maintain living standards.

Using the same equivalency scales, 1972 federal OASDHI and income tax levels, and an estimate for state income taxes, Henle has made more detailed estimates (for five levels of preretirement income) of the proportion of preretirement income necessary to maintain living standards in retirement. "At the lower income levels, the calculations indicate that a replacement rate of about 80 percent would be necessary if the retiree were to maintain his preretirement command of goods and services. At higher income levels, this rate drops slightly to 70 percent" (Henle, 1972).

The BLS equivalency estimates upon which both estimates are based are themselves based on rather arbitrary assumptions; in addition, they do not take into account the whole range of expenditure activity. Unfortunately little if any other emperical research has been done on this question. Nevertheless the point remains that pension programs based on the earnings replacement concept must take the needs factor into account.

The second relevant factor is the role played by a particular system in the general income-maintenance plans of retirees. John McConnell has succinctly summarized the commonly voiced view as to the relative roles of public pensions, private pensions, and personal savings in the United States:

> When the Social Security Act was passed, the purpose of old-age insurance was said to be the provision of a floor of income support. It was expected that individual savings would supplement the basic OASDI benefit. Following the rapid expansion of private pension plans during and following World War II, it became quite common for both the proponents and opponents of old-age insurance to refer to the American system of income maintenance as a three-legged stool, or a three-layer cake, although the pitiful nature of the income received by most older people from all sources made the analogy of the

cake seem something of a mockery. It is quite clear that the spread of private pension plans has confused the role of OASDI and of private pensions and savings. There is a tendency to argue that OASDI should provide only minimum subsistence, and that private pensions will supply enough when added to OASDI to equal an adequate income. Private saving will assure a comfortable existence. (McConnell, 1968)

Thus in deciding on the appropriate replacement rate for, say, the social security system, allowance can be made, if desired, for an assumed role for private pension and/or personal savings. If such allowance is made, then the required replacement rate does not have to be as large as when social security is designated to carry out the entire replacement job.

Finally, the third factor arises from the question whether one particular replacement rate is appropriate for all earning levels. In cases, for example, where the social security system assumes part or all of the job of providing minimum income to the poor, the appropriate replacement level for persons with very low preretirement income will often be over 100 percent. Alternatively, a pension system may assume the ability to save increases at higher levels and therefore reduce replacement rates at high income levels or impose maximum benefit ceilings.

Pension Adjustment during Retirement

Adjustment of pensions during retirement for price changes is necessary if the standard of living achieved at the time of retirement is not to deteriorate during the ensuing years. A more debatable issue is whether pensions that are generally adequate at the time of retirement should be improved as a result of economic growth. On this question, the United States Senate Special Committee on Aging Task Force, for example, observed:

The income gap between the retired group and the working group will widen in a period of national economic growth. With more years spent in retirement, this gap becomes even more significant. The retirement life span for [U.S.] couples is now approximately two decades: a man with a wife several years younger who retires at age 65, must now count on providing for himself and his wife for 13 years followed by another 6 or 7 years for his widow. Over a period of this length, the consumption level enjoyed by younger workers would approximately double, assuming earnings rise at a rate of four percent annually . . .

(U.S. Senate Special Committee on Aging, 1969)

A pension system that adjusts for economic growth before retirement need not continue to do so during retirement; in fact, most systems do not.

TABLE 14

Adjustments Made to Pensions during Retirement Period
for Selected Countries, 1971

Automatic Price Adjustment Only[a]	Earnings Index[b]	No Automatic Adjustment
Belgium[c]	Austria (semiautomatic)	Czechoslovakia
Canada	Canada (beginning 1976)	Hungary
Denmark	Fed. Rep. of Germany	Ireland
Finland	(semiautomatic)	New Zealand
Israel	France	Poland
Italy	Netherlands	Switzerland
Sweden	Norway	United Kingdom
United States[d]		USSR
Yugoslavia		

[a] Most countries specify a minimum amount (2–4 percent) of inflation before adjustment is to be carried out.
[b] The nature of this adjustment varies considerably from country to country.
[c] New legislation was passed in 1973 which provided for an earnings-index adjustment for those retiring *after* 1973.
[d] New legislation was passed in 1972 which established automatic price adjustment of benefits beginning in 1974. Later legislation in 1973 revised the starting date to June 1975.
Source: United States Social Security Administration (1971).

Table 14 summarizes practices in twenty-three countries. Current social security systems adjust in three basic ways:

1. Automatic price and growth adjustments.

2. Ad hoc price and growth adjustments.

3. Automatic price adjustment with ad hoc growth adjustment.

While about two thirds of the countries automatically adjust pensions for increasing price levels, only about a quarter automatically adjust for growth.

Pechman, Aaron, and Taussig (1968) summarize the issues to be considered as follows:

> Automatic adjustment for changes in money wages implies a judgment that retired workers should share fully in the productivity increase occurring after they leave the labor force. However, it may be argued that the preretirement income of the beneficiary is more likely to determine his style of life, which is, perhaps, a more relevant standard for setting old-age pensions. Furthermore, the desirability of additional public expenditures on social security must be weighed against other public spending and against private spending by tax payers who would benefit from tax reductions (or smaller tax increases) . . .

In countries where it is generally recognized that pensions *at* retirement are in need of significant improvement, the improvement of pensions *during* retirement will probably seem of secondary importance when deciding on imposing additional financing costs on the working population.

TWO ADDITIONAL ISSUES

In addition to the four basic questions associated with the development of pension programs which are both adequate and equitable and discussed in the prior section, there are two broad, underlying issues that are usually central in the political discussions of pension-program development. These issues are, first, how to pay for the programs and, second, determining the ideal combination of private and government operated programs.

Financing Pensions

As for the first question regarding financing, it is not simply a matter of having to pay more to get more or, in other words, only getting what you or somebody else pays for, although this rather fundamental homily is constantly ignored by some elderly people and their advocates crassly looking for something for nothing. The issue of who pays is even more complicated. Almost all public-pension programs and many private ones involve a certain amount of intergeneration financing with one generation transferring income to another.[20] We find today, however, that the success of this pension-financing technique has been complicated by the relatively recent phenomena of "aging populations." In a small but growing group of countries the proportion of aged persons in the population has been increasing relatively rapidly and promises to continue increasing in the near future. Thus there are currently at least twenty countries (see Table 15) with 8 percent or more of their population over the

TABLE 15

The Proportion of Aged in Selected Countries, 1968–1970

Country	Data Base Year	Proportion of Total Population	
		Age 60 or More	Age 65 or More
Australia	1969	12%	8%
Austria	1969	23	16
Belgium	1968	18	13
Canada	1966	11	7
Denmark	1968	17	12
Finland	1968	13	8
France	1968	19	13
Fed. Rep. of Germany	1968	18	12
German Dem. Rep.	1969	22	15
Greece	1969	15	10
Italy	1968	15	10
Japan	1969	10	7
Netherlands	1969	14	10
Norway	1969	18	13
Portugal	1969	13	9
Spain	1960	12	8
Sweden	1969	19	13
Switzerland	1969	17	11
England/Wales	1970	18	13
Yugoslavia	1968	12	7
USA	1970	14	10
USSR	1969	11	7

Source: United Nations (1971).

---

20. Readers not familiar with the literature on this point should see Turnbull, et al. (1967), pp. 155–159, for a succinct discussion.

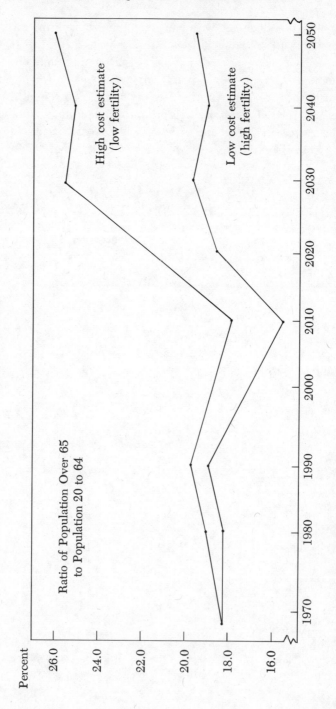

FIGURE V
Projected Cost Ratios

Source: United States Social Security Administration (1966b); also reproduced in Advisory Council on Social Security (1971).

age of 64 and about half of these countries with a percentage of aged greater than 12 percent.

The Long-term Problem. The nature of the long-run social security financing problem that is developing (and has already developed) in some countries—can be illustrated by the situation for the United States. Figure V shows the ratio of persons over age 65 to those age 20–64 as projected by the United States Social Security Administration (1966b). The ratio rises until about 1990, drops sharply to a low around the year 2010, and then rises dramatically over a twenty-year period to an historic high, as those born during the high birthrate years following the Second World War reach retirement age. Assuming low fertility rates, the projection indicates that as much as one quarter of the population over age 19 will be aged during the middle years of the twenty-first century (as compared with about 19 percent currently).[21]

But why should we worry about these high ratios that will occur so far in the future? One answer is that the recipients of those future benefits are just beginning their working career and have started to pay into the old-age security program. Their tax rates would be much lower if they did not have to pay for the aged who periodically receive improved old-age and medical compensation based on small amounts of prior contributions. For example, the chief actuary of the Social Security Administration from 1947 to 1970, Robert Myers, recently took the position that we should not increase old-age pension benefits without first carefully considering the long-term financing consequences:

> Over the long-range, the costs have been made to appear low by neglecting to take into account the current trend toward immediate-ZPG [zero population growth] and by assuming that the nation's productivity will continue to increase into the indefinite future at an annual rate of about 2% to 2¼%, as it did in the past, certainly far from a sure thing in light of the shift of public emphasis toward ecological goals rather than year-after-year production increases.
>
> Nevertheless the cost burden seems bound to rise on the working population. Under the deferred-ZPG assumptions used in the cost estimates of the Social Security Administration, the cost of the present level of Social Security benefits (kept up-to-

---

21. See also United States Bureau of the Census (1972c).

date with future changes in prices) will likely be as high as
about 15½% of taxable payroll in the decade of the 2010s. Under
immediate-ZPG conditions, this figure would rise to about 20%
of taxable payroll.

Assuming that we will very likely have immediate-ZPG conditions and that the country believes this to be desirable, it
seems essential that we should recognize its effect on the Social
Security program. If we do so, we should then be hesitant about
over-expanding the program at the present time, when it is in a
low-cost condition due to demographic elements that will most
certainly be different in the future. Not to consider this situation
will place an unduly heavy burden on our present younger
generation and on generations to come.   (Myers, 1972)

With the above considerations in mind, it is interesting to note
what happened when the very large increase in social security was
being considered in 1972. During the House debate on the proposed
increase, Congressman Byrnes stated:

Regarding the [proposed] new method of financing that has
produced the "windfall" that now is going to be used for the
20 percent benefit increase . . . not one word of testimony in
public or executive session has been received on this subject.
This fundamental change in the criteria by which the soundness of the Social Security trust fund has been measured for
one-third of a century is being adopted willy-nilly by the Congress without even a cursory review . . .   (Byrnes, 1972)

The lack of debate on financing that characterized the 1972
Congressional debates is somewhat atypical. Since the 1930's, there
has been frequent debate in the United States as to the intragenerational equity of both current private and public pension systems
(Projector, 1969). For example, the Nobel prize-winning economist
Paul Samuelson, representing the views of one group of economists,
argued in 1967 that because of *population* growth and continued
economic growth, windfall gains will continue for future generations:
"The beauty about social insurance is that it is actuarially unsound.
Everyone who reaches retirement age is given benefit privileges that
far exceed anything he has paid in. And exceed his payments by
more than ten times as much (or five times, counting in employer
payments)!" (Samuelson, 1967).

In contrast to the Samuelson view is one held by the noted

conservative economist Milton Friedman and a number of other economists:

> [Social security] combines a highly regressive tax with largely indiscriminate benefits and, on the average, probably redistributes income from lower to higher income persons . . .
>
> What . . . working people are now doing is paying taxes to finance payments to persons who are not working. The individual worker is in no sense building protection for himself and his family—as a person who contributes to a private vested pension system is building his own protection. Persons who are now receiving payments are receiving much more than the actuarial value of the taxes that were paid on their behalf. Young persons who are now paying social security taxes are being promised much less than the actuarial value that the taxes paid on their behalf could buy in private plans.
>
> (Cohen and Friedman, 1971)

The problem of intragenerational equity arises not only as a result of paying benefits to people who have a relatively few years of participation in the "pay-in" part of the system; it is created also by the numerous and frequent changes in pension formulas, benefit levels, benefit calculation procedures, and many other aspects of the pension system—changes which occur so frequently in almost all countries. All these changes make it difficult to analyze the relationship between the taxes paid and the benefits received by the current generation of retired people and make it almost impossible to make accurate predictions about future generations. Yet given the large number of social security systems in the world today whose benefits are fundamentally related to contributions (taxes) based upon earnings, it is mandatory that serious consideration and study be given to both *intra*generational and *inter*generational equity matters. With regard to intragenerational equity, a considerable body of literature has been developed and testifies to the complexity of the subject (Samuelson, 1958; Chen, 1967; Brittain, 1967; Campbell, 1969; Atkinson, 1970; Prest, 1970; Toldin, 1970).

Short-term Considerations. In addition to the question of equity among future generations of social security recipients, there is another reason for being concerned about present and future ratios of the older to younger population. There is the important question of equity between the current working population and the retired population. As the financing requirements of social security benefits increase, the equity aspects of financing by means of employer/employee contributions (i.e., the payroll tax) become more important. Higher contributions required in the future (as predicted, for example, by Myers) will add to the problems already of concern to many critics of the present financing mechanism:[22]

> The regressivity and other inequities of the payroll tax, rather than its stabilization and allocative-efficiency effects, are the grounds for considering it inferior to the personal income tax. The major differences that exist between the two taxes—the exemptions, the personal deductions, and the broader income concept under the personal income tax—argue in favor of the personal income tax rather than the payroll tax. The payroll tax bears too heavily on low-income persons and on those with heavy family responsibilities.   (Pechman, et al., 1968)

> The rise of the payroll tax has been a quiet drain on low- and middle-income Americans. For middle-income workers, payroll tax increases have more than offset the much vaunted reductions of personal income taxes of 1964, 1969, and 1971. Combined Social Security and individual income taxes for a family of four earning $10,000 in 1963 totaled 16.9 percent of their income. If the proposal to increase the Social Security tax rate to 12 percent is passed [enacted into law, Fall 1972], a similar family in 1973 will be paying 19.9 percent of income in taxes.

> For low-income workers earning $3,000, payroll tax increases have exceeded personal tax cuts. A worker with two or more dependents who is employed year round at the minimum wage is spared personal income tax because of his poverty, but he will pay $176 in payroll taxes himself in 1973 under present law; his employer also pays $176 . . .   (Aaron, et al., 1972)

Table 16 shows the payroll contribution amounts that result from the 1972 amendments to the United States Social Security Act and illustrate in more detail the problem discussed by Pechman, Aaron, and others. The tax burden would be distributed very differently if the present payroll tax method were abandoned or sup-

---

22. For additional criticism see Brittain (1972), Eckstein (1968), McClung (1969), Cruikshank (1970), Cohen (1972), and Atkinson (1972).

Past and Future Annual Social Security Contributions,[a]
by Earnings Class, 1972–2011 [b]

Earnings	1972	1973	1974–77	1978–80	1981–85	By 2011
$ 3000	$156	$176	$176	$182	$185	$219
4000	208	234	234	242	246	292
5000	260	293	293	303	308	365
6000	312	351	351	363	369	438
7500	390	439	439	454	461	548
8000	416	468	468	484	492	584
9000	468	527	527	545	554	657
10,000	468	585	585	605	615	730
11,000	468	632	644	666	677	803
12,000 and over	468	632	702	726	738	876

[a] Maximum contribution by worker, with employer paying a matching amount.
[b] Amounts shown here make no allowance for automatic increases in the taxable wage base due to future inflation, which the law now requires.
Source: Table in *U.S. News and World Report* (October 30, 1972), based on data from the United States Social Security Administration.

plemented by an alternative financing mechanism such as general revenue financing.

Although financing of social security is not a major focus of this book, it seems appropriate to make a number of general observations on the issue.[23] First, in trying to predict how soon and how great will be the economic burden of aging populations in various nations, we are faced with the difficulty that the key variables—fertility, pension levels, and the age of retirement—are in a state of flux and essentially unpredictable. This means that long-range planning becomes very difficult. However, at the same time, all these variables are subject to influence by national policy, and, therefore, the magnitude of future problems is subject to control—should a nation desire to do so.

Second, the increasing transfer costs of an aging population—

---

23. For a detailed discussion of the question see Brittain (1972).

together with rising social costs associated with urbanization and the economic production of a technologically oriented society—will make it increasingly difficult in the future to raise living standards during the working years in the highly developed nations of the world. In the United States, for example, the problems associated with or arising out of economic growth are creating a need for public expenditures which probably cannot be paid for out of the additional output or surplus of the economic growth itself (Schultze, 1971). Add to this the increased retirement needs of an aging population, and it is difficult to foresee how living standards in the middle years can continue to grow at past rates.

Third, the trend of a lengthening retirement period resulting from medical advances and, more importantly, from retiring at an earlier age needs to be watched closely. Serious thought should be given to reevaluating or, in many cases, establishing a national policy in this area. Perhaps the time has come when discussion of flexible retirement and job redesign can move from the academic and international organization arena to a meaningful dialogue including governments, labor organizations, and corporations.

Four, as the aging of a population develops, there will be a need for a greater awareness of the intra- and intergenerational equity considerations arising out of developing pension systems. As the national cost of income maintenance for the aged rises, greater attention to equity issues will be necessary in order (a) to maintain public confidence in and support for the systems and (b) to use with maximum effectiveness the retirement funds available.

Fifth, by briefly reviewing here some of the problems arising out of the changing demographic situation and the financing requirements of improved social security benefits, we do not mean to imply that major improvements in the adequacy of retirement income should be avoided or postponed. With the exception of Canada, all three of the other foreign countries studied in this book have aged populations which as a proportion of the total population are among the highest in the world. Despite this, they have been able financially to carry out the major pension reforms initiated, and to do this without major political problems or taxpayer rebellions. The actions of these countries indicate that much is possible if one is willing to pay the price. It is very important, nevertheless, to give consideration to the issues we have briefly raised in this section when considering major increases in pension expenditures.

The Mix of Public and Private Pensions

The second major issue that is almost always a part of the political debate over initiating and modifying pension programs is the appropriate mix of private and public provision. Despite the fact that the first pension plans were established about a century ago, there is still little agreement about the relative virtues of public versus private pensions and what the ideal mix of the two types should be.[24] There is great diversity in the mix of pensions existing in the various countries, with almost as many where public programs dominate as those relying primarily on private pensions.

This lack of agreement is different from the general consensus that has developed over time as to the need for some type of compulsory public pension or insurance arrangement to provide at least minimum economic security in retirement (and for other situations such as disability, illness, etc.). Although individual self-reliance and voluntary preparation for retirement—together with family interdependence—dominated the early discussions of old-age security provision, it is now generally accepted that this is not the appropriate cornerstone of an income maintenance policy for the aged. Instead, there is widespread support for relying on compulsory pensions.[25]

A number of prominent American economists have studied the rationale for compulsory pensions. In an excellent chapter on "Income Maintenance Policy," Kenneth Boulding concisely states the principal argument:

---

24. The first compulsory social insurance system was adopted by Austria in 1854. The German social security system (the first *comprehensive* plan) was instituted by Bismarck 1883–89. In the United States the American Express Company established a pension plan in 1875.

25. See Lubove (1968) for an extensive discussion of the debate over voluntarism versus compulsion which occurred prior to the passage of the initial social security legislation in the United States. See also Brown (1972) for a discussion of the proposed Clark Amendment to the original Social Security Act and why it was defeated. This amendment would have permitted approved company group annuity plans as substitutes for compulsory coverage under old-age insurance.

If everyone . . . were rationally motivated, [he] would be aware of the evils that might beset him, and would insure against them. It is argued, however, that many people are not so motivated, and that hardly anyone is completely motivated by these rational considerations, and that therefore under a purely voluntary system some will insure and some will not. This means, however, that those who do not insure will have to be supported anyway—perhaps at lower levels and in humiliating and respect-destroying ways—when they are in the non-productive phase of life, but that they will escape the burden of paying premiums when they are in the productive phase. In fairness to those who insure voluntarily, and in order to maintain the self-respect of those who would not otherwise insure, insurance should be compulsory.   (Boulding, 1958)

Richard Musgrave, writing on the role of social insurance, writes:

Insurance could be purchased privately, but becomes a matter of public concern only because [some] will not do so, while [others] will. Given their humanitarian premise, Calvin and Homer must bail out Jack should the contingency arise. They will require therefore that Jack should insure. Social insurance is now insurance in the technical sense, but its basic function (and especially the rationale for making it mandatory) is again to avoid burdening the prudent.   (Musgrave, 1968)

And finally, Pechman, Aaron, and Taussig in their book on social security, after an extensive discussion of the rationale for pensions, conclude that:

There is widespread myopia with respect to retirement needs. Empirical evidence shows that most people fail to save enough to prevent catastrophic drops in post retirement income . . . Not only do people fail to plan ahead carefully for retirement; even in the later years of their working life, many remain unaware of impending retirement needs . . . In an urban, industrial society, government intervention in the saving-consumption decision is needed to implement personal preferences over the life cycle. There is nothing inconsistent in the decision to undertake through the political process a course of action which would not be undertaken individually through the market place.
(Pechman et al., 1968)

Given widespread disagreement over the appropriate pension mix and the large number of political debates that have occurred in various countries on the question, one would expect to find a large professional literature devoted to this topic in various countries. Surprisingly, this is not the case. While there has been quite a lot of popular writing on the subject, and some writing on the question of compulsion (as cited above), very little has been written which attempts to approach objectively the question of the most desirable pension mix and accumulate data for evaluation purposes.

Information about and data on private pension plans in other countries are not readily available. For the project reported in this book, we tried to gather as much information as possible on private pension programs existing in the four countries. Our success, however, was mixed—ranging from nothing for Belgium to considerable information on schemes in Canada.

The next four chapters discuss the development of old-age pension programs in the Federal Republic of Germany, Sweden, Belgium, and Canada. The principal focus of each chapter is on the major pension reforms that have recently occurred in each country. The specific emphasis in each, however, is on the questions discussed above which relate to the adequacy philosophy, the replacement rate, and adjustments made at and during retirement. In addition, each country chapter attempts to summarize briefly the historical development of the pension program and the political events leading up to the pension-reform legislation. Finally, information on the financing of pensions and on the role of private pensions is presented to the extent that such information is available for each country.

Chapter 3

SWEDEN

SWEDEN has long had a reputation as a leader in the field of social welfare legislation. As Eli Heckscher (1963) has observed, in Sweden, "more than in most countries, social security has become an accepted institution." The Swedish citizen is currently covered by a broad range of programs which seek to provide protection from economic insecurity arising out of various social hazards, such as disability, death, old-age, unemployment, illness, and inadequate income.

Writing on the Swedes' conception and implementation of their welfare society, Ernst Michanek has observed:

> We have arrived at a gradually increased application of the principle of universality, i.e. that *all* persons should enjoy their share of a general welfare system . . . We laid a common foundation for the security of all citizens . . . The way we see it, our welfare policy has helped us create a democracy, in the true sense of the word. Everybody goes to the *same* public insurance society, be he a worker, a salaried employee, self-employed or a farmer . . . To draw on the services of the public employment service is becoming just as natural as opening the municipal water tap. For a long time it has been considered natural for all of us to enter the same public hospitals and to receive treatment from the best specialists available in these hospitals. (Michanek, 1964)

Sweden is Europe's third largest country, exceeded only by France and Spain, and is about the same size as the state of California. It has a population of about 8 million people and a private per-capita consumption level (in 1967) of $1666 (as compared to $2482 in the United States and $1095 in the United Kingdom). It is a constitutional monarchy with a Parliament that switched in 1971 from a bicameral assembly to one with only one chamber.

The rising economic prosperity in postwar Sweden did not dampen its enthusiasm for new and improved social programs. According to Michanek:

> All of us achieved a higher standard of living [after World War II]. Consequently we demanded that our social security system should ensure protection of our raised standards. Many of us already had higher pensions and higher income protection during illness, for instance, due to existing agreements. It became natural for everyone to claim protection for the standard of living he had achieved through his own work. We found it practical and natural that this individually adjusted protection should be organized for all by the community since it was our experience that this would ensure the most fair and efficient system. Furthermore, only a collective insurance, embracing the entire community, could afford to guarantee the constant value of social benefits, the need for which we had become familiar with during post-war inflation.

In response to this Swedish desire for greatly improved social protection, the Swedish Parliament has passed new social legislation in many areas during the last twenty years. One of the major areas of concern was the provision of adequate old-age income. In this area, the Parliament instituted in 1959 a major reform of the national old-age pension system. It is this highly innovative and comprehensive pension reform which will be the major focus of this chapter.

THE EARLY HISTORY OF SWEDISH PENSIONS

The first Swedish law to provide old-age pensions—the National Pension Act—was passed in 1913 and provided benefits for all persons over the age of 66. One part of this program was financed by individual contributions and was similar to a system of private insurance with "premium reserves." Benefits paid from this part of the system were related to contributions paid. A second part of the pension program, financed by taxation, provided a small "block" pension and a house or rental allowance; eligibility for this part of the program was determined by a needs test administered by the municipalities. There was also a national board to coordinate the program and oversee the operations of the local units.

The level of benefits paid out was wholly inadequate to meet the income needs of the aged: "many of the aged found it necessary to apply for welfare benefits to supplement the small old-age payments they received. As late as 1930, the average monthly benefit under The National Pension Act was only equivalent to seven United States dollars. The depression of the thirties, combined with inflation, resulted in great pressure for increased payments and an improved pension plan" (Rosenthal, 1967). Although benefits were low, the 1913 Act was very important, since it was the first time that the Swedish government accepted responsibility to help its citizens financially in old age.

Based on his study of Sweden's social security system, Carl Uhr (1966) concludes that this first pension was intended only as a regular supplement to other sources of old-age income maintenance, such as private savings, and that when no such private resources were available, it was to be a supplement to public relief. This early system was expanded in 1935 by the provision of additional tax-financed supplemental benefits. It was at this time that the name *Folkpension* (people's pension) was substituted for the term "insurance" (Carlson, 1966).

The main criticisms of the early pension program were directed at the means test and the inadequacy of benefits. Many people, including various government leaders, strongly objected to a means test for determining eligibility for a pension and housing allowance, arguing that the Folkpension benefit levels did not come close to meeting the needs of the aged. In response to widespread criticism, Parliament passed the National Pension Act of 1946, to become effective in 1948. The law provided for all single citizens to receive 1000 Kr. (about $200) per year (couples, 1600 Kr.) upon reaching age 67, regardless of prior or current income. In addition, when the legislation was adopted, it was generally acknowledged that there would be a periodic need to adjust pensions for increases in the cost of living and also for the real value of national income.

In the same year that this law was passed, however, the government appointed a high-level committee to study different possibilities for the establishment of an income-related, compulsory, and contributory social-insurance program that would provide more substantial benefits than the recent act. Uhr has concisely summarized the pension situation prior to the major reform which was to follow a decade of study by this committee and a succession of other committees:

> . . . one can characterize the Swedish old-age security system from 1948 to 1960, when certain far-reaching reforms enacted in 1959 gradually went into effect, as a system financed by a combination of a special pension tax and by appropriations from general revenues. It functioned without any attempt to accumulate any appreciable reserve. The pensions paid were in no direct way related to pensioners' past earnings . . . One can say that the aim of this system was to guarantee every aged citizen as a matter of right (without means test) a certain minimum consumption standard protected against price fluctuations and rising with the rise in real national income. The norm was one of providing a decency-and-dignity standard for the aged. At any rate, it was a standard above bare subsistence and superior to that afforded indigents on poor relief.
> (Uhr, 1966)

THE REFORM DEBATE

A tremendous amount of committee discussion and political debate preceded the social security reform act of 1959. As indicated above, a succession of government-appointed committees met throughout the decade to try to determine the best way of providing adequate financial security in old age. The various political and economic interest groups represented on these committees, however, could not reach agreement, their disagreement being reflective of the division of opinion which also existed among Swedish citizens themselves.

Debate during the fifties centered on three main issues:

1. Whether there should be private or public control of pension funds (reserves);

2. Whether the "supplementary" pension system to provide pensions beyond the basic pensions of the Folkpension should be government initiated and administered or established by collective bargaining between employees or their unions and employers or employer associations;

3. Whether supplementary pension coverage should be voluntary or compulsory.

There was general consensus in Sweden during the 1950's that pension levels should be increased significantly. Moreover, increasingly people began to talk about a pension that would enable every person to maintain a standard of living in old age which was approximately equal to his prior standard. The Folkpension, which gave the same pensions to every person, was obviously not an appropriate mechanism for maintaining prior living standards into old age. Supplementary pensions which were related to earnings and which, when added to the basic pension, represented a high percentage of earnings, were widely recognized as the answer.

By the 1950's supplementary pensions relating pension benefits to prior earnings existed to cover government employees and certain management/office personnel in the larger, more prosperous firms of the private sector. But very few production workers had such supplemental coverage, and as a consequence strong agitation had begun to make blue collar pension programs comparable to those for civil servants and for many of the white collar employees. Valdemar Carlson observes:

> There was no disagreement between employers and trade unions that production workers were equally entitled to supplementary pensions. The disagreement was about means, employers taking the position that pensions should be obtained through collective bargaining while Land Organization, the central bargaining agent for production workers, argued for government action . . . In the latter half of the 1950's, this issue was hotly debated in Parliament and the multi-party system of Sweden proved a cumbersome instrument for resolving the issue.   (Carlson, 1966)

Discussions with a view to achieving better pensions for Swedish workers had taken place in the early 1940's between the Swedish Federation of Labour (Land Organization) and the Swedish Employers' Association. These negotiations failed, with the Swedish Federation maintaining that nongovernment, private plans without legislated compulsion would inevitably fail to include many workers needing coverage. The National Pension Act of 1946 was, in part, a result of these discussions and in fact weakened interest in achieving any general labor-management agreement on private pensions. Discussion and analysis continued during the late forties, however, with the main work being undertaken by a pension commission appointed in 1947 by Commerce Minister Gunnar Myrdal. The work of this first government-appointed commission was inconclusive. On one point, however, all members of the commission agreed: "that pensions should be related to the employee's living standard, inviolable, and as far as possible part of a unified pension system" (Heclo, 1971). No agreement was reached on other issues.

Given the results of the commission's work, the Social Democratic government took no action on the pension question. The Swedish unions, however, would not allow the issue to be put aside:

> The powerful metal workers' union was by now firmly of the view that the employers' negative attitude on the matter pointed inescapably to the conclusion that a general superannuation plan would have to be legislated. At the 1951 LO [Swedish Federation of Labour] Congress, nine major motions were presented urging a speedy solution to the question and removal of the unjustified difference between workers and salaried employees . . . At the suggestion of the LO executive, the Congress declared itself for a speedy solution through legislation rather than employers' contracts. (Heclo, 1971)

A new investigatory commission was appointed. While it was completing its work, the Swedish Employers' Association presented to the unions a plan for developing workers' pensions by private contract. According to this plan, private pension plans were to be set up by collective bargaining agreements, with fees for the pensions to be paid entirely by the employers—pension funds being created in the companies concerned. There was to be no involvement of the government in the operation or supervision of these plans.

Representatives of the unions and employers met to discuss this proposal. However, "it soon became evident that LO [the Swedish Federation of Labour] preferred a state-organized system, and there is some evidence that some kind of agreement had already been made in 1953 between LO and the Social Democratic Party on this point, stating that the pension question should be solved by legislation in Parliament and not through collective contracts between employers and employees. The initiative of SAF [the Swedish Employers' Association], therefore, produced no results" (Molin, 1965).

The preference of the labor organizations and the Social Democratic Party for a governmental supplementary pension system appears to be based on a number of political and economic considerations. Some informed observers[1] argue that the most important reason for the unions wanting a government program was to ensure that the money arising from a growing pension fund would not "remain in the hands" (and, therefore, the exclusive control) of the employers. Many socialists argued that the amounts of money accumulated in the pension funds would be very large and therefore these funds should be invested centrally in order to influence "more rationally" the direction of the economy, rather than being scattered among a large number of employers.

Another argument made in favor of a governmental program was that this was the only way to cover all workers. Though Swedish industry was almost completely unionized, there were many low-wage industries and occupations where "because of foreign competition, low productivity or inefficient management, any considerable increase [in wages] cannot be achieved by collective bargaining" (Carlson, 1966). The unions therefore felt that it would be impossible to achieve through collective bargaining adequate supplemental pensions in these industries.[2] In addition, it was argued that the problems of nonunionized workers in various parts of the economy would not be solved by the Employers' Association proposal.

In 1955 the second pension commission presented a plan for an inflation-proof pension system to cover all citizens—not just employees. The majority plan called for a compulsory, state program and proposed to give each person a pension equal to about 50 per-

---

1. Based on interviews of public and private Swedish officials who participated in the private and public discussions during this period.

2. Carlson (1966) argues that the unions recognized that government taxes to finance pensions might cause bankruptcy or unemployment in these economically weak industries but that "this sequence of events would not adversely affect the prestige of trade unions and collective bargaining as a device to determine wages and working conditions."

cent of his average lifetime annual income. This plan met with favorable support from the Federation of Labour and the Social Democratic Party. But all other interest groups and political parties so strongly criticized the commission's proposal that the government (at that time a coalition of Social Democrats and the Centre Party) decided not to introduce in the Parliament a pension bill based upon it.[3] Instead, a third pension commission was appointed, with representatives from various political parties and interest groups. Again this commission was unable to reach agreement on any single recommendation and instead presented three separate proposals in the final commission report:

> Proposal 1: A system of compulsory supplementary pensions for *all* employees, financed by employers but *administered by government* authorities. This proposal was supported by commission members representing the Social Democratic Party, the Federation of Labour, and the Central Organization of Salaried Employees.

> Proposal 2: A system of *voluntary* supplementary pensions with a *maximum benefit* of 3,000 Kr., to be *administered by government* authorities. This proposal was supported only by the representative of the Centre Party.

> Proposal 3: A system of *voluntary* supplementary pensions *administered by a private institution* with a board chosen by employers and employees, with guidelines about the pension system to be determined by collective bargaining between the Federation of Labour and the Employers' Association. This proposal was supported by representatives of the Conservative Party, the Liberal Party, and the Employers' Association.

These three proposals were eventually submitted to the nation in a highly unusual national referendum. To understand why this referendum came about, it is necessary to understand the political situation which existed in Sweden at the time.[4] The Social Democratic Party and the Centre Party (formerly the Agrarian Party) had formed a coalition government in 1951, which continued to govern

---

3. Of the 89 organizations commenting on the report (43 of which were governmental units), only five were generally in favor of the majority position (Heclo, 1971).

4. The discussion which follows is based upon interviews by the author and the studies by Molin (1965) and Heclo (1971).

throughout the period when discussion of the pension question was at its height. Since both of the coalition parties lost seats in the general elections of 1952 and 1956 to the Liberal and Conservative parties, both were worried during this period about their political positions. The Social Democratic Party was especially sensitive to the fact that a decreasing share of recent votes had been cast for candidates of the two socialist parties (the Social Democrat and the Communist); in the 1956 election the "bourgeois parties" for the first time since 1930 received a majority of the popular vote. Political observers thought this development to be, in part, a result of the rising prosperity that occurred throughout the period and, in part, a result of the shift from blue-collar to white-collar employment developing throughout the economy. Thus the government was not anxious to get into a fight over the pension question when it was pressed by the trade unions (initially in 1955) to act on the problem. The Social Democrats, though willing to respond to the union requests because of strong and long-term political associations with the unions, were also worried about staying in power. Finally, pressed very hard by at least some influential unions, the Social Democrats agreed to attempt to pass pension legislation. It was then that the government appointed the third commission (referred to above) and assigned it the job of recommending a national supplementary pension system.

The inability of this third commission to achieve consensus created a dilemma for the government. Having lost a large number of seats in the 1956 general election and left with control of only the upper house of Parliament, the Social Democrats felt fairly certain that any legislation they proposed based on "Proposal No. 1" of the third commission's report would be defeated in the Parliament. Moreover, their coalition partner, the Centre Party, had taken a strong position against the compulsory pension scheme embodied in Proposal 1 and had supported their own voluntary and limited scheme as Proposal 2. Thus, with the Liberal and Conservative parties arguing that the pension issue was of such overwhelming importance that the entire nation should decide, the Social Democrats decided that essentially they had nothing to lose by calling for a referendum on the pension question.

The public debate over the merits of the three pension

proposals was not formally conducted by the various political parties. Instead, special committees composed of party and interest group representatives were established to take their cases to the people. Each committee was provided with public money to campaign. As indicated above, one of the principal issues debated was with regard to who should control the pension money:

> One argument in the political propaganda against Proposal No. 1 and particularly in favour of Proposal No. 2 was that the increased basic pension was quite sufficient for the needs of old-age people, and that the real purpose of the supplementary pensions scheme with its large State funds was to increase State control over the capital market. In the propaganda, Proposal No. 1 was often designated as "purely socialistic" by the opponents. (Molin, 1965)

A large number of the supporters of a government pension system apparently did in fact see a government system as a means of reducing the amount of economic power concentrated in private ownership. Carlson reports that in the summer of 1965 Hans Hagnell (member of Parliament and economist for the Metal Trades Union) argued that supplemental pension funds should be invested in common stock as a means of promoting and controlling economic growth.[5] "Hagnell's proposal created considerable attention in the press and was the subject of a television debate in which five members of Parliament, one from each of the five parties, participated. Whatever the merits of Hagnell's proposal, he . . . dramatized the problem of what should be done with growing social insurance funds that will not be paid out in benefits for many years" (Carlson, 1966).

The one factor that united opposition among the "bourgeois parties" seemed to be that Proposal 1 called for compulsory participation. The Centre Party, which was mainly composed of farmers and owners of small businesses, was adamant in its position that any supplemental pension program must be based upon individual freedom of choice. They argued that the self-employed provided their own pensions by plowing a part of their earnings back into

---

5. As will be discussed below, pp. 90, a choice was made to build up pension reserves to offset an expected drop in personal saving as a result of the improved social security pensions.

their businesses and that changing technology necessitated available funds to make such reinvestment in order to compete effectively.

The Conservative Party also criticized the compulsory nature of the system and initially argued that the only change in the national system should be an increase in the Folkpension. At the end of 1956, however, the party, in a move to help unify the opposition parties, decided to support Proposal 3, which called for collectively bargained supplementary pensions. When efforts to unify the nonsocialist parties proved unsuccessful, however, the party returned to its initial position of opposing any supplementary pension legislation and maintained this position both throughout the referendum debate and also during the subsequent pension reform debate in Parliament.

The Liberal Party, which was the leading opposition party during the 1950's, was basically sympathetic toward improving the pension situation but wished to change it in such a way as to facilitate the formation of a nonsocialist government. Thus the party was faced with the dilemma of favoring supplementary pension legislation but also needing the political support of the "right-wing" parties who felt very negatively about supplementary pensions. In meetings of the third pension committee the party supported a voluntary supplementary pension system, and supported Proposal 3 during the referendum debate. It saw Proposal 3 as essentially a compromise solution between the two extreme positions they thought were embodied in Proposals 1 and 2.

Advocates of Proposal 1, in addition to being concerned about who controlled the pension money, argued that a compulsory system was essential. They argued that "allowing persons to decide themselves whether or not they shall be taxed in their working years to provide annuities in their years of retirement is likely to result in a situation where those who are most likely to be in need of retirement pensions do not feel that they can afford to be taxed during their working years. A compulsory system covering all workers within a bargaining unit, at any rate, would have been equally necessary if collective bargaining had been utilized to provide supplementary pensions" (Carlson, 1966). It was further argued that compulsion would facilitate making adjustments in pension benefit levels for changing prices and changing levels of real national income.

Additional arguments in favor of compulsion centered in the ease and lower cost of administering such a system. It was maintained that if persons were given a choice, it would be necessary to establish a registry system that would show the "choice status" of each citizen. Administrative costs, it was argued, would be very high—especially given Sweden's small economic base. Also, the collection of pension revenues from employers would be much easier if the same percentage could be collected from large and small (prosperous and weak) companies. Some argued that employers were in a sense responsible for the welfare of all workers, not just their own workers, and that universal coverage embodied this principle.

But perhaps the one argument that had the most influence on the opinions of workers related to the fact that most workers at the time of the referendum had only the inadequate basic pension coverage of the Folkpension. Defeat of a national supplementary pension system would force these workers to bargain with their employer and to overcome in some way the expected plea from the employers that adequate pensions would be too expensive and would therefore require lower wages.

In addition, there was general recognition by the workers and their leaders of the problem of losing pensions when changing jobs. Many workers argued that they were entitled to pensions as good as those currently covering government employees and many white collar workers. The socialists particularly pointed to what they termed the discriminatory nature of the current pension situation.

In 1957 the nationwide plebiscite on the three proposals was finally held. Individuals could vote for one of the three or by leaving the ballot blank could vote against all. When the votes were counted, it was found that none of the three proposals had received a clear majority of the votes. Proposal 1, receiving about 46 percent of all votes cast, had the strongest endorsement. (Table 17 shows the voting results.)

After the referendum the Centre Party withdrew from the coalition, primarily over the pension issue, and the Social Democrats were forced to function as a minority government. The government entered into negotiations with the other political parties in an attempt to compromise, while at the same time preparing its own bill. On February 11, 1958, two days after the political talks broke

TABLE 17

National Pension Referendum, 1957

	Votes	Percentage	Percentage Excluding Blanks
Proposal 1	1,624,131	45.8	47.7
Proposal 2	530,576	15.0	15.6
Proposal 3	1,251,477	35.3	36.7
Blank votes	136,399	3.9	—
Total	3,542,583	100.0	100.0

Source: Björn Molin, Tjänstepensionsfragan, en studie i svensk parti-politik (Göteborg: Scandinavian University Books, 1965), p. 79.

up, the cabinet formally approved the state superannuation plan that had been prepared. Encouraged by the relatively strong support given to Proposal 1 in the referendum, the Social Democrats introduced a bill (which was similar to Proposal 1) to establish compulsory supplementary pensions for employees and employers.[6] The bill, however, was rejected in the Lower House by six votes, with the Conservative and Centre parties arguing against any kind of compulsory supplementary pension and the Liberal Party advocating compulsory pensions with free choice as to the level of benefits.

As a result of this defeat the Government dissolved the Lower House, and extraordinary elections took place in June 1958; the major election issue was clearly the pension question. In the newly elected house the Social Democrats held five additional seats, largely as a result of the fact that the Communist Party did not put up candidates in closely contested districts—withdrawing their candidates in eleven constituencies in favor of the Social Democrats (Molin, 1965). The Liberal Party suffered a serious setback, losing about one third of their seats to the Conservative and Centre parties.

---

6. One change from the original plan was made as a concession to opposition groups. Employees with existing collective pension contracts could contract out of the state program as a group but would be subject to strict government regulation.

In February 1959 the Government introduced another bill to establish compulsory supplementary pensions. Although the Social Democrats still held a solid majority in the Upper House, they were faced again with the probability of defeat in the Lower House. The votes were divided 115 to 115, which meant defeat for the bill if a vote were taken. In a dramatic move, however, one member of the Liberal Party (Ture Konigson) announced he would abstain from the final vote should it be a question of either voting for the government bill or having to support the Conservative/Centre parties' kind of bill. "According to his own account . . . the most important thing was in his view that a solution be reached on super-annuation; now that the electorate had rejected the Liberal approach, even cooperation with the Social Democrats was justifiable in order to reach a solution" (Heclo, 1971).

Thus the Social Democrats' pension bill passed in 1959 by a vote of 115 to 114, with one abstention.

Commenting on the political events that followed, Molin (1965) observes:

> The Conservative and Centre parties now made it clear that they did not accept this decision and that they intended to get the Act abolished. The Liberal Party, on the other hand, decided to accept the new system and in the 1960 general election, the Liberals fought with the Social Democrats against an abolition of the Act. The 1960 election resulted in a defeat for the Conservative Party and a success for the Social Democrats, who had reached a turning-point and were now near a clear majority in the Lower House. On the whole the position of the non-Socialist parties had changed for the worse. In 1960 the new Pension Act came into force, the first pensions being payable in January 1963. After the elections all parties accepted the system and did not attempt to have it abolished.

The Resulting Pension System

The pension reform legislation that was passed in 1959 is almost identical to the national pension system that exists today in Sweden.[7]

---

7. Discussion is limited in this section to benefit provisions. Financing aspects of the system are discussed in a later section. Details and

The Swedish pension system is divided into two basic programs: the National Basic Pension (Allmän Folkpension or AFP) and the National Supplementary Pension (Allmän Tilläggspension or ATP). The current basic pension system is a modified version of the original pension act passed in 1913 (see above, page 73); it currently consists of old-age, disability and widows' and orphans' pensions. The supplementary pension was added to the basic pension coverage by the law passed in 1959 and provides additional old-age, disability and widows' and orphans' benefits based on income derived from gainful employment in Sweden (i.e., it is a wage-related program). Both the basic and the supplementary pensions are paid in full at age 67—regardless of whether an individual is working or not. A person may begin receiving his pension starting at age 63, but the pension is reduced by 0.6 percent for each month by which the age of the insured falls short of age 67 when he first draws his pension. Alternatively, an individual may delay receipt of his pension and have his deferred pension increased by 0.6 percent for each month postponed up to age 70.

In order to understand the method of calculating Swedish pensions, one must be familiar with what the Swedes call the *base amount*. The base amount is an artificially designated money figure which (a) is used to calculate and adjust all pensions and, with regard to the supplementary pension, (b) is used to determine in constant monetary value the amount of earnings applicable for determining the supplemental pension benefit amount. The base amount was initially designated by the pension act of 1959 to be "4,000 Kr. a year in 1957 prices." At that time the base amount was about one third of average Swedish wages (Uhr, 1966). The law calls for this base amount to be automatically adjusted by the movement of the Swedish Consumer Price Index. Adjustments are made each month, but no change is made unless the price level has varied by at least 3 percent since the last change. As a result of this index adjustment, the base amount had risen from the original 4,000 Kr. to 7,300 Kr. by September 1972.

---

discussion of the Swedish system in this and later sections are based on interviews with pension officials and the following publications: Swedish Ministry of Health and Social Affairs (1971); Lagerstrom (1971); Holmquist, undated; and the Swedish Institute (1972).

The basic old-age pension (AFP) is paid to every Swedish citizen (living in the country) who reaches the eligibility age. The pension for an unmarried individual is equal to 90 percent of the current base amount (adjusted upward or downward for early or late retirement). Both partners of a married couple are entitled to separate pensions equal to 70 percent of the current base amount (or a total of 140 percent for the couple).[8]

The National Supplementary Pension (ATP) is more complicated to calculate. Each year after age 16 that an insured person works, his "pensionable income" is computed on the basis of his income from employment and "income from other gainful occupation."[9] Pensionable income consists of that part of total income which exceeds the base amount but is less than 7.5 times the base amount. In every year for which the insured person has pensionable income, he is credited with "pension points" equal to that year's pensionable income divided by the current base amount; the maximum number of pension points which can be credited in any one year, however, is 6.50. If pensionable income in any year is less than the base amount, the insured is credited with no pension points or "pension coverage" credit for that year. In order to be eligible for a full pension at a pensionable age, the insured must have accumulated pension points for at least 30 years.

To calculate the supplementary pension for eligible persons, the following formula is used:

Pension = .60 × Current Base Amount × "Average" Pension Points

where the annual average of pension points earned during the fifteen most favorable or best years of gainful occupation is used.

---

8. If any person drawing the basic pension is not entitled to a supplementary pension or if his supplementary pension is "insignificant," his basic pension is increased.

9. The term "income from other gainful occupation" refers to income from business, from farm property operated by the insured, and from remuneration—cash or in-kind in the form of board or lodging—for work performed for another person. This type of income is distinguished from other income because contributions based upon it are paid by the insured and not by an employer, and because the insured has the option of excluding himself from supplementary pension coverage with respect to this income.

If pension points have been earned for less than thirty years, however, one thirtieth of the full pension is deducted for each missing year. "The fact that the base amount is adjusted according to fluctuations in the cost of living guarantees a constant 'inflation-proof' value of pensions" (Lagerstrom, 1971). Special transitional provisions exist for persons born during the 1896–1914 and 1915–23 periods which reduce the number of years of creditable coverage required for a full pension benefit.[10]

With regard to widows, a national basic pension is paid before the age of 67 as a full widow's pension either to a widow who has one or more children under the age of 16 in her care or to a widow who has reached the age of 50 and who had either reached this age at the time of her husband's death or, failing this, still had a child or children under age 16 in her care when she did reach the age of 50. If a widow, at the time of her husband's death, had no children under age 16 in her care, she becomes entitled to a widow's pension only if her marriage to the deceased had lasted for at least five years. Eligible widows receive a pension equal to the amount of the basic pension paid to a single old-age pensioner.[11] In addition to the widow's benefit provided by the basic pension, widows of workers insured under the supplementary pension plan receive an additional pension that is either 35 percent of the relevant disability or old-age pension (if she has one or more children receiving a "child's pension") or 40 percent (in other cases).

CURRENT THINKING (A Look Backward and Forward)

The new pension system in Sweden has now been in operation for about a decade. As was indicated previously, although the national debate over the reform was extremely heated and bitter, all

---

10. For persons born during the 1896–1914 period, the thirty-year rule is replaced by a twenty-year rule. For persons born during the 1915–23 period, the thirty-year rule is replaced by a requirement of twenty years, plus one year for each year the person's year of birth exceeds 1914.

11. Widows who do not meet the age or child conditions specified get a pension reduced by 1/15th for each year by which her age at the determining date falls short of age 50.

political parties accepted the new system once it became law. During more than a decade of the system's operation, no political party has expressed serious dissatisfaction with the basic concepts embodied in the reform law as a result of the system's actual operation. In the words of Ernst Michanek, "we had a fierce political battle over the supplementary pensions scheme . . . Now that the fighting is over and the reform has been passed, no one recommends a return to the past" (Michanek, 1964).

The Compulsion Issue

What has happened in Sweden with regard to the fears and objections that were voiced initially by opponents of the present system? First, there was the objection to making the supplementary pension compulsory. In partial response to these fears, the final legislation made provision for certain persons and groups to opt out of the system. With regard to groups, the law provided that any group of employees with private supplementary pensions (or a group that intended to become covered) could by collective agreement request exemption from coverage by notifying the appropriate public authorities. This decision, however, had to be made during the first eighteen months after the date that the new law went into effect (January 1960). In actuality, no union or other collective organization elected to take this option, clearly indicating the favor with which workers and their representatives looked upon the new system at that time.

Individuals were (and still are) free to opt out of the system to the extent that their earnings are derived from self-employment. This provision permits farmers, various professionals, small-business entrepreneurs, and independent contractors an option with regard to pension taxes on the bulk of their income. It was these groups, especially the farmers and entrepreneurs, which had strongly opposed compulsion during the reform debates, arguing, first, that they provided for their own pensions by plowing their earnings back into their enterprises and, second, that they needed to use the bulk of their income for current investment in order to remain competitive. Uhr (1966) reports that only about 20 percent of those with income derived entirely or to a significant extent from self-employment have chosen to opt out of supplementary coverage.

The Funding Issue

The second major issue that dominated the prereform debate was the question whether the government would have a significant and undesirable amount of control over the economy's investment decisions as a result of the social security reserves that were projected. A deliberate decision had been made by the government to emphasize reserve funding of the new system, rather than place emphasis upon a pay-as-you-go type of system, the principal reason for this being to provide help for the chronic shortage of saving in the Swedish economy. Consequently, many feared that the accumulation of a large reserve fund would lead to an undesirable socialization of Swedish industry.

A parliamentary committee undertook extensive study of the funding issues connected with pension reform prior to the passage of the proposed reform legislation. The committee in a 1958 memorandum to Parliament recommended that contribution rates be set high and that the resulting surplus be put into a National Pension Fund.[12] Such action was necessary, they argued, in order to compensate for an expected decline in personal and business saving as a result of establishing the proposed national supplementary pensions.

The fears of critics who worried about central economic control and possible "socialization" effects on Swedish industry were supported by estimates prepared by K. O. Faxen for the parliamentary committee's investigation. Faxen estimated that fund reserves would reach within a few decades an amount equal to about one third of total assets in Sweden's credit and capital market and would be almost one third of gross savings by as early as 1970.[13] The committee, therefore, recommended decentralization of the fund. This recommendation was accepted by the Parliament and resulted in the establishment of three separate subfunds to avoid domination of the capital market:

---

12. *Promemoria med Forslag om Fondforvaltning M. M. i Samband Med en Utbyggd Pensionering* (Memorandum and Proposal Concerning the Administration of a Fund, etc., in Conjunction with the Further Development of Pensions).

13. It is interesting to note that, as reported by the Rikshauk, about 30 percent of total lending for 1970 in the Swedish credit market originated with public insurance institutions—as opposed to only 3.5 percent in the 1957–60 period (Allmänna Pensionsfonden, undated).

Subfund 1: to receive contributions from national and local governments in their role as employers. These funds can be placed in local and national government bonds or registered debentures of qualifying public agencies, but a certain proportion must be kept as a cash balance with the Central Bank.

Subfund 2: to receive contributions from private employers. These funds can be invested in corporate bonds and debentures, secured shorter term commercial loans, and loans to commercial, savings, and mortgage banks.

Subfund 3: to receive contributions from self-employed persons. Funds can be invested in a manner similar to that of Subfund 2.

Three different governing boards were established for the funds. Subfunds 1 and 2 have nine representatives, three each representing the employers, the workers, and the "public interest." Subfund 3 has seven members, representing organizations of the self-employed and the public interest. In 1972, for example, total contributions of 8489 million Kronor went into the three funds—29 percent, 52 percent, and 19 percent into Subfunds 1, 2, and 3 respectively (Allmänna Pensionsfonden, 1973).

During the early 1960's the fund began to grow and arguments against it continued, especially from the Conservative Party and businessmen. "During 1963 and 1964, arguments were increasingly heard that the state pension fund was diverting savings from the innovative, risk bearing sections of the economy; industrial spokesmen complained of the reduced savings and inadequate funds for industrial expansion" (Heclo, 1971). In 1965 the Conservative Party proposed that the "unexpected" accumulation of funds be used to pay people receiving very small or partial pensions; the proposal received little support.[14]

In contrast to the conservative efforts to abolish or at least reduce the state pension fund, labor spokesmen criticized the passiveness of fund use. They argued that the fund should be used as an economic tool to influence capital markets. This issue was carefully discussed at the Social Democratic Party executive meeting in

---

14. Contrary to conservative accusation, private savings in Sweden did not decline in the early 1960's. A study by the National Institute of Economic Research reported that personal savings rose between 1960 and 1964 and that corporate savings indicated no clear trend.

January 1967, where party policies were reviewed in reaction to the serious political setbacks of the 1966 election. At the meeting it was argued that "to provide the accelerated rationalization necessary in modern economic life, the state would have to provide a guaranteed and large supply of capital for industrial adaptations, as well as a labor market policy to ease the effect of these adaptations upon the workers" (Heclo, 1971).

Then on February 1, 1967, the Social Democratic Government proposed the establishment of a state-owned credit institution to finance "industrial rationalization" and development—the major source of funds to come from the bank's issuance of its own obligations and from the state pension funds. The Centre, Liberal, and Conservative parties all opposed the plan, but it was passed by the *Riksdag* in 1968.

Most recently, in the spring of 1973, a new fund (Subfund 4) was created by a parliamentary coalition of members from the Social Democratic and Communist parties. Authority is given to this new fund to buy shares in private companies. Money to do this is provided by thhe other three subfunds. The fund is governed by a board consisting of representatives of workers, employers, local authorities, and the government.

Table 18 shows the growth of total funds over the 1960–71 period. By the end of 1971 the fund was valued at 46,720 million Kronor (about $11 billion); net additions to the fund are currently equal to roughly 4 percent of the Swedish gross national product. In future years the growth of the fund is projected to decline (unless contribution rates are increased).

In general, the financing of social security in Sweden has been a politically controversial issue, especially with regard to the type of "funds" established. For example, Subfund 4—the most recent —was created amid bitter political debate over the merits of such an innovation. And debate continues in Sweden today over these financing issues.

The Role of Private Pensions

Another issue that was a part of the pension-reform debate was the appropriate role for private pensions. Many argued that the major part of retirement security should be provided on a business

TABLE 18

The Swedish National Pension Insurance Fund, 1960–1971

Year	Rate of Contribution	Fund Capital, Dec. 31 (mill. Kr.)
1960	3	480
1961	4	1210
1962	5	2640
1963	6	4670
1964	7	7300
1965	7½	10,500
1966	8	14,360
1967	8½	19,030
1968	9	24,880
1969	9½	31,340
1970	10	38,420
1971	10¼	46,720

Source: Allmänna Pensionsfonden (undated).

by business (or industry by industry) basis through separate agreements between employers and employees. It was argued that this would allow the resulting pension systems to be more responsive to the varying needs and preferences of different groups of workers.

Without doubt the establishment of national supplementary pensions for all workers in Sweden decreased the potential role to be played in private pensions and represented a major defeat for those wishing to accomplish the task through private pensions. This did not mean, however, that there were many large-scale cutbacks in existing private pension systems when the new pension system went into operation; there were simply not that many private pensions (set up to pay large benefits) when supplementary pensions were introduced. It did mean that future private-pension development was to be limited to a much more supplementary role.

Private pensions in Sweden are currently seen as having an important function, hence are growing in size.[15] They have been under continuous development throughout the past decade and are,

15. Over the 1957–60 period saving by Swedish private insurance institutions was 2.3 percent of gross national product; in 1961–64, 1.7 percent; in 1965–69, 2.0 percent (Allmänna Pensionsfonden, undated).

in the opinion of many pension experts, a model for other countries to study and perhaps emulate.

The reform of public pensions stimulated employer and employee groups into reassessing the role of private pensions and studying ways to unify the different systems that existed at the time. The first major result of the study and negotiations that took place was the creation of a private-pension plan for salaried employees (white collar workers) in industry and commerce. All businesses that were members of the Swedish Employers' Confederation joined in an agreement with the salaried employees' unions to supplement public pension benefits through a common private-pension plan.

The ITP plan, as it has been designated, provides additional old-age, disability, and survivor benefits to salaried workers. With regard to old-age pensions, it contains the following major provisions:

1. At age 65 (two years before the national pensions system pays full benefits) the employee receives a pension equal to 65 percent of his "principal final salary" up to a maximum of 10 times the base amount.

2. Employees with earnings over 10 times the base amount receive an additional pension amount equal to 32.5 percent of the additional salary (up to a maximum of 15 times the base amount).

3. The percentage used to calculate the pension is reduced at age 67 from 65 to 10 percent for that portion of salary up to 7.5 times the base amount.

Thus the ITP plan has three major functions: (1) it permits, financially, earlier retirement; (2) it provides additional pension remuneration for high-salaried employees whose earnings replacement would otherwise be relatively low; and (3) at age 67 it supplements the social security pension, so that the resulting pension approximates a replacement standard of 65 percent of the principal final wage.

One result of the social security supplementary pensions being based on the best fifteen years of earning is that the resulting pension is lower than if based on the final year's earnings. Parties to the pension negotiations estimated that the average value of the two national pensions would be about 55 percent of final earnings.[16] Therefore the ITP plan was set up to pay 10 percent and thereby to achieve the desired 65 percent replacement standard.

The benefits promised to employees under the ITP plan are (a) *immediately vested* and (b) *guaranteed* by requiring the participating employers "either to take out a pension insurance to cover his commitments, or to allocate in his balance sheet, to a liability account, a capital value corresponding to the purchase cost of an annuity from a life insurance company. With the latter alternative, it is an unconditional requirement that the employer must at the same time hold a credit insurance policy in the FPG [the Pension Guarantee Mutual Insurance Company]" (Federation of Swedish Industries, 1968).[17]

In June 1971 the Swedish Employers' Confederation reached another agreement with the unions, establishing for blue collar workers a pension plan similar to ITP. This new plan went into effect on July 1, 1973. Though details of the plan are somewhat different from ITP, the fund gives supplementary private pensions to blue collar workers which are quite similar to those currently received by salaried employees. One significant difference is that the private pensions are based only on earnings up to 7½ times the base amount —unlike the salaried pensions that take into account earnings above the social security pension ceiling.

Issues under Discussion

There are a number of issues concerning the granting of old-age pensions in Sweden which are under active consideration. In June 1970 the government appointed a committee to make recommendations regarding the questions (a) whether the eligibility age for benefits should be reduced, (b) whether pension level adjustments for economic growth should be added, and (c) whether the

---

16. In Chapter 7 we estimate the replacement potential of the two pensions for workers with various work histories. These estimates are consistent with the estimate (reported above) upon which the private pension negotiations were based.

17. Also, a 1967 law grants a certain right of priority for pension claims in the event of the employer's bankruptcy.

earnings ceiling, currently 7.5 times the base amount, should be changed.[18]

(a) Concerning the eligibility age for a pension, the committee has listened to presentations by medical experts dealing with the relationship between health and work or "not working." They have also investigated the economic consequences of lowering the retirement age, especially the effects on the costs of the social security system. One alternative proposed is to allow persons to retire at age 65 but subject to a retirement test similar to the current practice in the United States; not much public support has arisen for this proposal. Another proposal is to develop a flexible age scale that would permit retirement at varying ages but subject to a "true" actuarial reduction before the "normal" age, and a full actuarial increase for later ages; the current system does not reduce benefits by the full actuarial amount for early retirement, and late retirees get less than is actuarially justified.

Since the committee began its work, the unions for blue collar workers have negotiated full pensions beginning at age 65—similar to the earlier agreement for salaried workers. This has reduced union and employee interest in reducing the eligibility age for social security old-age pensions. One group (not covered by the new private pension agreements) that generally supports earlier pensions is the self-employed. As a consequence, the Centre Party has indicated interest in such a reform.

(b) In assessing the need for adjusting pensions to take into account economic growth, the committee has carefully studied existing adjustment mechanisms in various other countries—especially West Germany and Norway. The Swedes originally did not include such an adjustment mechanism, primarily because of the cost (both the amount and the difficulty of predicting the cost).

In prior discussions of the question, the government had publicly posed the question whether people would prefer lowering the retirement age or alternatively would like to see pension levels increased to reflect economic growth. Given the successful action

---

18. The committee was also asked to look at some social insurance issues not directly related to old-age pensions. At the time of this writing the committee had not yet made its report.

agreed on by the unions and employees in resolving the retirement-age question, such an either/or question now seems inappropriate.

(c) The "7½ times base" earnings maximum was established without any real research on the question of what should be the appropriate amount. At the time of the reform this ceiling resulted in the inclusion of more than 90 percent of all earnings. All the earnings for almost all blue collar workers fell under this ceiling, and 90–95 percent of the income of most salaried workers was included —the major exceptions being government "chiefs" and business executives. Over the years, however, these percentages have been eroded by the real growth of earnings, which is not reflected in the base amount.[19] In 1967 the Social Security Board (charged with making a report every five years) recommended that the ceiling not be changed at that time but also recommended that serious consideration be given to changing it sometime in the future.

Although most discussions on this question assume a future need to increase the ceiling, some trade union officials in recent years have questioned this assumption. They argue that pensions should be more equal for all—not being higher for persons with prior higher earnings. Once again, however, there does not seem to be much public support for any major weakening of the earnings-related principle embodied in the current supplementary pension system.

The Financing of Basic and Supplementary Pensions

The basic and the supplementary pensions are financed by two different provisions. The basic pension is financed by the combination of an earnings-related tax paid by the insured themselves and general revenue financing. The supplementary pension is financed entirely by employer contributions related to the earnings of their employees.

Looking first at the provisions for the basic pension, all persons between the ages of 16 and 65 pay contributions equal to 5 percent of their taxable income up to a maximum of 30,000 Kr. After age 65, no payment is required whether the person is working or not.

---

19. To reduce this problem some countries determine the earnings maximum as a percentage of actual average earnings.

In 1970, for example, this 5 percent tax raised revenues equal to 2.3 billion Kr. But in the same year it was necessary for the government to make a contribution of about 8 billion Kr. to meet the "basic pension" obligations that were paid out in that year.[20]

The supplementary pension system is financed by employer contributions and the contributions by individuals with self-employment income (who do not opt out). The contribution rate is set at a fixed percentage of remuneration paid by the employer to his workers—reduced (a) by the base amount multiplied by the average number of employees in his service during the year and (b) by any amount of remuneration paid to a worker which exceeded 7.5 times the base amount. The rate was initially set at 3 percent and has been increased yearly as follows:

1960	3%	1966	8%
1961	4	1967	8.5
1962	5	1968	9
1963	6	1969	9.5
1964	7	1970	10
1965	7.5	1971	10.25
		1972	10.5

In assessing the size of the tax, it is important to remember that when the supplementary system was developed and initiated, it was planned that a surplus would be generated and that a large pension fund would be created to be loaned out to the government and private business. Thus, for example, while about 6½ billion Kr. was paid into the supplementary system in 1971, only a little more than 1 billion Kr. was paid out in benefits. Contributions to the system could be much lower if funding were reduced.

---

20. A small part of this amount (.8 billion Kr.) was contributed by local municipalities, mainly to cover the costs of local housing supplements and wife's supplements. Data are from the National Insurance Board (1971).

Chapter 4

THE FEDERAL REPUBLIC OF GERMANY

On November 17, 1881, Kaiser William I, guided by Chancellor Otto von Bismarck, opened the German Reichstag with a speech that contained the following statement:

> The cure of social ills must be sought not exclusively in the repression of Social Democratic excesses, but simultaneously in the positive advancement in the welfare of the working classes . . . We should look back with the greatest satisfaction upon all the successes with which God has visibly blessed our government if we are able one day to take with us the consciousness that we left to the fatherland new and lasting sureties for its internal peace, and to those needing help greater security and liberality in the assistance to which they can lay claim . . . In order to realize these views a Bill for the insurance of workmen against industrial accidents will first be laid before you, after which a supplementary measure will be submitted providing for a general organization of industrial sickness insurance. But likewise those who are disabled in consequence of old age or invalidity possess a well-founded claim to a more ample relief on the part of the state than they have hitherto enjoyed.
> (Dawson, 1912)

Thus began in Germany, and in many countries soon to follow, the debate over, and development of, social security legislation.

The social security system instituted by Bismarck underwent many alterations over the years.[1] In addition to changes associated with various problems of administration, coverage, adequacy, equity, etc., the system was continually under development as an instrument of social control in both the Bismarckian and Hitlerian eras and was

---

1. For an excellent discussion of the history of German social security from Bismarck to the reform debates of the 1950's, see chapters 4 and 5 in Rimlinger (1971).

constantly being adjusted to overcome the problems created by periodic economic instability (inflation and depression) and war.

The early part of the post World War II years was spent trying to restore the old German social security system and dealing with the personal hardship resulting from the deaths, dislocations, unemployment, and many other problems arising from the war.

Rimlinger summarizes the situation as follows:

> As an almost inescapable consequence of patchwork legislation, there was much overlapping in benefit provisions, although important gaps in protection also existed. Cumulation of benefits (the simultaneous drawing of benefits from several programs) became a widely criticized symptom of the system's shortcomings. The real task of rationalizing social security on the basis of principles that were consistent and consonant with the existing economic and social order still lay ahead. In a declaration to the Bundestag on October 20, 1953, Chancellor Adenauer announced that a comprehensive social reform would be undertaken.   (Rimlinger, 1971)

After several years of study and vigorous debate, fundamental social security reform took place—establishing the system existing in the Federal Republic today (except for some minor modifications).

This chapter starts with a short summary of the current German pension program and analyzes the results obtained by the program after fifteen years of experience. After presenting this overview of the program, we review the main issues of the "Reform Debate" and follow with an evaluation of the present program and a summary of current thinking with regard to future change.

The German Old Age Pension System

A pension program that is part of a general social security system is usually complicated, especially since it has to take previous plans into account. The objective of the summary that follows is not to describe complicated details but to set forth the basic and more general features of the program for workers and salaried employees.[2]

---

2. A more detailed survey of the institutional regulations of the German social security system is given in Schewe, Nordhorn, and Schenke (1972).

The programs for these two groups are still separated institutionally, but there are no important differences. The existing programs for other groups of the population will not be taken into consideration in this summary.[3]

In Germany old-age pensions are financed essentially on a pay-as-you-go basis. Thus, during any specific period, the pension population (retired or working) receives transfer payments financed by the working population of the very same period.[4] The pensions are financed from the current national income and not from income of the past. The general level of the pension is related (by a mechanism described below) to the general level of income of the current working population. This mechanism makes it unnecessary to have any other adjustment for inflation, for productivity changes, or for other types of economic growth.

The pension programs of the Federal Republic of Germany have, therefore, two features which seem to be mutually exclusive but which are, in fact, combined in the system: (a) relating the pension to the present level of average income and (b) basing the pension on the former earnings of the individual during his entire earnings history.

In this book "pension" designates the payments originating from the old-age social security institutions called *Arbeiterrentenversicherung* and *Angestelltenversicherung*—although in German terminology these payments are referred to as "rents" (*Renten*). In Germany "pension" (*Pension*) refers to the payments made by the Government to its former civil servants. Civil servants are exempted from the general social security system and are not included in the discussions that follow. Payments we call "pensions" would not be so called in the German terminology. Also, we refer to the people covered by the *Arbeiterrentenversicherung* and the *Angestellten-versicherung* as "persons covered." The active persons who contribute to the system we call "working persons covered." The recipients of pensions we call "retired persons covered." The income concept used in the pension system is the concept of labor income or earnings. The base for calculating the size of pensions and contribu-

---

3. For example, miners and farmers each have separate programs.
4. There is no retirement test in Germany for workers.

tions in all cases is the "labor income" of the persons covered and not their total income. This labor income is defined as income before taxes.

Social security in Germany is a combined system where "old age" is only one of several reasons for the payment of a pension. Other protections included in the system are for invalidism, occupational disability, and general disability. In the following section we deal mainly with one program, old-age pensions.

In Germany the amount of old-age pensions is calculated in the following way: The pension P, of an individual, i, who retired at time t_r can be calculated for the year t_p (P_i, t_r, t_p) by multiplying his initial or original pension by the adjustment factor a_t for the years $t_r + 1$ to t_p.

Thus:[5]

$$P_i, t_r, t_p = P_i, t_r \cdot \prod_{t=t_r+1}^{t_p} (1 + a_t) \qquad (1)$$

The adjustment factor for any particular year is not determined automatically. The Bundestag votes on the adjustment annually after having received the Government's proposition together with the recommendation of the Social Advisory Council (*Sozialbeirat*). The adjustment rate is the same for all pensioners but is different for programs other than old-age. Historically these adjustments have paralleled very closely the trend of average wages for working persons covered by the system. This has resulted from the fact that, in practice, the actual adjustment rates each year have been the same as the increase in the "General Wage Base" of the previous year.[6] The relationship between wages and pensions over the 1958–73 period is shown in Figure VI.

---

5. In 1958 the value for a in the equation was zero: during the years after 1958 there was a lag of one year for the application of the adjustment factor. Therefore the actual situation might better be described by:

$$P_i, t_r, t_p = P_i, t_r \cdot \prod_{t=t_r+2}^{t_p} (1 + a_t)$$

In this equation the values of a are not equal to the values of a in equation 1.

6. The "General Wage Base" is a technical concept used in calculating the pension at the time of retirement and will be explained below.

FIGURE VI
Development of Wages and Pensions[a]

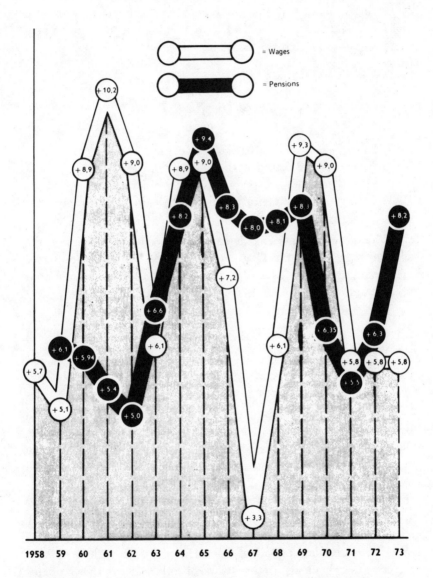

[a]This diagram presents the development anticipated in July 1970 from 1969
onward.

Source: Schewe, Nordhorn, and Schenke (1972), p. 78.

The size of the initial pension at the time of retirement is calculated by multiplying the "Personal Earnings Base" (*Persönliche Bemessungsgrundlage*), the "General Wage Base" (*Allgemeine Bemessungsgrundlage*), the number of years of coverage credits, and a constant factor (which varies depending on the type of pension program). For old-age pensions, the constant is currently set at 0.015.

Thus,

$$P_{i,\ t_r} = GWB_{t_r} \cdot PEB_i \cdot T_i \cdot C \tag{2}$$

Where:

GWB_{t_r} = General Wage Base in the year t_r

PEB_i = Personal Earnings Base of the individual i

T_i = The number of years of coverage credits for individual i

C = A constant factor which assumes a value of .015 for all old-age pensions

The General Wage Base is equal to the arithmetic mean of the average wages of the working persons covered by the program over the three-year period before $t_r - 1$. This average wage amount is very close to average labor income in the national accounts.

Thus the General Wage Base is calculated as follows:

$$GWB_{t_r} = (W_{t_r} - 4 + W_{t_r} - 3 + W_{t_r} - 2)/3 \tag{3}$$

Where:

W = The average wages of working persons covered by the old-age pension program

This averaging process over a three-year period results in a considerable lag between average wages and the pension base. During the years 1961 to 1970 this lag resulted in an average gap between average wages and the General Wage Base of the same year equal to about 25 percent of the General Wage Base. This, of course, results in lower pensions than would otherwise be the case.

The General Wage Base is used to relate all pensions to the current level of national income, while the "Personal Earnings Base" relates a particular individual's pension to his individual circumstances throughout his lifetime work history. For each year of this working history the individual's earnings are compared with the average wages for all covered working persons:

$$PEB_i = \frac{1}{t_r - t_s} \cdot \sum_{t_r - t_s}^{t_r - 1} \frac{e_t}{W_t} \tag{4}$$

Where:

t_s = The year the individual enters the program

e_t = The earnings of the person during the period t

$\dfrac{e_t}{W_t}$ has a maximum value of 2

It is assumed that the person was working during the entire period t_s to t_r. If the latter assumption does not hold, generally only the years during which the individual actually works are included in the average.[7]

The Personal Earnings Base ratio can take on a value below or above 1—indicating that over his lifetime the wages of an individual generally ranged below or above the lifetime average wages of all persons who worked during the same period of years.

It is a very important characteristic of the German pension program that the *absolute* values of the individual's income have no explicit influence on his pension benefit level. The *relative* position an individual's wages holds in the wage distribution is the sole determinant of the Personal Earnings Base. Another interesting feature is that all years of the income history have the same weight in calculating benefits. Work incentives, therefore, are distributed over the whole working cycle; work strategies by individuals to achieve high pensions by earning very high wages for only a few years are not possible in the German system.[8]

Whether an individual has relatively high relative earnings during his early years or shortly before retirement does not make a difference in determining the size of his Personal Earnings Base. It does make a considerable difference, however, with respect to the relation between the pension and earnings just prior to retirement.

The third factor involved in the calculation of the German pen-

---

7. There are, however, some exceptions to this general rule which will be discussed below.

8. There exists a supplementary pension schedule known as "higher insurance" (*Höherversicherung*), which allows individuals to receive higher pensions by paying special contributions. This supplementary system is based on private insurance principles.

sion is the length of time a person works in the system (*Versicherungsdauer*). This time factor is not equal solely to the time during which the individual actually worked and paid contributions. Periods during which the individual was unable or not expected to work because of special circumstances are also taken into consideration. For an individual the time of inclusion in the system, T, is equal to the following sum: the time of working and paying contributions (*Beitragszeit*), TC, plus the "substitution time" (*Ersatzzeit*), TS, plus the "excused time" (*Ausfallzeit*), TE. Thus,

$$T = TC + TS + TE \qquad (5)$$

The "substitution time" takes account of the fact that almost all individuals have public duties which may prevent them from working. Also, it takes account of political developments which make work impossible. Activities for which credit is given are specified in the law. The most important is substitution time based on military service during and after World War II. The justification for including this time in calculating credits is that the government should remunerate individuals by special legislation for damages caused by the various military activities of the government. The general revenue contribution the federal government pays in helping to finance the program is very often justified by this same reasoning.

The "excused time" takes into account periods during which individuals are in the labor force but unable to work for reasons beyond their control. The major reasons are illness, periods of health rehabilitation, and unemployment. For female workers periods of pregnancy are also allowable nonworking time.

To give incentives to individuals for undertaking additional education, periods of education after the age of 16 are also creditable. These educational credits are subject to a maximum number of years and are creditable only in cases where the individual begins working after having finished the education. The maximum allowable educational credit varies and is related to the "normal duration" of the particular type of education undertaken.

If an individual starts to work (or continues creditable education) at the age of 16, he will have accumulated forty-nine years of service credits when he retires at the normal pension eligibility age of 65. Multiplying these years by the pension formula constant of

0.015 gives such a person a pension equal to 73 percent of the product of the Personal Earnings Base and the General Wage Base. In practice, the number of years credited for retiring persons lies far below this maximum value. In 1970 the average number of years credit for male employees was about 35—an average of twenty-nine years of work time, three years of substitution time, and three years of excused time (Schewe, Nordhorn, and Schenke, 1972, p. 72).[9]

The old-age pension program is financed mainly by contributions paid by employers and employees. In addition, contributions are made out of general revenue, justified by the fact that the system has to carry a heavy burden resulting from the war. This financial contribution by the government, however, has decreased considerably (in relative size) during the last years; for example, in 1970 the government paid 15 percent of the costs of the pension program.

Over the years the pension program has had few surpluses. This is in large part due to the fact that rates of contribution were determined based on the financing principle of pay-as-you-go. In this regard, a valuable contribution has been made by the Social Advisory Council in planning for future financing requirements.

The total employer-employee contribution rate was fixed at 14 percent in the 1957 reform legislation. It was increased to 15 percent in 1968, 16 percent in 1969, 17 percent in 1970, and 18 percent in 1973. These increases were necessary because the proportion of working to retired persons in the German population has been declining. In a dynamic program of the German type (based mainly on the principle of income transfer) the demographic situation requires an increase in the rate of contribution.

Table 19 gives some information on the financial situation of the pension program and its size relative to the general economy. The data show that contributions by the state have been a decreasing proportion of the total since the later part of the 1950's. At the same time, the pension program's size in relation to the gross national product rose from 3.6 percent in 1950 to 7.2 percent in 1970.

Aside from the fact that differences exist in the financial situa-

---

9. The average is lowered because it includes persons who were part of the system for only a short time prior to retirement.

TABLE 19

Financing Old Age Pensions

	1950	1955	1960	1965	1970
Rate of contribution[a] (employer-employee)	10%	11	14	14	17
Expenses of the system (in millions of DM)[a]	3549	7058	17,883	28,708	48,130
Contribution of the state as a percentage of expenses	18.7%	35.1	25.0	21.2	15.0
Expenses of the pension program as a percentage of Gross National Product (Bruttosozialprodukt)[b]	3.6%	3.9	5.9	6.5	7.2

[a] Schewe, Nordhorn, Schenke (1972), pp. 84, 86.
[b] Bundesminister für Arbeit und Sozialordnung (1971), p. 72.

tion of the different institutions administering the pension system, the general financial situation of the system may be regarded as very good. Long-run projections by the government estimating future economic developments in the Federal Republic of Germany indicated that the pension program would generate a sizable surplus during the 1970's. The expected surplus has generated considerable discussion and has influenced the debates in Germany about changes in the program. As a consequence, a series of program revisions passed by the parliament in 1972 and 1973 (effective in 1973 and 1974) were scheduled to be financed in the short term largely by reducing this surplus.[10]

THE REFORM DEBATE

The German old-age pension program can be traced back to the end of the nineteenth century. At that time Bismarck tried to create a type of state socialism which would take care of the most urgent needs of the working population and reduce worker discontent—thereby stabilizing political conditions within the country. In a speech in 1889 Bismarck said: "I will consider it a great advantage

---

10. See below, pp. 121.

when we have 700,000 small pensioners drawing their annuities from the state, especially if they belong to those classes who otherwise do not have much to lose by an upheaval and erroneously believe they can actually gain much by it." [11]

This development of social reforms for political purposes is in large part responsible for the fact that the development of social security programs was regarded for a very long period as a means of repression by a large part of the labor movement. For example, the Communist opposition to such programs can be traced back to this historical situation.

By the end of the nineteenth century, ideas of a welfare state still did not dominate the thinking of most German leaders. Therefore the pension program was constructed mainly on principles of private insurance. Individual effort was to result in a pension directly related to this effort. The most important element of the public program was the introduction of compulsory coverage.

Bismarck's legislation in the social security area set an example for the whole world. But in Germany this legislation, to some extent, was seen very negatively, since it was closely connected with the political struggle against socialism. As a result, later pension developments were not greatly influenced by the specific provisions or principles embodied in the original legislation. Thus, although Bismarck made an important contribution to the development of social security around the world, the development of the pension reform in Germany in 1957 can be explained in large part by influences other than the precedents established by Bismarck in the early pension legislation.

After 1945 the situation changed considerably as a result of the tremendous number of economic and social changes which had occurred during the period between 1933 and 1945. For example, there was no continuity with regard to the value of money. The monetary reform of 1948 set up a completely new monetary system. Only assets kept in real form were not subject to the devaluation that occurred as a result of this reform. Assets kept in monetary forms were all devalued and at different rates, depending on their nature. The social security system's reserve fund was particularly affected by these changes.

---

11. Speech of May 18, 1889; cited by Rimlinger (1971).

This monetary reform, together with the other consequences of war (in particular the fact that several million people were expelled or moved from their birthplaces), gave rise to many social changes. The financial base for many people was completely destroyed. They lost their farms, their businesses, or their jobs. Many people also lost the assets they had accumulated for old age.

Beginning about 1945 there was general agreement that the currently existing regulations of the social security system were not adequate to meet the needs created by the social changes. The ad hoc measures undertaken to respond to the most urgent needs soon gave rise to a feeling that there was a necessity for some sort of "social planning." The starting point of the pension-reform discussions was Gerhard Mackenroth's call for the development of a German social plan. Mackenroth's basic idea was to separate the social security problem from the more general labor problem and to develop a comprehensive social security system based upon certain general principles governing the welfare of individuals covered by the system. While his specific contribution to the ultimate pension reform that was carried out in 1957 was not very large, Mackenroth did introduce the important idea that any social reform should be carried out in a systematic and comprehensive way, not focusing solely on separate parts of the social security system.

To understand the later reform of the pension system, one has to be aware of the fact that there was no political discussion devoted exclusively to the development and reform of the old-age pension program; instead there was the attempt to reform all branches of the social security system simultaneously. The discussion that follows is restricted to the reform of pensions, ignoring the debates of a more general character.

When one analyzes over fifteen years later the discussion which led to the 1957 Pension Reform, it is surprising to see how small the differences among the various points of view were. It is also surprising to see how broad a consensus there was on the basic principles of the reform. Less surprising, however, is the fact that not all forecasts, many of them by economists, were fulfilled.

The broad consensus with respect to pension reform is explained largely by the special situation existing in Germany during the postwar years and by the prior history of the German pension program.

The general feeling of solidarity that existed after World War II was compatible with conservative feelings based on both Bismarckian ideas and Roman Catholic thinking and with reformist social democratic traditions. The traditional view of German social policy was that the state was responsible for providing and responding to the needs of citizens unable to care for themselves. Although there had been considerable conflict between Bismarck and the Roman Catholics throughout the history of the old German Reich, Roman Catholic thinking eventually became dominant in the young German Federal Republic. The ideas of subsidiarity fit very nicely into this type of thinking on the role of the state. The Social Democratic position, however, went one step further: it was argued that the state should care for all its citizens.

A program based on the more conservative ideas prevailing in the 1950's in Western Germany could therefore be accepted very easily by the Social Democrats. Their own program was compatible with ideas of this type. The only major difference was that they wanted to increase the number of people included.

A very important element of the reform debate was a series of different plans and proposals prepared by various German scholars and politicians. It is impossible to report on all of them;[12] most relevant are the following:

1. The proposal by Gerhard Mackenroth (1952) for a German Social Plan.

2. The model for a social plan by Walter Auerbach (1952).

3. The Rothenfelser Memorandum (Rothenfelser *Denkschrift*), by Professors Hans Achinger, Josepf Hoeffner, Hans Muthesius, and Ludwig Neundoerfer (Achinger, et al., 1955). This memorandum—initiated by then Chancellor Adenauer—made suggestions for a new type of social security system.

4. The "Schreiber Plan," which developed the idea of "dynamic pensions" (Schreiber, 1955).

5. The "Social Plan for Germany" published by the Social Democratic Party (Sozialdemokratische Partei Deutschlands, 1957).

---

12. A very broad description of the reform process is given by Graefin von Bethusy-Huc (1965).

These plans and memoranda played an important role in the general discussions of the proposed new social security system. Only the plan by Schreiber, however, had an important impact on the details of reform of the pension program; his ideas were later summarized in a memorandum for the Government and had a considerable influence on the formulation of the draft law.

The crucial public and parliamentary discussions of the proposed pension reform were based on two draft laws—one issued by the Government and one proposed by the Social Democratic Party. At that time the Government was a coalition led by the Christian Democratic Party. Both draft laws had more in common than one would expect, given the considerable ideological differences that existed between both parties. It can be shown, however, that their seemingly different suggestions regarding the most important part of the reform, namely the pension formula, implied a similar result.

There was consensus on the following questions:

1. The necessity to have a reform of the whole social security system.

2. The necessity to adjust pensions to changes in real income.

3. The desirability of an earnings-related pension program.

4. The size of pension should be about 60 percent of the average income of the working population.

5. The necessity to adjust pensions in retirement for changes in both real income and prices, although the implementation of this point varied considerably in both drafts.

6. The need to finance the program essentially on a pay-as-you-go basis, with some contributions by the state (the latter interpreted differently by each party).

Differing views were held by the Government and the Social Democrats with regard to the following issues:

1. While the Social Democrats favored coverage of nearly all parts of the population, the Government draft wanted to restrict the pension program to all blue collar workers and only those salaried employees whose income fell below a certain limit. Although this difference seems to be merely a difference in degree, it is illustrative of the entirely different political ideology which underlay the different approaches.

2. The level of the pension was also controversial. This was again, however, a matter of degree. An opposition party (in this case the Social Democrats)—not responsible for the stability of the economy—is always inclined to suggest higher payments to the population than the party in power.

3. An important difference between both drafts was the approaches proposed with respect to the automatic adjustment of pensions during retirement. The Social-Democratic approach was to make all pensions dynamic in the same way; pensions were to be adjusted to changes in wages not only at the time of retirement but annually (in the same manner). The draft of the Government, however, specified adjustments for inflation and growth only at the time of retirement. The size of the pension was determined by the income development at the time of retirement. Every five years the pensions were to be readjusted to income developments. Automatic adjustments, therefore, would occur only when the calculation of the initial pension took place.

4. A final disagreement was over the share to be provided from general revenues by the state in financing the system. The Social Democrats favored a system in which state financing would carry a considerable part of the burden; whereas the Government preferred a system which was financed mainly by contributions by those being insured. Some Christian Democrats justified payments by the Government by the fact that the system had to pay benefits arising as a result of the war.

There were only a few groups in Germany who were against general reform. One group was the very conservative German Party (Deutsche Partei), and another was the Federation of Employers. There were subgroups of employers which did not share this general opposition to the reform. For example, the Federation of Roman Catholic Employers was strongly in favor of the reform, but their support can be explained in part by the fact that pension expert Wilfred Schreiber worked for the federation.

It would be inaccurate to account for the opposition of the Federation of Employers solely as a reflection of their generally conservative political and economic point of view. A major reason for the position of the employers was the fact that the proposals specified that the employers would have to pay half of the contributions to the pension system. Even if one argues that these contributions are in reality part of the wages (which is assumed, for example, in the German National Accounts), there is no doubt that an increase in the rate of contribution results in a "hidden wage increase" by the employer. If the rate of contribution is raised, the employer has to pay a large contribution to the pension system without the possibility (in the short run) of lowering wages. Therefore, the opposition of the Federation of Employers can in part be explained by their vested interest in the question.

Given the general consensus on most of the principal aspects of the pension reform, the discussion focused mainly on only two points:

1. The economic consequences of a "dynamic pension system" and

2. The economic consequences of basing the system almost completely on no reserve financing instead of a funded system.

The arguments brought forward, especially by economists, with respect to the economic consequences of a dynamic pension system were twofold. On the one hand, there were fears that a permanent increase in pensions would create permanent excess demand and consequently lead to a permanent inflation. Moreover, they thought that dynamic adjustment of pensions might promote an inflationary psychology in the population. If the state did not believe in the value of the money, it was argued, how could the citizen trust it? If inflation was assumed to be "normal," inflationary pressures of various kinds might be created.

Looking at those arguments fifteen years later, one can say that the dynamic pension system did not promote inflation in a significant way. However, one has to admit that the fears discussed prior to the reform were not without substance. No doubt a shift of demand from investment to consumption could have resulted in price movements within the consumption sector. This was possible, even though the increase in pension was to be financed by contributions; a part of the contributions was to be paid by the employer and was therefore directed from the investment to the consumption sector.

The size of the price change due to the shift in demand, however, depends on the nature of the adjustment process. In this regard, a valuable contribution was made by the Economic Council of the Ministry of Economic Affairs. The Council stressed that a lag of five years in the adjustment process (as proposed by the Christian Democrats) would produce "adjustment cycles" instead of diminishing the inflationary effect of the pension adjustment; if one did not want to have automatic adjustment, it would be necessary to at least decrease the adjustment lag for stabilization purposes. The Council's idea of an anticyclical adjustment procedure played an important role in the debate. The final solution, namely to have annual adjustments determined by parliamentary laws based on the recommendation of the Social Advisory Council, can be traced back to this idea.

It is very difficult to evaluate the fears regarding the promotion of an inflationary psychology in the population. Exaggerating, one could stress that this argument was itself a product of the population's strong opposition to inflation and that this opposition, in turn, contributed to the result that the dynamic pension system did not generate any sort of inflationary psychology. In the German situation, where a considerable part of the population had twice lost all its monetary assets by large-scale inflation, the fear regarding inflation was strong enough to prevent this kind of thinking. In general, it is very difficult to generalize this argument in one direction or the other.

The discussion regarding reserves and funding was also in many respects hypothetical. The previous German social security system had lost all its monetary assets. There was no possibility that assets could be sufficiently rebuilt to pay the pensions obligations due. At the time of the reform discussion the social security system did not contribute in any significant way to the financing of private or public investments. Only on a hypothetical basis, comparing the future world with a fictional world of the past (which never existed in pure form), could the argument be made that the introduction of a financing system without reserves would decrease investment.

One could argue the point more seriously with respect to private savings. If a public pension program provided a considerable part of the income necessary for old age, there might be no reason for individuals to save large amounts for old age. Many feared that life insurance and private pension plans would be seriously affected by a program that sought to provide pensions large enough to be regarded as sufficient.

One has to confront this argument with the realities existing around 1950. Private savings were very low. Moreover, private household savings were especially low, and business needs dominated the saving decision. Finally, there were very few private pensions.

Looking back, we see that the introduction of the new dynamic pension system based on nonfunded financing did not lead to lower investment rates. It can be shown that throughout the period German investment rates ranged far above the investment rates of comparable countries.

This short summary of the discussion cannot reflect very well all those points raised during the reform debate. It only gives an impression of general views and the main topics of discussion at that time.[13] It should be stressed once again that the special features of the 1957 reform of the old-age pension program were subject to little political debate. Although this reform represents a contribution to German social security development comparable to the pioneering actions of Bismarck, it was not one of the important controversies of that time. Rather, the reform was considered more a necessity long overdue than a significant change in the social legislation of the country.

Current Discussions

Today the program is widely accepted. There have been few if any political demands to change its basic principles. Instead, recent political discussion has centered mainly on three issues:

1. The need to achieve a better and "more honest" implementation of the system.

2. The need for flexible provisions to respond to the desires of people who need or want to retire before the age of 65.

3. The expansion of pension coverage to all segments of the population.

---

13. For additional details of the debate see Rimlinger (1971).

The issues that were important in the earlier reform debate no longer play a major role in the discussions. For example, the highly controversial question regarding the possible negative consequences of dynamic pensions on the price level is rarely discussed.

What is most surprising is that few people argue that the working population is unable to bear the burden of the high contribution rate necessary for the current system. In 1969 the schedule of contribution was fixed for the next years based upon a very pessimistic economic outlook. As a consequence, the contribution rate was fixed at 18 percent (starting in 1973). This rate turned out to be too high, and the system was projected to have considerable surplus in future years. One of the possibilities, given such a situation, would have been to lower the rate of contributions. But this option was, and is, very rarely mentioned in the political discussions. Discussions, instead, have focused on the question of what should be done with this extra money—how it should be used to improve the system. In Germany today hardly anyone considers the burden of the contribution on the working population to be so high as to constitute a reason to lower the rate.

The Early Retirement Provision

The main issue discussed in the new reform debate was the flexible age limit. Should an individual be allowed to retire earlier than the normal age of 65? Although there were some institutionally acknowledged reasons for early retirement, up to 1973 any individual in Germany who had a job and had good health had to work until the age of 65 to get his pension; workers could not take a lower pension and retire earlier unless "unemployed" at least a full year. Many arguments presented for liberalizing this policy were based on the fact that the abilities of people of the same age vary greatly. It was argued that there are people who are able to work (and/or want to work) beyond age 65 without difficulties; there are other people whose performance is poor (and/or prefer to leave their job) before age 65. It was argued by some that these differences between different people should be taken into account when the age of retirement policy is determined. Such people argued that a flexible age limit would be a significant structural improvement of the pension system.

Of course, the original 1957 pension system did contain a mechanism which would permit the introduction of a flexible retirement age if this was desired. The pension formula includes a factor based on the time covered by the program; each year of coverage is multiplied times the constant .015. If the system had permitted pensions to be paid at earlier ages, the pension of a person retiring before the age of 65 would have been lower (because of the lower multiplicative factor) than the pension of an individual who retired at the age of 65. This option would have permitted the individual to decide whether he wanted to have an earlier retirement with a lower pension or a higher pension later.

An unlimited flexible age limit of this type would have placed a considerable financial burden on the program, because the individual retiring one year earlier would pay contributions for one less year but would receive an additional year's pension. The difference would not be recovered by a deduction of 1.5 percent, since actuarially the cost is much higher.

Thus the discussion with regard to the flexible age limit centered on the question of whether (in the case of early retirement) deductions higher than the 1.5 percent should be specified in the applicable pension formula. The opponents were not against permitting persons to retire at an earlier age, but they argued that in such cases the pension should be diminished by the true actuarial cost of the earlier retirement. Such a deduction was considered by others as being prohibitive: retiring at 63 instead of 65 would reduce the pension by about 16 percent.

A further consideration debated was the effect that the flexible age limit would have on the labor market. It is uncertain whether this influence would be positive or negative. It is likely, however, that a flexible age limit would reduce the labor force, though the possibility does exist that a considerable number of individuals would choose a retirement age later than 65.

It was argued by some that earlier retirement in this age bracket might have a positive effect on the productivity of industry. Sometimes older persons find it difficult to adjust to structural changes in the production process. Given existing German labor legislation, it is difficult to discharge older people. As a result the current labor force of older people may contain considerable hidden unemployment. In such a case a flexible age limit might have positive effects on the labor market.

Despite the lack of positive evidence to substantiate the labor effects, most people have assumed flexible retirement would be economically advantageous. The discussions concentrated, therefore, on financial rather than economic questions.

If one accepts the principles of equal treatment and the existence of individual differences with regard to the aging process, the introduction of a flexible age limit together with the existing pension formula seems to be a reasonable approach to solve the problem. It is, however, a political question whether one considers such a structural reform more important than an increase in the level of pensions. Increasing the level of pensions affects more people immediately than would a structural reform of the age limit.

Eliminating the Lags

In recent years the Christian Democrats have argued that the projected surplus should be used for improving the benefit levels of the system. The Social Democrats, however, have argued for structural reforms, especially with respect to a flexible age limit.

The Christian-Democratic demand for a better implementation of the system was based mainly on the lower pension levels resulting from the adjustment process. The built-in adjustment lag of the system at retirement meant that the General Wage Base generally lagged behind any economic growth that occurred by at least two years. In addition, there was a lag in the adjustment process during retirement of one year, caused by the fact that pensions were not adjusted in 1958 due to financial consideration. As a result of these lags, it is argued that one main purpose of the program, namely to closely relate pensions to the rate of economic growth, had not been satisfactorily accomplished.

Different suggestions were made with regard to satisfactorily achieving the original goals of the program. The most modest and simplest recommendation was to adjust pension levels for the adjustment which was not carried out in 1958. This suggestion would have required no structural reform but would have given the pensioners an immediate benefit increase.

Based on the experience with the pension program during the

years since its introduction, another recommendation was to shorten the built-in lag. It was proposed, for example, that the General Wage Base be defined as average earnings *for the year before retirement.* Departing from the current practice of basing the General Wage Base on a three-year average would shorten the lag considerably and lessen the probability of anticyclical movement in pensions levels. In practice it became nearly impossible to explain to a pensioner during a boom that his pension was relatively low because the General Wage Base still included earnings from prior years of recession. Specifically, an institutional change of this type was proposed by the German Federation of Unions (DGB).

Another proposal in the same direction was to make the adjustment of existing pensions entirely automatic. The German experience with recommendations from the Social Advisory Council has shown that the idea of choosing the pension adjustment rate based upon varying economic conditions has not proved very successful. For political reasons the Social Advisory Council has always chosen an adjustment rate equal to the rate of growth of money wages. Given this experience, it was argued, it would seem advantageous to make the adjustment mechanism more straightforward. Then it would be impossible for vested interests to diminish the level of pensions by choosing some arbitrarily low adjustment rate.

Broader Coverage

The third area of discussion dealt with the coverage by the pension program of people who were not then eligible. These people are the self-employed—in small business or in professional practice —and housewives.

Recommendations were made by nearly all parties to open the program to the self-employed but without any compulsion. The question whether a housewife should be allowed to get her own pension was also proposed, but on this question there was substantial disagreement.

The main issue debated was the question of who is to bear the financial burden of beginning this new coverage. Some feared that the voluntary inclusion of such persons would lead to a self-selection of negative risks. Also, the possibility was pointed out that some people who are old now, as well as people who did not want coverage while they were young, would like to be included in the program at a relatively late point in life. In this case, it was asked, who would pay the very high compensatory contributions necessary to get an acceptable pension? Many people thought that these required contributions would be unacceptably high to the individuals. There were discussions whether these contribution amounts could be reduced. A reduction of contributions by the self-employed, however, was not generally acceptable to the employees. Most seemed to be of the opinion that the self-employed should pay at least as much as others.

The Resulting Changes

In 1972 and 1973 the issues described in the preceding section were resolved by new legislation which became effective in 1973 and 1974.[14] The principal reform was to replace the fixed retirement age of 65 with an option that gives a long-term worker the opportunity to begin receiving his pension as early as age 63. However, other important changes in the social security law were implemented at the same time that flexible retirement was introduced.

First, the new law permits workers with at least 35 years of insurance credit to retire "normally" with full pension at the age of 63. However, such workers are not allowed to work full time until they reach age 65.[15] Also, such workers lose an additional 1.5 percent per year of the basic pension that would have been received as a result of the additional years of work (*Versicherungsdauer*).

Workers who instead continue working beyond age 65 without claiming a pension receive their normal pension beginning at age 65 (as specified under the original 1957 law) plus the 1.5 percent of basic pension increment. In addition they now receive an additional

14. See Wang (1973) for a summary of the first part of this reform. Summaries of the whole reform are given in Jantz (1973) and Niemeyer (1973). See also the other contributions in *Bundesarbeitsblatt* 3/4 (1973).

15. "If they wish, they may concurrently engage in part-time employment, without effect on their pension, in one of two ways: (1) up to 3 months (75 work days) in each year without earnings limit or (2) regular work with earnings up to 30 percent of the contribution base" (Wang, 1973).

0.6 percent of the normal pension for each month they work between age 65 and age 67. Finally, as pointed out by Wang (1973), "the periodic adjustments to wage increases and other economic factors will make the deferred pension relatively higher than that paid at age 63." [16]

With regard to the problem of lags in the adjustment process, two important changes were legislated. First, given that pensions at retirement and also pensions during retirement were previously based on the national wage level of 2½ to 3½ years prior, the adjustment date was advanced by 6 months (reducing this lag by half a year). Second, since the goal of keeping pension levels at about 60 percent of a comparable income from work had not been achieved, and since the actual relationship had fallen historically as low as 42.5 percent of current average wages—the new law established an adjustment guideline. The law now states that the average pension earned after 40 years of coverage (assuming a personal earnings base of 100 percent and calculated in July of the adjustment year) should be about 50 percent of the national average wages of the year before. If the pension level is below this guideline during the succeeding years, the government must make suggestions for further adjustments.

The fourth change in the original pension plan is a liberalization of persons eligible to participate in the program. The two groups that were the subject of extensive prior discussion—the self-employed, not previously covered, and nonworking women—are the two principal new groups covered. In general the law provides for some self-selection of the rate of contribution to be made by these groups; benefits are reduced, however, if a lower contribution schedule is selected. And, with regard to the controversial issue of retroactive coverage, the new law permits (until 1975) newly covered individuals to make extra contributions for periods dating back to 1956. "Those nearing retirement age but without any previous coverage will get special assistance in making retroactive contributions" (Wang, 1973).

Finally, two changes not discussed in the previous sections were

---

16. Workers retiring at the normal age of 65 are allowed to work without any restrictions.

legislated: (a) retirement pensions for severely disabled persons were liberalized by a new calculation procedure, and (b) special minimum pensions are provided for low-wage earners with at least twenty-five years of compulsory contributions and with a personal earnings base below 75 percent.

Summarizing, it can be stated that in Germany today the general principles of the social security old-age pension program are widely accepted. Recent debate has led to some important changes, but these reforms are of the type which, by improving the program, will be a confirmation of its success. This does not mean, however, that all the social problems of the old-age population have been solved in Germany. As in other countries, there still remain relevant problems that cannot be solved by the pension program alone.

Chapter 5

THE WORKER AND SELF-EMPLOYED
PROGRAMS IN BELGIUM

Belgian Pension Legislation

The 1850 statute that created the *Algemene Lijfrentekas* (General Life Annuity Fund) is regarded as the first step in the development of pension legislation in Belgium; based upon the individual's voluntary prior deposits, old-age pensions were paid when he reached the retirement age. The next step in the development of pension legislation occurred in 1891, when the government made small discretionary contributions ("savings premiums") to individual accounts. Both these programs preceded and led up to the first general pension statute, passed by the Belgian Parliament in the year 1900.

The statute of May 10, 1900, set up a system of noncompulsory old-age insurance. Under certain circumstances,[1] the government was required by this statute to pay premiums from public funds as an encouragement to persons who made deposits to the *Algemene Lijfrentekas*. In such cases the amount of premium paid was 60 percent of the deposited funds.

The 1900 statute, however, did not produce the expected results. The major complicating problem was that most private, and therefore also public, contributions virtually disappeared during the First World War because workers lacked money to save. After the war several studies were undertaken by the government with the objective of recommending directions for a complete reform of the

---

1. See statute of May 10, 1900 (*Staatsblad*, May 14–15, 1900); requirements: nationality, age, premium level, fund, etc.

existing pension system (Commissie van de Kamer van Volks-vertegenwoordigers, 1923–24).

A temporary measure was passed in 1920 which guaranteed all workers a *minimum* retirement pension.[2] Then in 1924 and 1925 the first compulsory old-age insurance programs for blue and white collar workers were enacted (to come into effect on January 1, 1926).[3] Two types of benefits were paid: (1) a payment based on the workers' and employers' prior contributions and (2) a special payment to workers whose income before retirement was below a specified amount. The first type was financed in the same way as private insurance systems: contributions were placed in a fund; reserves were accumulated; and interest was credited. This method of financing the old-age pension programs by means of *individuele capitalisatie* (full funding) remained the major financing principle up until the Second World War. The means-tested benefit was financed out of general revenue.

In the decade prior to the War, a number of major changes in the law were enacted. In 1930 the individual capitalization financing was modified to introduce and allow some departure from full-funding financing. In 1937 the means-tested benefit was abolished.

Major Pension Reform

During the Occupation an *Ontwerp van Overeenkomst tot Sociale Solidariteit* (Scheme of Arrangement for Social Solidarity) was drafted by a group of Belgian employers, workers, and government officials.[4] This document, which discussed various social security problems, was instrumental in stimulating the passage of new pension legislation. Laws were passed in 1945 which set down separate pension provisions for (a) blue collar workers, (b) white collar workers, (c) miners, and (d) seamen.

---

2. *Staatsblad*, August 30–31, 1920.

3. Statutes of December 10, 1924 (*Staatsblad*, December 22–23, 1924) and March 10, 1925 (*Staatsblad*, April 1, 1925).

4. The first meetings took place during August 1941, with representatives of the two major trade unions (the Algemeen Belgisch Vakverbond and the Algemeen Christelijk Vakverbond), the organization of employers, and two persons who had been civil servants prior to the occupation.

Thus, in addition to the existing pensions financed by individuele capitalisatie, these new pension statutes made provision for financing an additional flat-rate pension benefit on a partial pay-as-you-go basis, thereby emphasizing an important financing principle which was to influence subsequent legislation. The individual's pension was no longer financed mainly by his own contributions; instead pensions were to be financed out of the total contributions allocated to the particular pension scheme by all workers.

A major reason for basing the new programs on this financing principle was the desire to deal with the problem of individual contributions that depreciated in value as a result of inflation. As a result of efforts to provide a pension of a "reasonable amount" and adjust for the rising costs of living, that part of the total pension program which was based on partial funding became over time a more and more important part of the total for all four groups. Over the years, therefore, the trend of pension legislation was away from reliance on "individual capitalization" and toward various forms of income redistribution through partial funding.

In 1953 Secretary of Social Welfare G. van den Daele proposed a bill to establish an earnings-related pension system with earnings replacement levels which, at least in theory, were to be very high. The bill was passed without much debate. Soon after this law was passed and before it could be implemented, however, a new government came into power. Acting for the Government, the new Secretary of Social Welfare, L. Troclet, immediately moved (for political reasons) to have the 1953 law abolished. The Government then proposed and passed new pension laws in 1955 and 1957, copying the major principles of the 1953 law.

It is interesting to note that there was an almost complete lack of debate over this reform. Since the trade unions had long favored an earnings-related system, they voiced no opposition to the details of the proposal. Similarly, no other interested party—employers' organizations, pensioners' associations, political parties—opposed the reform. In fact all three major political parties were, in an important sense, responsible for the reform: the 1953 law was proposed by an all Christian Democratic government and the 1955–57 reform was initiated by a Socialist-Conservative coalition.

The new pension statutes for blue collar workers in 1955 and white collar workers in 1957 (and the related laws for seamen and miners) contained important and innovative new provisions. *It was this legislation which introduced wage related pensions by establishing a pension formula that calculated the pension as a given percentage of prior earnings.* The law specified that a pension for an unmarried worker was to equal 60 percent of the worker's average lifetime earnings; in the case of a couple, a spouse supplement was to be paid, bringing the earnings replacement up to 75 percent of average lifetime earnings. Because, in most cases, the actual earnings prior to the new law had never been recorded and therefore were unknown, "flat wages" (similar for all years) had to be used in the calculation for the prior years. After a transition period of 45 years (ending in the year 2000), the calculated pensions were to be based entirely upon the workers' actual average lifetime earnings.

Adjustment of these pensions for changes in the cost of living were to be achieved in two ways: first, by revaluating the wages used to calculate pensions *at the time of retirement* and, second, by adjusting the pensions *during retirement* by means of a consumer price index.[5]

Two additional features of the reforms of 1955 and 1957 are of special importance: (1) the laws broadened the coverage of the social security system by liberalizing the definition of blue and white collar workers covered and (2) the government guaranteed the financial stability of the system.

The resulting pension system—the one in Belgium today—can be viewed as the most significant step taken thus far in Belgium toward achieving adequate retirement income. Its most important features—to relate pensions to the worker's lifetime earnings, a goal of high replacement, automatic adjustment provisions, and the introduction of pay-as-you-go financing—were a dramatic break from earlier pension provisions and will be discussed in detail below.

Establishing Minimum Pensions

Because the 1955/57 reforms involved a lengthy transition period, legislation was enacted in 1958 which established interim minimum pension benefits for all pension programs. These guar-

---

5. These provisions are described in greater detail below, pp. 134.

anteed amounts were subsequently increased in 1961, 1962, and 1965. Between 1958 and 1965 the minimum pension level was raised by about 47 percent for couples and 59 percent for unmarried individuals in the blue collar workers' system and by 36 percent and 48 percent, respectively, for white collar workers.[6]

Over the years the weight of actual wages in the pension calculations of retiring persons rapidly increased. Since the "flat wage" substitutes for real wages had been set very low, the shift in weighting resulted in higher pensions being paid to the more recent retirees. As a result of this development, the Government felt that the role of the minimum pension program should be reconsidered. To keep pension costs low, the Government decided that the minimum should be eliminated from pensions awarded after January 1, 1962.[7] An exception was made for miners' pensions, but since these pensions had always been based on flat earnings only, the guaranteed minimum was not abolished and continued to be applied up until December 31, 1967.

The abolition of minimum pensions lasted seven years. In 1969 new pension legislation was passed which guaranteed a minimum income to all aged Belgians—not only pensioners but all men and women above age 65 and 60, respectively. The receipt of this payment—up to 41,620 BF (in 1971) for a married couple and 27,746 BF for a single person—was made conditional on satisfying a means test.

Consolidation of Pension Programs

As indicated above, the Belgian pension system established in 1955/57 contained four separate programs. A new law passed in 1967 eliminated these four programs and brought all workers into one pension scheme. The major reason was to solve a serious problem: the ratio of pensioners to active workers in some of the programs had become unfavorable and made financing difficult. The general shift of workers in the economy from one category to another had caused the number of white collar workers to increase 46 percent from 1956 to 1965, the number of blue collar workers to increase

---

6. "Evolutie van de Ontvangsten en Uitgaven van de Sociale Zekerheid tussen 1958–1965" (1967).

7. See below, Chapter 7.

only 9 percent, and the number of miners to decrease 44 percent. By 1965, the proportion of pensioners to active workers had reached 21 percent in the program for white collar workers, 34 percent in the blue collar program, and 132 percent in the program for miners.[8]

This situation resulted in (a) the white collar workers' pension program developing considerable reserves; (b) the miners' program no longer being able to guarantee pensions without receiving large state contributions, and (c) an inability to finance further pension increases in the blue collar workers' and seamen's pension programs. Some sort of consolidation was a necessity.

When the Government proposed that the financing of the four programs be consolidated, there was considerable opposition from the trade unions representing white collar workers. These unions feared that the proposed consolidation would be counter to their interests because their pension reserves, in effect, would be used to pay the pensions of workers in other occupations. In exchange for their agreeing to the consolidation, the minimum pension for white collar pensioners that had retired before 1962 was increased much more than for those in other occupational groups.

The resulting consolidated scheme did not mean that contributions and benefits were immediately and completely equalized for the four different categories of workers. Differences with regard to the calculation of these pensions and the retirement eligibility age remained.[9] But clearly the legislature did intend that this would be a step toward the long-run establishment of a uniform pension system.

In addition to the financial consolidation of the four programs and the introduction of relatively uniform regulations, the legislature sought to improve the administrative structure of the pension system and to raise pension levels. This latter objective was achieved primarily by increasing the level of the "flat wages" used in the pension calculation.

---

8. Because of the decreasing numbers of miners (50,351 in 1968) and seamen (about 3,000 in 1968), we will not deal further with their pension schemes in this book.

9. Eligibility ages are: 65 for white and blue collar workers; 60 for seamen; 60 for miners above ground; 55 for miners underground; at any age for miners underground with 27 years of service.

Between 1967 and 1972 the pension system did not undergo any major changes. The parliament raised pensions for the retired aged in 1969, 1970, 1971, 1972, and 1973 (by 4, 5, 5, 5, and 7.96 percent respectively) to reflect increases in average real wage levels. Although these pensions were being automatically adjusted by a consumer price index, ad hoc increases were instituted primarily as a result of the increasing disparity between the level of price-adjusted pensions and the wage incomes of active workers.

Then in March 1973 a major change in the pension benefit calculation was legislated. Beginning in 1974 both earnings used to calculate initial benefits and also pensions paid throughout retirement were adjusted by both a price index and a "productivity adjustment"—instead of the earlier price index (see page 134).

Pensions for the Self-Employed

In addition to the improved and consolidated pension program for workers discussed above, a compulsory pension system for self-employed workers was introduced in 1956. The basic principles of this program were the following: the system was to be based mainly on the reserve fund model; its main objective was to guarantee a minimum pension that could be supplemented by private insurance and saving; pension benefits were to originate mainly from capitalized contributions (originating from individual payments of the self-employed), complemented by a flat-rate pension financed on a partial pay-as-you-go basis. The receipt of the flat benefit was initially dependent upon satisfying a means test; between 1955 and 1971 the test incorporated into the flat-rate pension was gradually liberalized, however, until finally in 1972 legislation was passed to eliminate it by 1975.

In contrast to the workers' system, the flat-rate pension for self-employed persons is based only upon the person's occupation and not upon his actual income.[10] This pension is therefore the same for all self-employed persons.

With regard to benefit levels, Belgian pension legislation seeks to make a clear distinction between the role of public pensions for workers versus their role for the self-employed. For the former the

---

10. Contributions to the program, however, vary with the level of income.

intent is to preserve the workers' average lifetime standard of living; for the latter, the legislation seeks merely to establish a guaranteed minimum pension.

THE REFORMS OF 1955, 1956, 1957, AND 1973

As indicated in the previous section, major Belgian pension reform occurred in 1955 for blue collar workers, in 1956 for the self-employed, and in 1957 for white collar workers. We speak of this legislation as a major reform because it significantly changed the ability of the pension system to provide adequate pensions. To do this, the pensions were based on the "assessment principle": a system of "collective capitalization." This principle assumed that there was strong solidarity between different categories of workers and their employers.

Because of the importance of the 1955 and 1957 laws, they receive close attention in the discussion that follows. The discussion will not exclude, however, some description and analysis of later laws voted in the early and mid sixties, especially the major changes in 1973.

The Current Old Age Pension System

At the present time there are three public old-age pension programs in Belgium: (1) the Government Employees Program, (2) the Self-Employed Pension Program, and (3) the Workers System. The Workers System consists of four programs—for blue collar workers, white collar, miners, and seamen. While these four programs share many similar provisions and the financing for all has been combined, each program has some special or unique aspects.

Pensions for blue and white collar workers are paid at age 65 (for men) and age 60 (for women) and are equal to 75 percent (for couples) and 60 percent (for single persons) of the employee's average earnings throughout the working career—each year's earnings being adjusted by an earnings index for changes occurring between the year of receipt and the year of retirement. This *full* pension is paid to all workers who work a "full career" (normally 45 years) and reduced by 1/45 (1/40 for women) for each year less than a full career. Although there is no maximum pension for blue collar workers, white collar workers are taxed on and credited for gross earnings up to the "earnings ceiling"—which is currently equal to about 80 percent of average earnings.[11]

Pensions may be requested up to five years before the age of normal retirement but are reduced by 5 percent for each year of early retirement. If pension receipt is delayed, the pension award is increased by 1/45 for each year of later retirement (up to a maximum of 5 years).

Until December 1973 pensions were adjusted during retirement only for changes in the price level. Beginning in 1974, however, this price adjustment was replaced by an earnings index that adjusts pensions at and during retirement for changes in average wages. (See page 220.)

There is a widow's benefit equal to 80 percent of the couple's benefit.

The Pension Formula

To better understand the Belgian system and the major reforms instituted, the pension formula needs to be traced through its successive changes.

Belgian workers' pensions are currently based upon a formula first legislated as part of the pension reform legislation of 1955/57.[12] Algebraically, the old formula can be written as follows:[13]

$$\frac{1}{X}(aM + brE_A) + Z = P_w \tag{1}$$

where

P_w is the workers' pension amount,

x denotes the number of credited years required for a "complete career," hence full pension; x equals 45 for men and 40 for women. [14]

---

11. The latter regulation already constitutes a built-in inadequacy, the earnings ceiling being so low.

12. Many of the details in this section are based upon Spitaels and Klaric (1968).

13. This formula was the same for both white and blue collar workers.

14. The law of 1955 specified that a male and female worker would be credited with a "volledige loopbaan" (complete career) if they started working at the age of 20 and retired at the ages of 65 and 60 respectively (the normal retirement ages for men and women).

a is the number of years worked before January 1, 1955.

b is the number of years worked after January 1, 1955.

M is a guaranteed minimum pension amount that is specified by law; its amount varies depending on white versus blue collar status and a couple's versus an individual's pension.

r is 75 percent in the case of a retiring worker who has a spouse (a) who has also stopped all professional activities (except those permitted by law) and (b) who does *not* receive herself any social security benefits; r is 60 percent in all other cases.

E_A is the average of the worker's gross earnings (adjusted for price changes) earned from January 1, 1955, until the date of retirement; if gross earnings in any particular year are less than M, the value of M is substituted for that year's earnings. In the case of white collar workers, only gross earnings up to the maximum taxable earnings level specified by law may be credited.

Z is equal to a pension calculated using private insurance principles. That is, the recipient who lives the average life expectancy is entitled to his principle paid in plus interest accrued less administrative expenses. The amount depends upon the pensioner's contribution history before 1955, during the period when the old-age pension system was running on an "individual capitalization" or fully funded basis.

As one can observe from formula 1, the workers' gross earnings before 1955 were not taken into account in the pension calculation. The formula did provide, however, for a substitute in the form of a "guaranteed minimum pension" amount specified in the law. This procedure was necessitated by the fact that the pension administration did not have any record of a worker's earnings prior to 1955. Thus, although the new system was called an earnings-related pension system, it in fact turned out to be a two-tier system—since the total pension included both a flat minimum amount and an earnings-related payment based on the workers' gross earnings after 1954.

The first change in the 1955/57 formula was legislated in 1962. The law of April 3, 1962, provided for an increase in the guaranteed minimum. However, in order to avoid a possibly excessive deficit in the old-age pension account, the method of calculating the average of gross earnings after 1954 was changed for new awards; in calculating the pension, M could no longer be substituted for gross earnings less than M for any year after 1954.

The legislation also modified the x in the pension formula representing the length of a "complete career." The value of x was made equal to the number of years between the year of retirement and 1926, the latter being the year in which the first Belgian contributory pension program was made compulsory. Also, a in the formula was to be set equal to the number of years worked between 1926 and 1955.

The next major change in the benefit formula was legislated in 1967.[15] The pension law of October 24 was particularly important because it integrated the four pension systems; however, it also specified some changes in the pension calculation. The guaranteed minimum pension was replaced by "flat wages" in the calculation of all new old-age pensions, and all earnings (flat and actual) were to be multiplied by the appropriate value of r (75 or 60 percent).

Finally, on March 28, 1973, the adjustment of earnings (beginning in 1974) was changed to include a productivity adjustment in addition to the price adjustment. The productivity adjustment is based upon a coefficient determined by law. The 1973 and 1974 adjustment coefficients, for example, were 1.0325^n and 1.035^n—n being equal to the number of years between the year preceding the year of retirement and the year of earnings receipt. Workers who retired prior to 1974, however, do not benefit from this new provision.

Modifying formula 1 in the light of these various changes, we arrive at the pension formula that is used for workers retiring after 1973:

$$P_w = r \frac{1}{X^*} (a^*F^* + bE_A{}^*) + Z \qquad (2)$$

where

X^* is the number of years between the year of retirement and 1926 (up to a maximum of 45),

a^* is the number of years between 1955 and 1926,

F^* is a flat amount chosen as a proxy for the real but unknown wages before 1955. This flat amount is adjusted to reflect productivity increases.

---

15. The application of these new regulations started on January 1, 1968.

$E_A{}^*$ is the average of the worker's gross earnings (adjusted for price and productivity changes) earned from January 1, 1955, until the date of retirement. Such earnings are subject to a minimum and maximum, as described above.

P_w, r, b, and Z have the same meaning as in formula 1.

The Formula for the Self-Employed [16]

In 1956 the social security system was expanded to include self-employed persons; this self-employed pension program was based on the following four general principles:

(a) the system was to rely heavily on funding; however, government contributions were to be made;

(b) the social security provisions were to cover only the minimum needs of these persons;

(c) various organizations representing the self-employed workers were to take an important part in the management of the system;

(d) pensions received were to be subject to a means test.

The original pension program for the self-employed had two parts: an individual account and a partial pay-as-you-go group plan which (1) paid pensions according to need, (2) paid minimum pensions to the self-employed without prior contributions, and (3) was used to adjust payments for inflation.[17] Three fourths of a self-employed male's pension contributions and three fifths of a female's goes into the individual account. When a self-employed person reaches retirement age—65 in the case of men and 60 in the case of women—he or she has an unconditional claim on the "capitalized interest amounts" resulting from these contributions.[18] Of course, these amounts are currently very small since the legislation, which made such contributions compulsory, was inaugurated less than two

---

16. For details of the program we rely on the descriptions provided by De Gadt (1971) and Vergauwen (1971).

17. These functions were modified in 1972 and will be further discussed below.

18. The operation of this part of the program is similar to the General Life Annuity Fund for workers, but separate financial reserves and administration are maintained.

decades ago. Theoretically, this capitalized interest (called *rente* in the Belgian pension literature) can accumulate to quite a substantial amount. For example, the amount paid in the year 2016 would be 70,000 BF ($1800) per year, if a self-employed person began working at age 21 years (in 1971) and contributed the maximum amount of pension contributions during his entire employment career. Self-employed persons who are currently retiring have participated in this compulsory pension program for a maximum of only eighteen years (1956–74) or about one third of a complete career. The result is that their capitalized interest account currently represents only a small part of the total pension amount. It is certainly not a sufficient amount to make a significant contribution toward the goal of adequate retirement income. It should be noted, however, that the capitalized interest amounts are adjusted yearly for inflation occurring after, but not before, retirement. The adjustment is paid for out of group plan funds.

Realizing the current inadequacy of these interest payments, the sponsors of the 1956 law also provided for a group plan—operating on the "assessment principle"—as a mechanism for dealing with this problem. There exists a major difference between this group program and the program for workers. The pension amounts for the latter are basically earnings-related. In contrast the self-employed pension amount paid from the group plan is unrelated to income earned during a person's active life; instead it is related to the financial need of the person. The total pension amount is paid to everyone who has worked as a self-employed worker throughout his entire career. Persons working fewer years in self-employment receive a pension that is a fraction of the full amount. The denominator of the fraction used to determine how much is paid depends on the number of years between the retirement year and January 1, 1926; the numerator is equal to the number of self-employed years during the same period. (An example will be given below.) The adjustment mechanism is identical to that applied in the workers' pension system.

The special characteristic of the original pension program for the self-employed was its means test. This special regulation was adopted principally to keep down costs. Since the institution of the pension program was not enthusiastically supported by the self-

employed themselves, the Government had to set a very low contribution rate and seek ways to economize on the benefits paid out.
One way to save money is to restrict the payment of pensions only
to people who need them. As in other countries, there are a large
number of self-employed people in Belgium who earn very high
incomes during their working years and who are able to accumulate
large stocks of assets which would permit them to enjoy a relatively
high standard of living during retirement.[19] Many thought that the
payment of large old-age pensions to such persons would create an
inequitable situation.

Also, because of financial reasons, the flat pension received by
persons meeting the means test was set at a rather low level. Critics
have argued in recent years that the established benefit level was
inadequate for self-employed persons who were earning only modest
incomes—for whom it is an almost impossible job to accumulate
personal savings for old-age.[20]

The self-employed pension formula established in 1956 was:

$$P_s = \frac{n}{d}(F - [I - C]) - R \qquad (3)$$

where

P_s is the self-employed person's pension,

n is the number of years of self-employment (a maximum of 45),

d equals 45,

F is the flat pension amount legislated by law,

I is yearly income from other designated sources,

C is a predetermined (deductible) ceiling, and

R is the yearly "capitalization" amount to which the
person is unconditionally entitled.

We can apply formula 3 to a person who, for example:

(a) worked 30 years in a self-employed capacity,

---

19. For example, medical doctors, pharmacists, owners of large
businesses, etc.

20. For example, hairdressers, grocers, shoemakers, bakers, small
businessmen, etc. (See Table 20.)

(b) can count, during his retirement, on a yearly income from various assets of 40,000 BF,

(c) is entitled to a yeyarly interest amount of 4000 BF,

(d) retired in April 1971, and

(e) is married.

In this case the pension is calculated as follows:

$$P_s = \frac{30}{45}\,(45{,}529 - [40{,}000 - 21{,}000]) - 4000 = 13{,}679 \qquad BF$$

The above calculation uses the flat pension and deductible levels that were in effect in April 1971.[21] The person's total pension is equal, therefore, to the sum of the pension formula result (13,679 BF) and the capitalization amount (4000 BF) or a total of 17,679 BF.

Since the initiation of the self-employment pension program, the flat level amount has been changed frequently. Table 20 shows

TABLE 20

Flat Pension Amounts for the Self-Employed
and Percentage Changes in These Amounts

Date of Change	Couples' Pension Amount	Individual's Pension Amount	Increase in Flat Amount	
			Couples' Pension	Individuals' Pension
1/1/1956	18,000 BF	12,000 BF		
1/1/1960	21,000	14,000	16.6%	16.6%
1/7/1963	24,600	16,400	17.1	17.1
1/1/1965	26,926	17,952	9.4	9.4
1/4/1966	30,705	20,470	14.0	14.0
1/1/1968	36,750	24,500	19.6	19.6
1/7/1969	39,780	26,520	8.2	8.2
1/7/1970	44,686	30,137	12.3	13.6

Source: Flat pension amounts are reported in J. De Gadt (1971), pp. 66–67.

the various amounts and the percentage increases from change to change. The table shows that the flat pension amounts have grown

---

21. In the case of a single person, this deductible amount equals 14,000 BF.

considerably since 1956 (both for couples and individuals): an average of about 13 percent per year.

Table 21

TABLE 21

Comparison of Self-Employed Couples' Pensions
for Blue and White Collar Workers
in Manufacturing, 1957–1971

Year (1)	Self-Employed (2)	Blue Collar Workers (3)	White Collar Workers (4)	(2)/(3) (5)	(2)/(4) (6)
1960	21,000	38,862	50,464	.54	.42
1966	30,705	54,065	67,890	.57	.45
1971	49,882	75,859	100,450	.66	.50

Sources: De Gadt (1971), p. 67, for self-employed pensions; pensions for blue and white collar workers are for hypothetical workers.

Table 21 shows how the level of self-employed pensions has improved relative to those for blue and white collar workers. Columns 5 and 6 in the table show that flat pensions for the self-employed improved much faster than those of the worker pension system.

The progress made in the last 15 years in improving the level of self-employed pensions is not likely to come to a halt in the near future. In 1970 an important law was enacted by the Belgian Parliament which contained a "social plan for the self-employed." This new law provided for minimum pensions in 1975 of 60,000 BF and 48,000 BF [22] for couples and individuals respectively.[23] These new levels represent an average real growth of the pension level between 1971 and 1975 of 6 percent and 12 percent. The higher percentage increase for individuals was a deliberate action to bring the non-married pension up from 66 percent—as is presently the case—to 80 percent of the couple's pension level.

---

22. Note that these amounts are linked to the consumer price index.

23. In a later section we discuss measures of minimum need. Most authorities writing in the Belgian social security field assume that about 5000 BF per month meet this minimum. We argue below, however, that 5000 BF is insufficient and should not be used in formulating social security policy.

A second innovation is that starting July 1, 1971, the means test was not applied to those years in which the self-employed person made any contribution to the system. Most self-employed workers' organizations objected to this change, arguing that it did not go far enough. Instead, they advocated complete abolition of the means test. Recent legislation, overriding the new law, took account of these objectives by providing for the gradual abolition of the means test.

Finally, starting in July 1972, flat pensions were set at 60,000 BF and 45,000 BF for a couple and an individual, respectively, and on January 1, 1975, these amounts are scheduled to become 81,180 BF and 64,944 BF respectively (about $2000 and $1600).

In general, we think that these new changes improve the self-employed pension program. However, the reforms still do not make the pension program entirely earnings-related. We think this is a major disadvantage. In addition, the present program fails to give adequate pensions to the self-employed with very low incomes.

Financing the System

The Belgian social security pension program for workers is financed primarily by contributions paid by workers and their employers, although the Government also contributes. In addition, a very small proportion of the funds is derived from the interest on pension fund investments, the receipts of extraordinary taxes,[24] and transfers from other social security administrations. Table 22 shows the statutory tax rates for workers and employers.

The justification given in the official pension literature for the Government's contributions is that it is "a necessary way to guarantee a sound financial functioning of the pension programs." It should be noted, however, that as the workers' pension program has grown, there has been less and less need for government financial support —reflecting the growing self-sufficiency of these programs at prevail-

---

24. For example, "cyclical taxes," which are taxes that are levied on consumption and investment during a boom period.

TABLE 22

Contribution Rates, Workers' Old Age Pension Programs
July 1974

Type of Worker	Contribution Paid by		Maximum Taxable Earnings
	Worker	Employer	
Blue Collar	6%	8%	None
White Collar	5.75	8	24,550 BF [a]

[a] This amount is linked to and adjusted regularly by an earnings index.

ing contribution levels. Table 23, for example, shows for various years the declining ratio of the government's contribution to total receipts.[25]

TABLE 23

Ratio of Government Contributions
to Total Pension Receipts

Year	Ratio
1959	26.33
1960	25.65
1961	25.41
1962	25.92
1963	24.97
1964	22.58
1965	21.51
1966	19.36
1967	19.37
1968	18.64

Source: Ministerie van Sociale Voorzorg (1970).

Officially, the *workers'* contributions are announced as taxes that give financial support to the pension system but also reflect a "solidarity" among the workers. On the other hand, some people

25. We disregard here funds originating from sources other than the worker, employer, and government contributions.

view *employers'* contributions as special aids or gifts to the workers. Deleeck (1966) has argued, however, that the employers' contributions are in fact financed out of the real wages of labor.[26] Deleeck arrives at this conclusion by showing that the rise in social security contributions in Belgium has not led to any increase in the real share of total wages (direct wages plus contributions for social security) in the national income.

Unlike Deleeck, other Belgian writers have assumed that employer costs rise with an increase in social security taxes. It has been argued, for example, that an advantage of financing the largest part of the pension fund by means of social security taxes based on wages is that an incentive is built into the contributory system to "save" as much labor as possible. Entrepreneurs, it is argued, regard such a financing system as one that increases their production costs and therefore puts a downward pressure on profits. Indirectly, therefore, through this stimulation to increase capital intensity, economic growth in enterprises is encouraged (Frank, 1964; Kervyn, 1964).

Others argue that the major disadvantages of the present financing method is that not all enterprises have the flexibility or the resources to achieve a higher degree of capital intensity every time indirect labor costs increase. In fact, firms that are already characterized by a high degree of capital intensity would be favored because they will have relatively minor problems in absorbing an increase in the direct labor cost. Hence, it is possible that a contributory system leads to a reduction in the degree of competition in the economy. E. S. Kirschen, for example, has argued that employers' contributions are not based on the value added by a firm's product but on the enterprise's total wage bill; this implies that labor-intensive enterprises are at a disadvantage in relation to firms with proportionately less manpower (Kirschen, 1964).

In Belgium, no major empirical studies have been undertaken to investigate the possible shift in the burden of social security taxes to workers' wages. Until further empirical evidence regarding this question is presented, one cannot make a definitive statement on the matter. In the United States recent studies by Gordon (1971) and Brittain (1972) conclude that the U.S. social security tax burden falls almost entirely on wage income in the long run.

---

26. See also Delperee (1962).

Financing the Self-Employed Program[27]

The contributions of the self-employed in a certain year are based on the income these persons received during the third calendar year that preceded calculation of the contribution; the income in this year is then adjusted by a price index. For example, the required contributions for 1970 were on an income base calculated by multiplying self-employment income received in 1967 times a coefficient of 1.15—which adjusts for the 15 percent increase in prices that occurred over the three-year period.

The law further specifies that the first 71,999 BF of income are exempt from taxation, after which there is an "intermediate" ceiling of 206,470 BF and a maximum ceiling of 354,705 BF.[28] Any person with an income that equals or exceeds the latter amount pays a maximum contribution. Other self-employed persons pay 5.75 percent on any income above the exemption but below the intermediate amount and 2.1 percent on that part of income which exceeds the intermediate ceiling. Income above the maximum ceiling is not taxed.

The 2.1 percent contribution is called a "solidarity" contribution rate because its yield is allocated to help finance all social security programs for the self-employed, in contrast to the contribution of 5.75 percent, which is a specific pension tax rate. In other words, the contributions resulting from this specific pension tax rate are directed uniquely to the pension assessment scheme, whereas the yields from the application of the solidarity rate are spread over the funds of all schemes, viz. the pension, sickness insurance and family benefits schemes.

Recent legislation calls for a change in the various financing rates and ceilings. Table 24 indicates these scheduled changes.

Current Thinking

The first part of this section discusses important research that has been done recently on the economic status of the aged in

---

27. Only the financing system applicable to the persons who are self-employed full time is described.

28. These are the amounts as of January 1971, when the price index was 148.5.

TABLE 24

Planned Changes in Financing the Self-Employed
Pension System

Provisions	July 1, 1972	January 1, 1975
Exempt amount	80,000 BF	100,000 BF
Intermediate ceiling	225,000	325,000
Maximum ceiling	420,000	420,000
Contribution rate on income between the minimum amount and the intermediate ceiling	6.3%	6.8%
Solidarity rate	2.5%	4%
Government contribution	2.97 billion BF	7.815 billion BF

Source: Ministerie van Sociale Voorzorg.

Belgium. The end of the section presents the opinions of some Belgian pension experts regarding needed improvements in the current Belgian old-age pension system.

The Economic Status of the Aged

Deleeck (1966) reports in his doctoral dissertation that a significant redistribution of social security funds occurs from the active contributing Belgian population to the aged. He calculates that 28 percent of the total gross redistribution of social security funds in 1961 (12 billion BF) was transferred to the aged.

One should not conclude from this fact that the Belgian aged population is currently well off. It has been shown in previous sections that the current old-age pension system provides, on the average, inadequate replacement in terms of achieving a living standard in retirement similar to one just prior to retirement.

A number of articles have been written on the extent of poverty among elderly people in Belgium. (La Cité, 1967; Centre de Recherche et de l'Information Sociales et Politique, 1967; Mertens, 1971; Nationale Actie voor Bestaanszekerheid, 1969; Schoetter and Spitaels, 1966; Versichelen, 1970.) Some of them are of special interest and should be discussed.

In 1966 P. Schoetter and G. Spitaels published the results of an analysis of five randomly chosen Belgian "welfare bureaus." These bureaus had been created by Parliament in order to provide relief over and above the existing social security aid provided to people who were found in need. Schoetter and Spitaels found that 59 percent of the people who were requesting help from these bureaus were age 65 or older. If one includes women pensioners between the ages of 60 and 64, the proportion rises to 66 percent. Twenty-five percent of the aged included in the sample had a monthly income of less that 1000 BF ($25), 15 percent had monthly incomes in the range of 1000–1999 BF ($25–50), and 12 percent had incomes between 2000–3499 BF ($50–88). Using a poverty line of 4000–5000 BF ($100–125), one can see that a very high proportion of the aged in the five municipalities surveyed were poor. Another interesting finding was that 66 percent of all the poor in the five municipalities were pensioners.

The Centre de Recherche et de l'Information Sociale et Politique (CRISP) (1967) estimated the number of aged people in each pension category in 1965 who received less than 4000 BF (in the case of couples' pensions) and 2500 BF (in the case of individuals' pensions).[29] Their study reported that 86,700 couples and 305,150 individuals (i.e., 32 percent of the total aged population) fell below these poverty lines. The researchers of CRISP qualified these findings, however. They observed that their estimates did not take account of:

(a) income from property;

(b) any earnings received by pensioners;

(c) supplementary private pensions;[30]

(d) the fact that about half of the pensioners owned their house or apartment.[31]

---

29. The analysis was limited to pension schemes in the private sector (i.e., the pension schemes for all workers excluding civil servants).

30. According to CRISP, 80 percent of white collar workers are covered by private pension schemes.

31. This statement is supported by the results of a questionnaire sent to 8500 pensioners living in the southern Belgian provinces by the *Union Nationale Chretienne des Pensionnes*. Of the 7632 pensioners who answered the survey investigating the ownership of housing, 4543 (55.4 percent) declared that they owned the house or apartment they were living in.

CRISP estimates that if these additional factors were considered, about 43,500 couples and 152,500 single pensioners fell below the poverty line. Finally, CRISP estimates that when poor pensioners from the nonprivate sector are included, a total of 300,000 pensioners (20 percent of the total aged population) could not achieve a satisfactory minimum standard of living in 1965.

A more recent inquiry into the economic situation of the aged has been reported on by J. Mertens (1971). It is more comprehensive than most other studies, analyzing the distribution of pension income from all types of pensions.[32] In order to get a more reliable and realistic estimate of the number of poor among pensioners, Mertens also tries to correct for possible double-counting.[33] Mertens makes estimates of the income position of couples.[34] He discusses the income situation of the "working" aged and the incomes the aged received from sources other than social security. He adjusts his figures for additional benefits that a number of pensioners receive, mainly veterans' benefits and "supplementary old-age interests."[35] Unfortunately, because of inadequate statistical material, he could not take account of income from work and from private pension benefits, and this is a serious shortcoming of the study.

Using a poverty line of 5000 BF and 4000 BF for couples and unmarried persons respectively, Mertens estimates that there were 25,000 poor aged families and 100,000 poor individuals (i.e., 9.5 percent of the total old-age population) in the year 1969.

The studies summarized above have added to our knowledge about the economic status of the aged in Belgium. They have contributed to the rising awareness among the population and the government that much of the old-age population cannot count on

32. Workers', survivors', veterans', and civil servants' pensions.
33. Some pensioners qualify for two or more pensions, which are then reported separately.
34. One obtains a biased estimate of the number of poor aged if one does not make an estimate of the income position of married aged couples. The latter cannot be easily estimated from the available statistical data, since these data contain separate information about the pensions of men and women who are married.
35. This is a special provision regulated by the law of February 12, 1963, whereby interest is awarded if one has contributed to a special scheme on a voluntary basis.

adequate income in retirement. As a result of these studies, many Belgians conclude that the aged are not receiving a just share in the wealth of the nation. To accurately determine the extent of this possible injustice, however, a comprehensive survey of the aged is needed in Belgium, similar to those recently carried out in the United States.

Another of our major criticisms of prior estimates of poor, aged persons in the total aged population is that the measure of poverty used (the "poverty line") is very low. The measure used by Schoetter, Spitaels, and Mertens was based on a minimum budget for only three items—food, clothing, and housing. Judging this measure to be too low, we have calculated a monthly "sociovital" budget for both a family of two and a single person. This budget incorporates such items as the cost of a modest vacation, recreation, transportation, and certain services (items omitted from the poverty measure discussed above). In 1971 the cost of this budget was 8600 BF for a couple and 5000 BF for an individual (Werkgroep voor Alternatieve Economie, 1972).

Extrapolating backward and assuming a nominal average growth rate of 6 percent, we propose for a minimum standard of living 7654 BF and 4450 BF for a couple and an individual, respectively, in 1969, and 6064 BF and 3525 BF for a couple and an individual, respectively, in 1965. In contrast, the poverty lines used by CRISP are 4000 BF and 2500 BF (1965) and by Mertens, 5000 BF and 4000 BF (1969). With this new poverty line the estimates of aged poverty increase by about 50 percent.

Current Opinions

In 1971 we sought the opinions of a number of Belgian experts in the pension field by means of a written questionnaire. These experts were asked about the adequacy of pensions in Belgium.[36] All of those answering the questionnaire agreed that an *adequate pension* should be defined as one that enables the pensioner at least to maintain the same standard of living in retirement which he had be-

---

36. The questionnaire was sent to ten experts. Only five answers were obtained: three from civil servants, one from a trade union official, and one from the employers' association.

fore retirement. Furthermore, they agreed that the pension system should guarantee a basic minimum to everybody.

Some experts stressed that the adequacy of the pension should be evaluated not only on the basis of the adequacy of individual pensions but also on the basis of the collective result. In fact, they argued, a pension system can only be considered adequate when the population as a whole and every pensioner is sufficiently protected.

A simple linking of benefits to the price index was considered insufficient for several reasons. The current way of calculating this index was criticized, and some pointed out that there is a considerable lapse of time (generally three months) before the index fully influences the pension amount.

All the experts were convinced that pension levels at and during retirement should be linked to an earnings index[37] However, they were aware of the fact that such a reform would encounter many practical problems. For example, the Belgian civil service pension used to be linked to wage changes beginning in 1955. But after large wage increases occurred in 1963, this practice had to be discontinued for financial reasons.

The experts, asked if they thought pensions should be related to the earnings gained during the whole professional career, typically answered that the amount should be at least in proportion to a representative part of the career. The current objective—that the pension should amount to 75 percent of average lifetime income—was questioned by some who argued that the 75 percent goal was initially established at a time when all professional activities were prohibited after retirement and work expenses were estimated to amount to 25 percent of wages. In view of the recent improved opportunities for working after retirement, one of the experts thought that the pension amount could be reduced to about 65 percent, regardless of the marital status of the beneficiary.[38]

---

37. The experts were surveyed two years prior to the passage in 1973 of the legislation instituting a productivity adjustment.

38. In contrast, recent opinion polls of Belgian workers and employers show that the pensions currently received are considered inadequate by the beneficiaries themselves and that their first priority, not surprisingly, is a large increase in the pension amounts. According to the

The experts did not advocate abolition of the existing differentiated systems based on occupation, and they thought that the guaranteed income for elderly people should be set at a higher level.

Every expert emphasized that the private pension schemes were being developed to compensate for the inadequacies of the social security system, given that it does not enable beneficiaries to maintain their former standard of living. Consequently, the experts stressed that these schemes would probably always have an important complementary role—especially for white collar workers whose social security pensions are based only on earnings below the maximum earnings ceiling.

All experts agreed that almost nothing is known about the private pension schemes currently in operation in Belgium; there is absolutely no statistical material currently available.

Finally, they warned of dangers arising from the existence of these private systems; they saw these plans as decreasing worker solidarity and resulting in the overprotection of some groups to the prejudice of others. In addition, one expert observed that the expansion of the private schemes has undoubtedly retarded the development of the social security system.

Proposed Changes

In the preceding pages, we have summarized the discussion of certain experts regarding important pension issues. Many of these questions are also the subject of public discussion. Here we will briefly summarize and complete the list of such questions generally under discussion.

Various groups or individuals have proposed the following improvements in the programs for the aged:

(a) *Increasing the minimum level of pensions.* This would be one of the measures that could eliminate poverty among the aged, provided that the minimum was a reasonably adequate amount. It is the opinion of the Kristelijke, Bond van Gepensioneerden (Christian Pensioners' Association), for instance, that the current pension

polls, higher pensions are considered more important than decreasing the eligibility age for pensions.

system should be replaced by a two-tier system (i.e., one in which a basic minimum is distributed to everyone but supplemented by an earnings-related component).

(b) *Increasing the pension level to 75 percent of average earnings throughout the preretirement period (instead of lifetime earnings).* In fact, in 1968 Deputy R. Hicguet proposed a bill which would base old-age pensions on 75 percent of the average earnings of the last five working years or of the best ten working years, whichever is greater. No action was ever taken on this bill, however.

(c) *Linking pension levels in some way to the general level of current earnings.* Over the years this reform has been strongly advocated by a number of trade unions, certain government pension experts, and all the pensioners' organizations. Although the new price and productivity mechanism for adjusting pensions during retirement was a major change which will greatly increase pensions for future retirees, restricting the productivity adjustment at retirement to post-1973 retirees widens the gap between those who received their first pension before 1973 and those retiring in the years thereafter. This gap constitutes again a new political problem. Already many of the elderly have criticized the new adjustment mechanism as discriminatory, and protest meetings have been held in various Belgian cities.

(d) *Changing the eligibility age for pensions.* Some argue that the difference between the eligibility ages (for males 65, and for females 60) are no longer equitable. They also argue that the retirement age should be viewed as a function of the character of the job, not of the beneficiary's sex. Others argue that the number of early retirement exceptions (such as the current ones for miners, seamen, and some other categories) should be increased but that the general eligibility age should not be lowered.

(e) *Eliminating differences between the pension amounts paid to married versus unmarried pension recipients.* Such a difference does not exist in the present pension program for civil services. However, some argue that if the difference is to be meaningful, the housewife's domestic work role should be credited toward her entitlement to a pension of her own.

(f) *Unifying the pension programs.* After the 1967 pension reform, some people argued that a logical step was to go further and establish complete harmony between the pension systems of workers, self-employed people, and civil employees—thereby encouraging greater solidarity among them. Thus far no definite proposal has been made.

Chapter 6

THE THREE-TIERED CANADIAN SYSTEM

IT was not until 1966 that Canada added an earnings-related pension program to its system of income maintenance for its older residents—an action taken in the United States and many other industrialized countries decades earlier. As a result of this late start, Canada has been able to draw upon the experiences of the rest of the western world and, by combining these inputs with its own unique experiences and problems, give an important new approach to the problem of income maintenance for the elderly. An understanding of the Canadian experience may help to improve the income maintenance system elsewhere. Furthermore, pursuing the Canadian case can help us to understand the formation of public policy in a pluralistic democracy. As one observer has said, "The progression of Canada's old-age benefits, from a means test assistance to a complex and sophisticated three-tier system . . . is a classical case of the emergence of a social welfare program" (Morgan, 1970).

The three-tier system of income maintenance for the elderly, as it is called, is composed of three separate yet interconnected parts. The first consists principally of a universal flat grant payment or "demogrant" which is paid to all elderly inhabitants of Canada who meet residency requirements under the Old Age Security Act; however, the Old Age Security Act also provides for income supplement payments to impoverished elderly Canadians. The second part is an earnings-related government-administered compulsory pension system (similar to our OASDI program) known as the Canada Pension Plan (CPP) with a similar but not identical version in the Province of Quebec known as the Quebec Pension Plan (QPP). The third tier is the income provided by private pension plans.

The first tier or universal payment is provided under the authority of the Old Age Security Act, first enacted in 1951. As it currently stands (1973), it provides $100 per month to each resident of Canada who meets certain age and residency requirements. The age requirement is met by all Canadian residents at least 65 years old. There are three methods of meeting the residency requirement. Any person who has resided in Canada for forty years after reaching age 18 is eligible. Secondly, any person who has resided in Canada for the ten years prior to approval of application for benefits under the above act is eligible. Lastly, any person having "been present in Canada, after reaching age 18 and prior to the 10 years mentioned above, for periods which equal, when totalled, at least three times the length of . . . absences during the 10 year period, and (having) resided in Canada for at least one year immediately preceding the approval of application," can obtain benefits. (*Your Old Age Pension,* Information Canada, Ottawa, 1971.)

In addition to the universal pension, there is a second payment within the first tier made to some of those over age 65, a guaranteed income supplement (GIS). The GIS is a negative income tax for the low-income elderly. It, too, is paid under authority of the Old Age Security Act. This program, instituted in 1967, was originally viewed as an attempt to provide income for those unable to qualify for significant benefits under the newly instituted CPP because of their advanced age and/or short contribution period under the plan. In 1970, however, the expiration date on the program was removed, and it is now a permanent program. As of 1974, it provided —as a supplement to the universal pension—$70.14 per month to elderly individuals and $62.30 to each partner of an elderly couple who have no income other than the $100 per person demogrant. This benefit is also provided at reduced amounts to those with small additional incomes; for every two dollars of additional income, the GIS declines by one dollar. Thus, under the current schedule of payments, an individual with income between zero and $24 *per year* receives the full supplement of $70.14 *per month,* while an individual, for example, with an annual income between $1368 and $1392 receives only $13.14 per month. Those with incomes beyond $1704 receive no monthly supplement. Similar schedules exist for

couples who are both pensioners and couples where only one partner is a pensioner. As a result of the supplementation program, the
minimum income of each elderly individual in Canada meeting the
previous age and residency requirements is $170.14 per month, or
$2042 per year. The comparable figures for an elderly couple meet-
ing the same requirements are $285 and $3420.

Although the income so provided is not sufficient to provide a comfortable middle-class standard of living, it is above
the levels defined officially both in the United States and Canada
as "poverty level income." For purpose of comparison, under existing United States welfare programs, the average monthly benefit
paid to elderly persons in Massachusetts (a state paying compara-
tively high welfare benefits) was $127 in January 1973. The amount
of the GIS monthly supplement is adjusted annually to account for
some of the increase in the cost of living. In 1976, when the ten-year
CPP transition period ends, it will be adjusted on the basis of an
earnings index along with the CPP pension.

The CPP pension, which is the second tier of the system of income maintenance for the elderly in Canada, provides an earnings-
related pension supported by contributions from wage earners, employers, and the self-employed. The CPP (and its twin in Quebec)
provide a pension approximately equal to 25 percent of "pensionable earnings." Pensionable earnings, a complex measure of the lifetime earnings of an individual, is intended to reflect the relative position of the total lifetime earnings of the individual with regard to
the standard of living current at the time of retirement. Thus the
earnings of past periods are adjusted so that the dollar amounts
measure not what past income could buy at current prices, but
what it could buy at past prices. This adjustment process is explained in detail below, page 178.

Although the plan is designed to provide 25 percent of pensionable earnings, it also puts a ceiling on these earnings. The intention
is to have a movable ceiling that reflects the average earnings
prevalent in the economy over time. The maximum pension that
any worker can receive under this plan is 25 percent of those average earnings. This is consistent with the stated Canadian policy
goal of providing a public pension that keeps individuals above

poverty.[1] Any additional retirement income under this policy is to be provided by private sources such as savings or private pensions —the third tier of the system.

HISTORICAL ANTECEDENTS[2]

In order to understand the evolution of the public old age pension in Canada, it is useful to place it within the context of the changes that the society was undergoing during that evolution. The period in question, from the turn of the century until the present, was one in which Canada, along with the rest of the western world, was undergoing industrialization and urbanization. The tensions between the style of life created by the experience of the Canadian frontier and agricultural past and the needs created by the social organization of the industrial era were constantly at the root of the proposals and counterproposals of those in decision-making capacity in Canadian society and government. As one student of Canadian pensions has put it, "public pension policy in Canada has been the product of the conflict between an emerging environmental want and the market ethos" (Bryden, 1970). The term "market ethos" connotes the philosophy of individual self-reliance which was the product of the Canadian experience until the turn of the century. During the period from then to the present, the growth in nonagricultural output and urbanization has been rapid and significant. For example, though as late as 1926 almost 20 percent of Gross Domestic Product was derived from agriculture, by 1967 this had fallen to less than 5 percent. Similarly, in 1921 slightly less than half of the total Canadian population was urban, but by 1961 this proportion had risen to almost 70 percent (Bryden, 1970). These

---

1. A model social security system "must combat poverty by seeking to assure to everyone an acceptable minimum income, whether that income comes through employment or savings (social and private insurance), or whether, in the case of people who are unable to work or to find work, that income comes from government" (Government of Canada, 1973).

2. This summary of the history of public pension developments in Canada relies extensively on an excellent study made available to us by Dr. K. W. Bryden (1970).

trends can be extrapolated back to the turn of the century and before. In predominantly rural and agricultural Canada "communities were largely self-contained and there was a tradition of reliance on the family unit in time of need" (Kelly, 1969). Industrialization and the concomitant urbanization process brought with it the breakdown of those familial and community structures which gave individuals that measure of self-reliance which is supportive of the market ethos. An important result of the disintegration of built-in social welfare structures in the social reorganization which accompanied the industrialization process was that the government had to recreate these structures in some formal way. As life style and its attendant philosophy tend to be the product of past experience, it should not therefore be surprising to find these two forces grappling with each other as the new social welfare institutions are brought into being. It is partly because of this conflict that social policy change must of necessity be a slow process.

Though Canada has moved at a slower pace than other parts of the western world with regard to many aspects of governmental income maintenance for the elderly, it does not necessarily follow that the history of such endeavors in Canada is shorter. In fact the first attempts to provide income for the elderly in Canada extend back to about the turn of the century.

The Government Annuities Program, 1908

The first governmental attempt to provide for the income needs of the vast majority of elderly in Canada came to fruition with the passage of the Government Annuities Act of 1908. It allowed the Dominion Government to sell both deferred and immediate annuities to residents of Canada. The justification of the Act was that it was "in the public interest that habits of thrift be promoted and that the people of Canada be encouraged and aided thereto so that provision may be made for old age" (Clark, 1959).

Although the impact of the program has been steadily on the decline since 1967, when the federal government decided that "government annuities were no longer a necessary public service" (Kleiler, 1970), an understanding of the history of the program is helpful in understanding the evolution of the existing Canadian public pension system. This is the case because many of the forces acting to create and later modify the annuities programs were also important in shaping the present program.

A good formal definition of Canadian Government Annuities given by one observer is as follows:

> A Canadian Government Annuity is a yearly income of not less than $10 and not more than $1200 payable in monthly installments (unless otherwise stipulated) for the life of the annuitant or for the lives of joint annuitants with continuation to the survivor, and it may alternatively be paid for a term of years certain, not exceeding 20 years, or for life, whichever period be the longer. Annuities may be deferred or immediate. Deferred annuities are generally for purchase by younger persons desiring to provide for their old age by monthly, quarterly, or yearly premiums or by single premiums. Immediate annuities are mainly for purchase by older persons no longer gainfully employed who wish to obtain immediate income in return for their accumulated savings.   (Clark, 1959)

The introduction of the 1908 program can be viewed as a statutory manifestation of the growing recognition that there was a need to provide income for the elderly. It would not be until much later in the century, when the industrialization process was further along, that a more inclusive program would have to be developed. By 1908, however, the pressures of industrialization were such that the problem of income for the elderly had to come before Parliament. In the parliamentary debate that preceded the enactment of the program, both the proponents and opponents operated from a similar conventional wisdom. Both felt that unless a *contributory* plan were introduced, the result would be to encourage idleness and thriftlessness among the general population.

Sir Richard Cartwright, the author of the plan, "conceded that few Canadians had taken advantage of the opportunity already open to them to buy annuities from private insurance companies" (Bryden, 1970). He argued that this was the case because people of limited means were not willing to entrust their life savings to private companies; rather they preferred the government whom they implicitly trusted. In addition, the government had the flexibility to do things which private companies could not do. "The Act provided not only that there would be no profit on government annuities but also that administrative costs would be defrayed out of the public treasury" (Bryden, 1970). The interest rate on the annuities was set at 4 percent. This represented a further subsidy, since that rate was slightly above the rate on long-term government borrowing (which we can take as a measure of the then prevailing interest rate).

Senator Donald Ferguson, who opposed the plan, argued "that working people would not voluntarily buy annuities, for the simple reason that they could not afford them no matter how favourable the terms" (Bryden, 1970). Future events were to prove him correct. "A 1915 analysis of a random sample of annuity contracts revealed that purchasers were mainly people in the lower paid professions (notably teachers and clergy), clerks, skilled tradesmen, farmers and small businessmen. 'Labourers' accounted for only 4 percent of sales" (Bryden, 1970). Additional surveys done in the 1920's revealed a similar pattern. Not only was the population that was served different from that intended, but it was also quite limited. As late as 1930–31 there were fewer than 12,000 individual government annuity contracts in force (Bryden, 1970).

In order to ensure that the rich would not exploit the program, the maximum annuity was set at $600, raised in 1913 to $1000. Initially the program's administration was entrusted to Cartwright. During the fiscal years 1910–11 and 1911–12, contracts issued exceeded 1000 (Bryden, 1970). With a change in governments, administration of the program was transferred to the Post Office, and sales promotion was halted. At the same time, rising interest rates also contributed to a considerably lower rate of sales.

In 1920 the ceiling on annuity contracts was raised to $5000.

An imputed interest rate of 4 percent may have made government annuities unattractive to prospective purchasers but to the finance minister of 1920 it was attractive. In order to corral more of this cheap money, he had the Act amended to increase the ceiling to $5,000. He did not indicate how he arrived at the conclusion that the public would buy large annuities under conditions which were not inducing it to buy small ones in significant volume. At any rate, the increased ceiling had no appreciable effect on sales.   (Bryden, 1970)

With another change in government, in 1922, administration of the program was again transferred, this time to the Department of Labour. With the transfer in administration a small sales force located at key locations across the country was established. Establishment of this sales force and, more importantly, use of the 1893 Annuitants Table of Great Britain as a basis for premium rates, increased sales. The use of an out-of-date mortality table has the effect of subsidizing a population whose life span has increased. "In the 1927–28 fiscal year new contracts issued passed the 1,000 mark for the first time since 1911–12, and in 1930–31 they reached 1,722" (Bryden, 1970).

The increase in sales did not go unnoticed by the life insurance industry, which by that time had developed "a profitable sideline in annuities and they viewed government competition with disfavour" (Bryden, 1970). As a result of the pressure brought by the industry, the Government reduced the ceiling to $1200 in 1931, and it has remained at that amount ever since. Although the insurance industry hailed the change as a victory, the sales situation remained unchanged. Not only were contracts in excess of $1200 a very small fraction of total sales, but the depression of the 1930's drove the general rate of interest in the economy down and served to make the 4 percent rate on the annuities far more attractive. As a result, sales rose quite dramatically during the 1930's.

The next response of the life insurance industry was to bring pressure to bear to change the mortality basis and thus force government premiums closer to those of private industry. This was accomplished through the establishment of a parliamentary committee with close ties to the insurance industry. As a result of the committee's work, the mortality basis was revised in 1938. Prior to the development of new mortality tables, however, the premium rates were raised 15 percent in 1936, and with the development of the new mortality tables the rates were again raised.

Offsetting these price hikes was the fact that the interest rate remained at 4 percent and the administrative costs were still paid from general revenues. "Moreover, in 1940 the regulations were changed to give the branch greater freedom of action in underwriting group contracts, a type of business which was then on the verge of rapid expansion" (Bryden, 1970). As a result of these favorable conditions, sales of individual and group contracts continued to grow. In fiscal 1946–47, for example, sales totaled 43,585 individual contracts and certificates under group contracts.

Once again the success of the plan brought with it a counter-attack from insurance interests outside and inside the Government. On the outside the attack was led by the Chamber of Commerce; on the inside it was the Department of Insurance and the Department of Finance. In large measure the thrust of the argument was that the program was not in accord with the principles by which a private profit-seeking company would administer an annuity program, resulting in a subsidy to those participating in the program. At no time was this argument countered with any argument pertaining to policy decisions to subsidize the elderly.

The logic of profit-seeking was unchallenged, largely because those who stood to gain were a diffuse group as opposed to the distinct special interest group that could mobilize pressure. Resulting changes in the program were to prove fatal to it. In 1948 the interest rate was lowered from 4 to 3 percent, and the mortality figures were rated down three years. This action caused a dramatic drop in sales.

During the period of the late forties and early fifties, proposals to revive the program through greater flexibility were consistently beaten by the pressure of the insurance industry, leading to a further sales decline.[3] In 1962 a government commission, "accepting uncritically the mythology which the insurance industry and its allies had been promoting for a generation, recommended that the sale of government annuities be discontinued" (Bryden, 1970). Another government commission made a similar recommendation, and finally, on November 3, 1967, the Labour Minister took action that was tantamount to extinction of the program. He announced a "drastic reduction of field services in the annuities branch and cessation on November 30 (of that year) of promotional activities. Existing contracts (would still be) serviced, but new contracts (were) issued only to those who (sought) out the branch, and it now (had) little of benefit to offer them" (Bryden, 1970).

The demise of the Annuities Program must be considered within the context of the goals of existing public policy concerning

---

3. The original Social Security Act in the United States contained a provision for voluntary purchases of additional annuities, but the provision was defeated by the insurance industry before enactment (Merriam, 1973).

income maintenance for the elderly in Canada. The existing program has the goal of providing sufficient support to ensure that the elderly are above poverty. It encourages those who can, and wish to, provide additional income for themselves to do so. As Bryden (1970) has pointed out:

> This was stated repeatedly even in relation to the Canada Pension Plan, which in itself is a form of supplementation of the basic old age security pension. With expansionist rather than restrictive policies, the Government Annuities Act could have become a companion piece to the public pension programs, providing groups and individuals with the opportunity for supplementary protection at more favourable rates than private companies could offer. The government would thereby have made a major contribution to realizing an objective which it said itself was important and, in the process, it would have been provided with a growing volume of interest-free money. Private carriers, however, would have found their opportunities in this field severely restricted if not entirely eliminated. In the end their interests prevailed.

The Means Test Pension, 1927

Although we can trace some of the philosophical roots of the earnings related CPP back to the Government Annuities Act, the universal or demogrant portion has its roots in another aspect of the history of old-age income maintenance in Canada. The annuities program did provide some old-age income for those able to purchase such annuities, but it could do nothing for those without sufficient income in their working years to purchase such annuities. This latter group included an uncomfortably large and growing portion of the elderly population. There had been pressure in Canada, going back to the turn of the century, for the provision of non-contributory pensions to the elderly, although this was somewhat diffused by the Annuities Act. In fact, as late as 1915 it was possible for an observer to state that "the agitation for old age pensions has persisted in spite of the establishment of the government annuity program; but it is an agitation kept up by a few enthusiasts, aided by partisans, and has no grip on the public mind" (quoted in Bryden, 1970). As the century moved forward, however, the pressures of industrialization and urbanization forced the issue to a crisis. By the end of the 1920's the pressures reached sufficient proportions to bring about action by the government.

One of the earliest and most persistent proponents of old-age pensions in Canada was organized labor. For example, as early as 1915 the Trades and Labor Congress of Canada decided that old-age pensions should be an issue of high priority. This advocacy was important in shaping public opinion.

The period from the end of the First World War through the depression was characterized by a growth in union activity and much left-wing political action. Out of these political pressures and activities grew the demands for social welfare legislation which began to take root throughout Canadian society. For example, a federal commission established to look into the causes of industrial discontent that plagued Canada in the post World War I period recommended "immediate inquiry by expert boards" into "state insurance against unemployment, sickness, invalidity and old age."

MacKenzie King, who was to become Liberal Prime Minister of Canada in a few short years, wrote in 1918:

> That insofar as may be practicable, having regard for Canada's financial position, an adequate system of insurance against unemployment, sickness and dependence in old age and other disability, which would include old age pensions, widows' pensions and maternity benefits, shall be instituted by the Federal Government in conjunction with the Governments of the several provinces . . .   (Bryden, 1970)

Although King personally desired such a program, when he became Prime Minister in 1922 the political balance in Parliament created by the election precluded any action in that direction. A major source of support for the King Government came from 65 Quebec MP's, "most of them highly conservative in their social outlook" (Bryden, 1970). Bryden describes the potential situation at the time as follows:

> King's main preoccupation was simply with staying in office. To do this he had to keep the support of at least some of the 65. . . . Keeping their favour without creating intolerable tensions in his Quebec wing was a tactical enterprise which left little scope for new policy initiatives.

Despite the inability of the government to act on the pension issue, it continued at both the provincial and federal levels of government to be important over the next four years, finally coming to a head quite rapidly in 1926. At the opening of the 1926 session two Labour members who had long been advocates of old-age pensions petitioned King (a Liberal) about the issue. "King's initial response was to invite the Labour members to discuss the matter with him privately. In the negotiations which followed he agreed to proceed with old age pensions . . ." (Bryden, 1970). Though King was favorably disposed to proceed, he needed to convince his Cabinet that the move was politically necessary. "A convincing demonstration was provided on January 14 when the House divided on the first non-confidence motion of the session. The motion was defeated by only three votes (120 to 123), with Woodsworth and Heaps (the two Labour members advocating old age pensions) supporting the government. If they had voted the other way, it would have carried by 122 votes to 121" (Bryden, 1970).

A bill to establish old-age pensions was quickly passed by the House of Commons in March, but the upper House (Senate), in which the Conservatives were strong, defeated the bill. The arguments were the old ones: it rewarded thriftlessness; it destroyed family responsibility and private charity; it did not differentiate between those deserving and those undeserving; and there was no public demand for it. The principal argument, however, was that a federal program providing pensions to the poor aged would infringe upon provincial rights.

A scandal caused the Government to resign in September, and in the general elections that followed, the pension issue proved to be important. Many Conservatives in the Senate who had opposed the bill were defeated. The 1926 bill was introduced once again in February 1927 and passed both houses by March.

The program that emerged represented a compromise between the needs of the elderly poor to avoid destitution and the objections of Conservatives to the establishment of programs which they perceived would undermine vital social institutions. It was clearly not the more comprehensive kind of pension which those of the Liberal-Labour Left had been advocating. The Old Age Pensions Act of 1927 authorized the Government to enter into agreements with the provinces, providing for the reimbursement of half the cost of pensions paid under provincial legislation if the legislation met the requirements of the federal act. Under the 1927 Act, pensions were payable to those who (a) were 70 years of age or over, (b) were British subjects or widows of aliens who had become British subjects before marriage, (c) had resided in Canada for 20 years and in the province concerned for five years immediately preceding commencement of benefits, and (d) had not transferred property to qualify for pension. Indians as defined by the Indian Act were excluded.

The 1927 Act allowed for a pension of $240 per year, subject to a means test. Under the means test a pensioner was permitted additional income up to $125 per year or a total income of $365. Any income over the $125 was completely taxed away by a commensurate reduction in the pension. Any individual with an income over $365 per year was ineligible for the pension. Although the ownership of assets in and of themselves were not a reason for disqualification, income value imputed to the assets in a manner prescribed in the regulations was considered in determining eligibility under the act. The house in which a pensioner owned an interest and resided was not included in the asset calculation if the pensioner's interest was assigned to the pension authority. If the pensioner died or moved, the authority could sell the assigned interest and retain an amount equal to the amount by which the income value of the house would have reduced pension payments plus 5 percent compound interest. In addition, local pension authorities were allowed to recover from the estates of deceased pensioners up to the full amount of any pensions paid plus interest at 5 percent annually compounded. An exception was made in the case where the beneficiary of the estate was another pensioner or a person who had contributed what the authorities considered a reasonable amount toward the support of the pensioner for three years prior to the pensioner's death.

The 1927 Act was designed to provide no more than subsistence for the most destitute portions of the elderly Canadian population. While modifications were made in the act during the Great Depression and Second World War, the modified design was still far short of providing living levels for the elderly which approached the minimal middle class comfort envisaged by many of the advocates of old-age pensions throughout the years. In addition, the act was not popular with most of the citizenry. The means test ensured that it was to be looked upon as a handout to those incapable of providing for themselves. And the amount paid provided a bare subsistence for those in the most dire straits.

Despite the plan's lack of popular support, necessity made it widespread, and by 1950 the program supplied income benefits to more than 40 percent of Canadians over 70 (Kleiler, 1970). A significant portion of the remaining elderly fell between two stools, however. They were above the point of out-and-out destitution, yet far below an income level that would provide decent housing and nutrition in old age. As a result, the year 1950 saw the formation of a parliamentary commission to reassess old-age pensions and recommend alternatives. In the following year a new approach to the problem was introduced. This 1951 approach is still an integral part of the present three-tier system.

Universal Pensions: Shaping the First Tier

Inherent in the means-test approach to pensions is a certain irony. A principal justification for the means test is that it helps to ensure the conservative policy goal that only those truly in need will receive benefits. By ensuring that what is regarded as charity is limited to the needy, the virtues of self-reliance and thrift are protected. Surely if such benefits were made available to all, the argument goes, no incentive would exist for the general population to prepare for old age. However, the actual working of the means test ensures precisely the opposite result: unless one has substantial financial resource for one's old age, the means test acts as a disincentive to small savings or other income-creating activity because it brings about either a reduction in benefits or total ineligibility.

Consequently the means test, in addition to its degrading feature, is simply not a good vehicle for implementing a philosophy of the market ethos. Neither the Left nor the Right in Canada was really pleased with the workings of the 1927 Act. As a result, throughout the 1930's and 1940's there was a great deal of political and social pressure to reform the old-age pension system. The pressure existed despite the fact that the Depression and Second World War made major changes impossible at that time. As indicated above, this pressure culminated in the formation of a special legislative study commission in 1950, and the work of this commission resulted in two acts passed in 1951: the Old-Age Security Act and the Old-Age Assistance Act.

The Old-Age Security Act established a universal pension payable at age 70 to all who met the residency requirements of the Act. These requirements were essentially the same as those used in the 1927 Act (i.e., 20 preceding years of residency subject to offsetting earlier residence for any absence).[4] The pension provided under this plan was $40 per month. The Old-Age Assistance Act allowed the federal government to contribute, along the lines of the 1927 Act, to provincial means-tested plans for those between 65 and 70 years of age. The limits on allowable income were increased. The new limits were $720 for individual pensioners and $1200 for couples. In cases where a spouse was blind, the couple was eligible for $1320.

In attempting to formulate alternatives to a means-tested pension, there are two basic approaches open to policymakers—contributory pensions and universal ones. A contributory pension is one in which the benefit paid is related to a contribution made by the beneficiary; a universal pension does not tie the benefit to a previous contribution. Any particular pension takes either one of these approaches or some combination of them.

The climate of opinion in Canada during the Depression, the Second World War, and the postwar period was such that an observer at the time would have concluded that a contributory pension was inevitable in 1951. Yet it would not be until 1966 that such a pension finally came into existence. In the interim, the Canadians relied upon a universal pension. Because this universal pension (which emerged from the public policy debates of the late forties) formed a basis upon which the CPP of the mid-sixties firmly rests, it is important to understand something about the evolution of the Old-Age Security Act.

There were many attacks upon the means-tested pension during the Depression and the Second World War, and the conditions of the time clearly placed old-age pensions at the bottom of the priority list. In addition, the very nature of the problem—support

---

4. One change was that Indians became eligible under the 1951 Act.

for a segment of the population beyond its productive years—is such that societies consider the issue only when there is sufficient output beyond that needed to keep the socially productive machine in operation. It was therefore not until the period of economic expansion after World War II that the issue of sustaining the old-age population became a matter of priority.

During the Depression articulate support for a contributory pension plan could be found in two key places in Canadian society: the government and the business community. Based upon population projections alone, government officials were alarmed at the projected growth in expenditures for the means-tested pension over the next few decades—figures which did not even take into account an increase in the size of the benefit. Based on these projections, cost-conscious officials became advocates of a contributory scheme.

For similar reasons business groups like the Canadian Manufacturers Association also advocated such a plan. In addition, a contributory plan recommended itself to business types because it was consistent with the philosophy of self-reliance which they tended to espouse. Whatever support there was for universal pensions at the time tended to be concentrated in the left wing of the labor movement and was not very widely articulated. Even the moderate faction of the movement, the Trades and Labour Council, supported only an increase in the benefit payment of the means-tested pension.

Immediately after the War there was much support all across the political spectrum for broadening social welfare programs. During this period labor came out more clearly for contributory pensions, with the exception of the labor Left, which consistently advocated universal pensions. One point on which all the labor groups (and practically everybody else) did agree was that the means-tested pension had to go.

The late forties saw even more consolidation around the need for a contributory pension. In 1948 the governing Liberal Party reaffirmed a position it had been developing since the 1930's in favor of contributory pensions. Thus by 1950 it seemed to informed observers that Canada was on the verge of adopting a contributory pension.

The pressure for abolishing the means test was strong at the end of the decade of the forties, and the Liberals were going to have to act. Unfortunately, they did not have an implementable alternative plan. In order to placate public opinion and buy time, they established, during the 1950 legislative session, a joint parliamentary study commission. Virtually all the witnesses who testified before the commission agreed upon two points: first, the means test must go and, second, the Government should assume financial responsibility for whatever form the particular alternative took.

The additional time which the study commission was able to buy for the Government was not sufficient to bring forth a contributory plan. Indeed, as shall be seen when we discuss below the development of the CPP, it took almost three full years to work out all the tax and other financial complexities inherent in such a plan.[5] As a result of these difficulties the commission was forced to bring forth recommendations which called for a universal pension.

The universal pension, as a compromise, had support from a diverse cross-section of the political spectrum. Even the insurance industry found itself in support of the plan and somewhat out of step with other business interests. In the case of the insurance industry, however, there were mitigating circumstances. At this particular time the industry was busy fighting the Annuities Program; it feared that a contributory plan would take business away from itself as well as undermine that other fight. Yet the industry, knowing that something had to be done, supported a universal benefit, though at a very low level.

A benefit level of $40 was the uppermost limit that insurance interests considered acceptable. The Government, too, for cost reasons wanted a low-benefit level, and it also wanted to keep the age of eligibility at 70 despite much popular pressure to lower it. As a result the compromise that came out of the commission was for a $40 universal benefit payable at age 70 and a means-tested, federally and provincially administered $40 pension for those between 65 and 69.

The 1952 Old Age Security Act was modified in terms of benefit size and eligibility limits a few times between its initial passage and the beginning of the process (in the early 1960's) that created the CPP. In 1956 the Liberals increased the benefit amount 15 percent,

---

5. It should be noted that it took three years despite the Government's hope of producing such a plan in about sixty days!

from $40 to $46 a month. While such a small increase was economically a correct move (given the state of the economy), it was politically incorrect. Partly as a result of this blunder as well as a few others, the Conservatives came to power in 1957. One of the first pieces of business of the new Government was to raise the benefit level to $55.

In 1960, the eligibility rules were relaxed so that alien residents who had lived in Canada at least 25 years after their 21st birthday would also be eligible.

Finally, on the eve of the 1962 election, the Conservatives raised the benefit level another $10, to $65 per month. Further modification was bound up with the development of the CPP and will therefore be discussed in that context.

THE CANADA PENSION PLAN: THE SECOND TIER

Beginning in January 1966, the Canada Pension Plan (CPP) and its companion Quebec plan (QPP) began providing earnings-related retirement, disability, and death benefits to the Canadian population. It is currently estimated that well over 90 percent of Canada's citizenry are covered by the two plans. Since the CPP and QPP are virtually identical, further reference in the main text will be made to the CPP only; however, important differences resulting from recent changes in the QPP will be noted in footnotes.

The CPP provides pension income related to earnings to all those eligible over the age of 65. This income is in addition to that provided under the first tier by the demogrant and the Guaranteed Income Supplement. While the plan also provides disability and death benefits, we will only concern ourselves with the income-providing features for the aged of the plan—the major focus of this book.

The Reform Debate, 1951–1963

Establishment of universal pensions for the elderly in 1951 took pressure off the Government for a while but avoided the more basic issue of decent living standards for those past working age. The universal pension was not sufficient to prevent a drastic drop in the standard of living of those retiring from the work force, nor was it intended to prevent such a decline. As inadequate as the demogrant available was to those aged 70 and over, it tended to be better than the means-tested provincially administered pension available to the 65–69 age group. It was as true in 1950 as in 1970 that the vast majority of workers, who during working careers usually earned enough to cover basic necessities and perhaps a bit more, never had sufficient income to save for their retirement. Thus throughout the fifties the elderly and organized labor placed continual pressure upon the Government for reform of old-age pensions, although there was no widespread agreement upon the shape of alternatives.

Reform was also sought by other segments of Canadian society. Within the Government, the Department of Finance in particular seemed to see the handwriting on the wall with regard to the need to expand benefits. Its concern during the period of time when public debate over alternatives occurred was to see that whatever plan emerged would be one in which firm control over costs would be achieved. This concern also manifested itself within a broad spectrum of the business community.

The desire of many to improve upon the performance of private pension plans also generated support for a Government-administered contributory public pension plan. Anticipated dissatisfaction with private pensions plans centered on their poor portability and vesting provisions.[6] It was argued that the combination meant that even workers who earned sufficient sums to participate in a company-sponsored pension plan often had nothing to show at the end of a long work career because of employment changes necessitated by the normal functionings of the job market. The establishment of public pensions was seen by some as a means of forcing improvement in private pensions through comparison.

Support for an earnings-related plan could also be found within organized labor. The Canadian Congress of Labour, in its submission to the 1950 joint committee which prepared the 1951 reforms, proposed a two-level program which piggy-backed an earnings-related pension onto a universal pension. The Canadian Congress of

6. "Portability" refers to ease with which a worker can transfer accrued pension benefits from one employer to another. "Vesting" is defined as the point at which a worker achieves legal title to sums invested in a pension fund on her or his behalf by an employer.

Labour reiterated this position in 1960 when it sought an input into the shape of the then-emerging pension plan.

The convergence of the interests of the elderly, labor, government officials, business, and pension reformers resulted in a de facto broad coalition for change in the nation's pension system during the years 1951–63. Furthermore, the support was clearly colored in favor of an earnings-related contributory system.

The impetus for public pension reform was so widespread in the 1950's and early 1960's that it was a significant issue in the election campaigns of 1957, 1958, 1962, and 1963. In the 1957 election campaign Conservative leader John Diefenbaker was able to use the pension issue successfully as he won control of the Government from the Liberals. The Liberals, it should be remembered, had just passed a $6 increase in the universal pension, from $40 to $46. A $6 instead of a $10 increase had the effect of making the Liberals appear cheap. As a result they earned themselves the derisive label of "the six dollar boys."

In campaigning, Diefenbaker was able to exploit the popular discontent by promising a more substantial increase. Indeed he later put through a $9 increase to raise the total monthly universal pension to $55. However, he was concerned that the pension issue could become very costly as each political party attempted to outbid the other in raising pensions to obtain votes. In order to stop the escalation he proposed that Canada establish a social security system similar to the one in the United States and promised, if elected, to investigate the United States system as a possible model for Canada. He honored his election pledge in February 1958 by appointing Professor R. M. Clark, an economist at the University of British Columbia, to make a comparative study of the two systems.

The two-volume Clark study suggested that the adoption of the United States system by Canada would be an almost impossible task because of the very different structure of social welfare institutions. However, it did inject the question of death and disability benefits into the issue of pensions for the elderly. These additional benefits ultimately became part of the CPP, although they originally were not.

After the elections of 1957 and 1958, the Liberal Party found itself in the unaccustomed role of the official opposition. As the party out-of-power, it went through a massive reorganization, with a shake-up in leadership. New programs and policies emerged in all areas. With regard to the problems of income maintenance for the elderly, there was a plan for a means-tested pension for those between 65 and 69, a universal pension for those over 70, and an additional earnings-related plan providing survivor and disability benefits.

By the time the elections of 1962 and 1963 came around, the Liberals, Conservatives, and New Democratic Party (with strong labor ties) had all committed themselves to the principle of contributory, earnings-related pensions. The elections returned the Liberals to power. One of their campaign slogans had been "60 days of decision"—indicating that they intended to act immediately on many pressing matters. One of these matters was of course an earnings-related old-age pension. As they were to find out, however, the technicalities of the plan were such that when combined with the political reality of interprovincial relations, nothing approaching a plan was possible in 60 days.

Although there was widespread support for the implementation of such a plan when the Liberals came to power, the support was by no means unanimous. Immediately after the election the life insurance industry paid a visit to the new government to find out if they were really serious about a Government plan. When they found that they were, the insurance people joined with their allies in the Chamber of Commerce (who had previously supported them in opposing the Annuities Program) to mount a campaign against it. They were never able to gain much support, and with the handwriting clearly on the wall, the Chamber eventually changed its stance in order to have a voice in arranging a "fiscally sound" plan. Since they had large profits at stake, the life insurance industry remained bitterly opposed to the end.

In response to the attack from the insurance interests, organized labor (most importantly the Canadian Labour Congress) launched a postcard and letter campaign. The campaign, although not widespread, did neutralize some aspects of the anti-pension drive. In the final analysis, however, it was the broad spectrum of business, labor, and welfare group support which ensured that the Government would move forward and produce a plan.

Shaping the Final Design, 1963–1965

Even though the Liberals, upon coming to power in 1963, had committed themselves to a contributory pension, that was far from the end of the battle. Indeed, in many important respects it was only the beginning. While the plan which finally emerged in 1965 as the CPP was philosophically close to the initial Liberal description, many of the details were different, and as a result the actual workings of the plan can only be understood within the context of the decision process during .the three years in question.

One of the most important innovations that this period produced was the Guaranteed Income Supplement (GIS). A major 1963 Liberal campaign promise had been to increase the universal pension. This promise had been made contingent upon the adoption of a contributory pension scheme. The Liberals were reluctant to act upon the pension increase until the entire CPP financing package had been developed. But they found themselves under considerable pressure from the opposition, some members of their own party, and most especially from the elderly to redeem their election pledge. Although the Liberals ultimately acceded to the pressure and raised the pension to $75, the political pressures did not abate. Rather, those who had been pushing for an increase began to ask for a pension of $100 per month almost immediately after $75 was instituted.

This continuing pressure was in reality masking a more fundamental issue. If a pension scheme that tied benefits to contributions was to be enacted shortly, those too old to have contributed in any significant way to the plan would receive little or no income under it. It was this fear which motivated the elderly and their supporters to press for increases in the universal pension. But the difficulty with this strategy was that even if it succeeded in raising the absolute level of benefits, it would not lessen the relative differential between those people receiving only a universal pension and those receiving substantial additional benefits under an earnings-related plan. Furthermore, from the standpoint of social policy, continual increases in the universal portion of the pension were recognized as a very inefficient way to deal with the special income problems of a part of the population which would be decreasing over time.

In response to these problems a special Senate Committee,

which met during the early part of 1963, developed a compromise. The Committee proposed that the Government pay income supplements to elderly persons and couples whose income fell below certain levels. This simple proposal eventually evolved into the GIS, which became law on January 1, 1967. Initially the GIS was viewed as a temporary program to run during the ten-year period of the CPP phase-in (scheduled to end in 1976). The program has thus far proved to be so successful and popular, however, that the ending date was removed in 1970, and the GIS is now a permanent part of the Old Age Security Act.

A second thorny question which policymakers had to face concerned the age of eligibility. There was official reluctance to lower the eligibility age because of the resulting increased program costs. On the other hand there were pressures from organized labor, the elderly, and other supporters for lowering the eligibility age. While many ages had been proposed, the most universally agreed-upon lower age was 65. The combination of heavy labor force competition for available jobs and the fact that the system of old-age income was being significantly overhauled probably contributed to the Government's willingness to accept a compromise on this issue. Thus the age of eligibility for a pension was lowered from 70 to 65 over a five-year period which commenced on January 1, 1966, the date on which the CPP was instituted. The impact of this compromise was to remove the last vestige of the means-tested benefits for the elderly by de facto phasing out the Old Age Assistance Act, half of the 1951 package.

Another important issue discussed during the 1963–65 period was the question of provincial federal relations (with all the implicit problems of French Canadian Nationalism). Under Canadian constitutional provisions, provincial authority takes precedence over federal authority in the area of welfare programs. If a province decides to establish its own program, the federal program is to be inoperative in that province. Thus if the two largest Canadian provinces decided to develop their own programs, any federal program would be effectively worthless—which was the situation the Liberal Party faced in the period 1963–65.

The provinces of Ontario and Quebec were planning to initiate programs of their own to provide for the income needs of the elderly. Consequently, if any meaningful plan was to come from the federal government, the wishes of these two provinces would have to be given careful consideration. Indeed the final version of the federal plan bears the imprimatur of the Quebec plan in many significant aspects, and the Ontario plan also affected the legislative outcome (but in a more subtle manner).

The dominant approach to adequate income for the elderly in Ontario was to improve the workings of the private pension system. The principal provisions of Ontario's Pension Benefits Act dealt with the problem of achieving uniformity in vesting and portability among the private plans of the province. The Act called for the mandatory establishment of a pension plan by any employer with fifteen or more workers. The plan was to ensure that every worker received a minimum income of $80 per month.

With the passage of the CPP these two provisions in the Ontario Act were removed. In deference to Ontario, however, the federal government established an amending procedure for the CPP which effectively gave Ontario a veto over any proposed change in the CPP. This procedure required that any amendment had to be approved by two thirds of the provinces with two thirds of the population. Since Quebec had established its own plan and the province of Ontario has over one third of the total population outside of Quebec, the amendment procedure was tantamount to giving Ontario a veto over all amendments.

Quebec developed its own plan. Through a series of intense negotiations with the federal government, however, the two plans were made identical with a provision for easy transfer from one to the other as workers moved during their careers. The initial Quebec proposal was far more extensive than the federal one, and one of the most important results of the negotiations was to produce a broader federal plan.

There were three principal changes brought about in the CPP as a result of the federal/Quebec bargaining process. The first was to make coverage under the plan compulsory for the self-employed. This modification was added to the federal plan because of a fear that farmers would not voluntarily join, resulting in a large number of persons without adequate old-age pensions.

A second Quebec-initiated modification was the establishment of a fund and a funding program that would supplant the pay-as-you-go technique. This modification did not affect the benefits of the plan to those participating, but it did provide the provincial government with a pool of low-cost investment funds—important to a province intent upon following an independent course within the confederation. The result of this change was a slightly higher rate of taxation to finance the pension plan.

The third important modification was the inclusion of disability and survivors benefits in the CPP. Although these inclusions reflected the concern of Quebec, it should be borne in mind that organized labor had also been strongly in favor of their inclusion.

In addition to these three major changes, there were a few other alterations made during the period which had an important effect upon the final plan. Principal among them was the development of a procedure for calculating ceilings on pensionable earnings and pension rates. In addition, an automatic cost-of-living adjustment was added to the plan, so that pensions would be continually adjusted to offset the upward drift of prices over time. These two changes were brought about principally through the support and urging of organized labor.

Labor, however, did not get all the adjustments that would allow retirees to receive increased pension income reflecting increases in general productivity in the economy. Business interests raised strong opposition to such adjustments, arguing that they would be highly inflationary.

Out of this period of debate came a public pension plan for the entire nation, to be administered by the federal government. Only Quebec chose to administer independently its own plan, which was identical to CPP up until 1972. Although the level of income of this new plan was insufficient to maintain a middle-class standard of living, it was at least a basis upon which such a standard could be built.

THE CPP PENSION

In this section we will look at the actual workings of the income portion of the CPP with an eye toward the long-run performance of the plan. Provisions designed to operate during the ten-year phase-in period of 1966 to 1975 will be ignored; instead, the plan will be described and then analyzed in terms of the features that will be operational after December 31, 1975.

Officially, the CPP provides a monthly retirement pension which is equal to 25 percent of "average monthly pensionable earnings" (AMPE). This does not necessarily mean, however, that a retired worker receives 25 percent of average lifetime earnings. Indeed, in almost all actual cases the precise percentage of average lifetime earnings will be different from 25 percent. In order to understand the replacement rate embodied in the pension program, we must look at a complex of factors which affect the replacement determination.

AMPE is calculated as the average of "total pensionable earnings" (TPE) divided by the number of months of the worker's contributory period. The TPE and the contributory period are generally defined as a full career measure of earnings. That is, the relevant period of time in which earnings are calculated is the period between a worker's 18th and 65th birthdays. TPE, however, does not refer to all earnings which a worker receives but only those *below a specified ceiling*.

The total amount of pensionable earnings which a worker earns between his 18th and 65th birthday is divided by the amount of time between those dates less 15 percent; in other words, forty years of the forty-seven-year period are used in calculating the pension. At the time of retirement, the worker can drop any seven years from the overall calculation.[7] Presumably, the worker will drop the years in which earnings were low or zero. The remaining earnings and time are then used to calculate the average. The 1973 limit on pensionable earnings was $5600.[8] By 1975 the maximum was scheduled to increase to $7800. Thereafter, the ceiling was to be adjusted on the basis of an "earnings index."

---

7. If a worker elects to work beyond age 65, each additional month of work can be used to replace a month of earnings prior to 65. In no case, however, can this substitution process be carried beyond a worker's 70th birthday. After 70 a worker receives a pension based upon his best forty years, regardless of whether he continues work or not.

8. The QPP was amended in 1972 to establish a different schedule of ceilings: $5900 in 1973, $6100 in 1974, and $6300 in 1975.

The pension calculations thus far can be shown algebraically:

$$P = .25 \, (AMPE) \tag{1}$$

$$AMPE = TPE/480 \tag{2}$$

where

$$P = \text{monthly pension}$$

The 480 in the denominator of the ratio in equation 2 is based on a forty-year work history (forty-seven years less 15 percent), which is equivalent to 480 months.

The moving ceiling on pensionable earnings is designed to ensure that pensionable earnings will move along with increases in prices and productivity in the Canadian economy. When the program went into effect in 1966, the ceiling was set at $5000, the average earnings in the economy at that time. During the 1966–75 phase-in, the ceiling was to be adjusted upward with increases in the consumer price index. These upward increases were to be restricted to 2 percent. This restriction reflected the conventional wisdom of 1963–65, when inflation was not a serious problem.

The Canadians, however, badly underestimated the inflation that was to occur. As a result, the ceiling has to a large degree failed to keep pace with the actual increase in prices and wages which have occurred in Canada. By 1970, average wages had reached $6400, while the ceiling of the plan was at $5300. In order to correct for this, the federal government proposed in 1970 a new schedule of ceilings reaching either a maximum of $7800 in 1975 or the average wage at that time, should it be above $7800.[9]

Beginning in 1976 an earnings index—which will reflect both price and productivity changes through the effect of these changes upon wages—will be used to adjust the ceiling. The earnings index is defined as the ratio of average wages during the eight-year base period 1966–73 to the average of "average earnings for the eight years ending with the second year preceding that year" for which the ceiling is to be adjusted. The measurement of average earnings is done with respect to wages and salaries as defined by the Income Tax Act. These relationships can be shown as follows:

---

9. Assuming Provincial acquiescence (except for Quebec) to this new schedule, the analysis below will be based on the assumption that $7800 is the prevailing ceiling in 1975.

$$E_t = A/B \tag{3}$$

$$A = \sum_{j=t-10}^{t-2} A_j/8 \tag{4}$$

$$B = \sum_{k=1966}^{1973} B_k/8 \tag{5}$$

where

E_t = the earnings index for the tth year.

A = the average of actual earnings for the "eight year period" ending two years before the tth year.

A_j = the actual earnings for the jth year in the "eight year period."

B = the average of actual earnings for the base period 1966–73.

B_k = the actual earnings for the kth year of the eight-year base period.

Using the earnings index, the ceiling on pensionable earnings for each year commencing in 1976 is then calculated by multiplying the 1975 maximum by that index and then rounding down to the nearest multiple of $100. For example, if the 1975 maximum was $7800 and the earnings index for 1976 was 1.05, the 1976 ceiling would be $8100 even though $7800 × 1.05 = $8190. This ceiling is officially called the "Year's of Maximum Pensionable Earnings" (YMPE). Algebraically, we can define the YMPE for any particular year as follows:

$$YMPE_t = YMPE_{1975} \cdot E_t \tag{6}$$

where

$YMPE_t$ = the year's maximum pensionable earnings for the tth year.

$YMPE_{1975}$ = the year's maximum pensionable earnings for the year 1975.

At the time an individual retires, his pensionable earnings for each working year are adjusted by a factor that attempts to convert the past purchasing power of those earnings into dollar amounts which reflect the prices and standard of living at the time of retirement. The factor used to accomplish this adjustment is the ratio of the average of YMPE for the year of retirement and the two preceding ones to the YMPE for each year of pensionable earnings counted in calculating a worker's retirement income. The pensionable earnings for each year are multiplied by this adjustment factor in order to compile the worker's TPE (total pensionable earnings). Algebraically, these relationships are as follows:

$$F_i = \frac{YMPE_n + YMPE_{n-1} + YMPE_{n-2}}{3} \Big/ YMPE_i \qquad (7)$$

$$TPE = \sum_{i=1}^{n} W_i \cdot F_i \qquad (8)$$

where

F_i = the adjustment factor for the ith year

n = year of retirement

W_i = the individual worker's pensionable earnings in the ith year.

Private Pensions: The Third Tier

The drop in living standard after retirement reflected in the above replacement rates is significant, but the CPP and demogrant were never intended to replace all or even most of the preretirement earnings of the Canadian work force. They were intended as a floor located somewhere above poverty but below the standard of living reflected by current average earnings. Responsibility for the additional income needed to achieve any higher living standard is regarded as the responsibility of either the individual alone or jointly with his employer. Thus private pensions are the third tier of the Canadian scheme for providing income to the elderly. This approach to income maintenance is consistent with the marketplace values espoused by those involved in the policy-making process in Canada. The tendency toward a market-based solution to the problems of income maintenance for the elderly can be seen in the recent history of some important private pension regulations in Canada.

As mentioned previously, during the period of time in which the CPP was being finalized, the province of Ontario attempted to develop an income-maintenance system which would be almost solely based upon private pension funds. Although the attempt was not successful in light of massive nationwide support for a government sponsored plan, it did contribute to the development of better portability and vesting provisions in private pension plans throughout most of Canada.

Responding to pressure for the development of income maintenance programs for the elderly which began to build to high intensity during the 1950's, the Prime Minister of Ontario established the Committee on Portable Pensions in 1960. As a result of the work and recommendations of that committee, the Ontario legislature enacted the Pension Benefits Act, 1962–63. It was the intention of this legislation to establish a privately based system of retirement income for the vast majority of workers in the province.

There were four major features to the Act as passed at that time. The Act called for the mandatory establishment of a pension plan by any employer employing fifteen or more people. The Act stipulated that plans so established had to provide certain minimal retirement benefits. The second major and perhaps best-known feature of the Act was its vesting provision. Under the provisions of the Act, 100 percent vesting took place for each worker with eighteen months of service past the age of 30. The third significant feature concerned portability. It provided that in the event a worker left a particular job prior to retirement, either he should receive an annuity payable prior to age 70 which represented the value of his vested share in the pension plan, or the vested portion was to be transferred to a central pension fund authorized under the statute to receive, hold, and disburse pension funds. A final major feature of the legislation was the establishment of funding requirements. This feature meant that an employer could no longer promise pension benefits without providing the contributions to pay for the benefits. These four provisions taken together, it was felt, represented a rather complete system of private pension coverage for most workers. How well the system would have worked out in actual practice we shall never know, as the law was amended shortly after passage.

With passage of the CPP imminent, the Ontario legislature modified its pension law in 1964, making it less stringent. The provision that all employers with fifteen or more employees establish a pension with minimum specified standards was repealed. The vesting provision was changed so that 100 percent vesting now takes place after age 45 and after ten years of service with the particular employer or ten years participation in the plan. A new feature of the 1964 amendments ensured that the pension funds could own no more than 30 percent of the common stock of any particular company nor more than 10 percent of the assets of the firm providing the pension. There were also restrictions on the lending of pension funds to parties associated with the fund. The intention of these new features was to ensure the long-run stability and solvency of the funds.

The modified Ontario pension act of 1964 served as a model for almost identical legislation by the federal government and the provinces of Quebec, Saskatchewan, and Alberta. While uniform pension legislation now covers only the federal government and four of the ten provinces, nonetheless the large populations in these provinces result in about 75 percent of all Canadian workers covered by private pension being in plans covered by government pension regulation laws. This regulation, although not as strong as the original Ontario act, still provides a relatively firm basis for building a significant third tier of income protection, completing the Canadian pension system. Only time will tell whether this will in fact be the case.

Perhaps the most significant aspect of the private pension laws is their vesting provision. The laws require that both employer contributions *and required employee contributions* remain locked-in in order always to provide the employee with a deferred pension. While the legislation required some employers to upgrade their vesting provisions, the locking-in provision also was of crucial significance; it prevented employees from forfeiting a vested pension in order to obtain a refund of their contributions. Indeed, even before enactment of the legislation, many plans had more generous vesting provisions than the legislation required, but the effectiveness of this vesting was seriously impaired because most plans permitted departing employees to take a refund of their contributions in lieu of a vested deferred pension.

Of course, a deferred benefit may be more apparent than real, especially during times of long-term severe inflation. An individual might be better off spending a refund in the present than waiting a decade or two to receive a deferred pension, the purchasing power of which would be seriously eroded over time. As we argue in Chapter 8, this dilemma is one of the most important that private pension development must face in the ensuing decades.

The effectiveness of the Canadian vesting standard is open to question on other grounds as well. That many employees work for a number of employers during their work careers means that it would be difficult for these people to meet the ten years of service and age 45 requirement. In the case of employees covered under "unit pension plans," even when they do not change jobs and remain with one employer, they do not receive much in the way of a locked-in employer contribution. This is because under unit plans it is not until an employee is well into his 40's that the employer contribution purchases all or a large portion of the accrued pension. (In 1970 38 percent of all pension plans were unit plans.)

At present, the extent of private pension coverage in the Canadian economy is quite limited. Whether the development of more awareness about the limited extent of present CPP coverage will generate more interest in the more extensive development of private pension coverage or merely more pressure for the extension of the CPP remains to be seen. In 1960 there were 8920 private pension plans in Canada. By 1970 this number had grown by approximately 81 percent to 16,137.[10] The largest portion of this growth, however, was between 1960 and 1965, prior to the CPP, when the number of plans grew 53 percent to a total of 13,660. The growth from 1965 to 1970, after the inception of CPP, was slight: about 18 percent.

In 1960 the 8920 plans covered 36 percent of the paid work force. Despite the considerable increase in the number of plans, only 38 percent of the paid work force was covered by 1965, and by 1970 this figure had increased to only 40 percent of the work force.[11]

Not only is the proportion of the work force covered by private pensions far below that of the combined CPP and QPP—it appears also to be narrowly concentrated in a few industries. In 1970, 55 percent of those workers covered by private pension plans were in just three industries: public administration and defense, construction and community business, and personal service. In fact, better than one out of every four covered employees could be found in public administration and defense (26.9 percent).

10. The statistics for this paragraph come from published and unpublished documents of the Pension Section of Statistics Canada.
11. It should be noted that this coverage figure is very similar to estimates of coverage for the United States (discussed in Chapter 8).

On the other hand, the available evidence suggests that for workers covered by private pensions, the coverage is significant. In 1969 contributions to private pension plans amounted to $1.7 billion. This exceeded the combined contributions to both the Canada and Quebec pension plans for that year. Furthermore these private pensions represent an important vehicle for the mobilization of workers' savings for Canadian economic development, since about three out of every four plans involve employee contributions. This is in part stimulated by the fact that such contributions are deductible from income taxation.

Though it appears that private pensions will be an important part of the system of income maintenance for the elderly of Canada, it is also the case that about half the workers covered by the CPP are without such third-tier protection. It would seem, therefore, that despite the advances made in the development of government-sponsored income maintenance for the elderly in recent years, a fundamental issue regarding the potential role of private pensions must still be faced if a satisfactory income system for all of Canada's elderly is to be developed.

FINANCING THE INCOME MAINTENANCE SYSTEM

The first two tiers of the Canadian system of income maintenance for the elderly are supported from taxes. The demogrant and GIS are paid from a tripartite tax. Initially, this tax was known as "the 2-2-2 tax." When the Old-Age Security Act was first passed in 1951, a 2 percent tax upon sales, personal income, and corporate income was levied. The only restriction on this tax was the limit on the personal income portion of the tax. The 2 percent personal income tax was paid only upon the first $3000 or, in other words, was limited to $60. This tripartite tax supported not only the federally administered demogrant but also the portion of provincially administered means-tested pensions given to those between 65 and 70 years of age.

In 1959 the tax was raised to a "3-3-3 tax" to cover the cost of the increases in the demogrant given in the late 1950's. The personal tax limit was extended commensurately to $90. Despite the increase in benefits granted in 1962, the tax was not raised at that time. In 1974 the basic tax was approximately the same and also supported the GIS. The only change is that the rate on personal income taxes had been raised to 4 percent while the other taxes have remained at the 3 percent level.

Although from time to time there had been discussions about abolishing these special taxes for the purpose of supporting the elderly, the official sentiment has been that it is better to let the public be aware of the cost of these programs and any increases. This position is especially supported by the insurance industry and other business interests, who hope that awareness of costs will help to keep the public demand for increases in such programs to a minimum.

The CPP is a contributory pension and is thus paid by the potential beneficiaries and their employers. The present rate is 3.6 percent, split evenly between employer and employee (1.8 percent each). The tax is paid on all earnings between $600 ($700 for QPP) and up to and including whatever the current earnings ceiling happens to be at the time. For self-employed individuals the full 3.6 percent rate must be paid, except that incomes below $800 are exempted. According to official government estimates,[12] despite the proposed increase in allowable pension levels, it will not be necessary to raise the basic rates until 1985 at the earliest, for the increase in the ceiling will automatically generate more revenue over time.

CONCLUSIONS

The system of income maintenance which has arisen in Canada over the last seven decades is complex. The complexity does not by itself mean that the elderly will over time come to enjoy a standard of living which will approach the average for the rest of the population. That will depend upon the interaction of complex factors— most particularly work incentives, roles assigned to different age groups in the population, the productivity of the entire economy, and the values by which the total economic output is distributed. The process by which these factors interact and work themselves

12. *Income Security for Canadians*, Department of National Health and Welfare, Ottawa (1970).

out will in turn naturally occur in the political arena. It is possible, then, to speculate upon the long-term operation of the system by looking at the political process.

The elderly, in desiring higher incomes, will generally look not to private pensions or adjustments in them to provide that income but rather to the public sector. Unions, workers, and others will also look in that direction. The principal reason is that to achieve a higher standard of living, given some level of productivity, implies some sort of income redistribution from the larger society to the elderly. Private pensions based upon principles of private profit and actuarial soundness by their very nature cannot provide real, as distinct from monetary, higher incomes to those already retired. Nor can they do much about giving the rest of the work force real higher incomes through redistribution, as they must charge a premium that reflects the present discounted value of these future earnings. Therefore, it is only through the public sector that any effective redistribution of income from the larger society to the elderly can take place. This happens when the Government raises taxes on those in the work force to provide higher incomes for those retired from the work force.

Thus, while it may happen that private pension plans by becoming more flexible and attractive through better vesting and portability do attract increased participation, this will not take the pressure off the public sector from unions, welfare groups, and the elderly to expand public pensions. For it is only through public pensions that any effective redistribution of income is likely to occur unless providers of private pensions are willing to assume a loss by subsidizing the elderly through charging actuarily unsound premiums. We cannot, nor should we, expect such to be the case.[13]

---

13. The issue of the public/private pension mix is discussed at greater length in Chapter 8.

Chapter 7

ANALYSIS OF FOREIGN SYSTEMS

In Chapter 2 we presented and discussed a set of four questions that are crucial to understanding any pension system which relates benefits to earnings and which seeks to also relate living standards in retirement to the standard prevailing during some portion of the preretirement period. Chapters 3–6 discussed the historical development of old-age pension programs in four countries where major pension reform has recently occurred.

In this chapter we look more closely at the nature and implications of the reforms in these countries, using the framework introduced in Chapter 2. In the sections that follow, each of the pension programs in the four countries is discussed in relation to the four questions previously posed.

The Philosophy of Adequacy

Two basically different approaches to this question are represented by the countries studied. Sweden, Germany, and Belgium have specified relatively high adequacy goals in an attempt to maintain living standards in retirement, primarily through a national pension system. Canada, in contrast, does not place reliance primarily on social security; it has established a multitiered system that explicitly limits the role of social security pensions for other than workers with relatively low earnings but also recognizes the resulting role required of private pensions by establishing minimum standards for them.

Sweden

The very first old-age pensions introduced by the Swedish government were considered to be supplements to income provision in old age through private means (or, in the case of the poor, supplements to public relief). It was not until after World War II that public policy began to shift away from government old-age pensions being merely supplements or a special kind of welfare payment. The aim of the National Pension Act of 1946, according to Uhr, "was to raise pension payments . . . to a level tentatively set at 1,000 Kr. per year for single pensioners and 1,600 Kr. for couples, so that the aged who had no other resources would be able to live on their pensions without having to apply for means-tested and relief related supplements." [1]

In the 1950's, however, the principal objective of old-age income maintenance to be achieved through public and private programs changed significantly. The objective that began to gain general acceptance was to provide persons with a standard of old-age security that was at least equal to the standard of living which persons had attained during their best years of active work. In Sweden this is expressed by the phrase "the principle of compensation for decline in earnings from work" (*inkomstbortfallsprincipen*).

The retirement pensions system was not the first program of the social security system to embody this principle. A compulsory program of cash sickness benefits came into force in 1955. Employed persons who become ill and as a result are unable to work are entitled to cash payments related to prior earnings. The amount of payment established by the legislation was set at a level that was to be sufficient to maintain prior income levels based on earnings. After allowance for reduced expenditure needs that result from not working, benefits were established to provide 65–70 percent of the average daily earnings for persons whose earnings were at a level equal to the national average.

This replacement concept was again embodied in the national pension reform legislation. When the government introduced this legislation in 1958, the Minister for Social Affairs told the Riksdag representatives that the principle of providing only a "minimum standard" for retirement through the basic pension should no longer be the appropriate standard. Instead, the government's minister

---

1. According to Uhr, even this pension was reduced according to a graduated scale for pensioners whose income from other sources, or whose net worth, exceeded certain stipulated ceilings (Uhr, 1966).

argued that the standard should be based on the "principle of lost income," which required that benefits be based on earnings prior to retirement.

In order to maintain prior living standards into retirement, pension programs must replace a high proportion of earnings. But as we have discussed before, replacement of which earnings? The Swedish answer was to base the supplementary pensions on the earnings of the best fifteen years of work history.

Labor unions rejected suggestions that the pensions be related to the last year or most recent years of work history and urged that "best" earnings be used. This was mainly because existing evidence indicated that actual earnings for many workers went down during the period just prior to retirement. Labor was anxious, therefore, to avoid the pension inequities that would be created between persons with their "best" earnings at different points in the lifetime earnings pattern. They saw this problem as being particularly disadvantageous to blue collar workers.

With regard to the choice of *fifteen* years, the objective was to achieve some sort of income averaging that would avoid the basing of pensions on abnormally high earnings and also would avoid creating incentives for persons to create high earning years for pension purposes. In the words of one Swede instrumental in developing the reformed social security system, "some strange results would certainly be obtained if the pension could be based on high incomes during a few years of the pensioner's active period. Furthermore there would be a risk that salary scales would be developed which would produce pensions which were disproportionately high" (Broberg, 1973).

As will be discussed in the next section, basing pensions on fifteen years of work history (roughly one third of a full work history) results in a standard to measure "prior living standards," which does not explicitly take into account the general growth in the economy (hence the rise in average earnings) which occurs between the years of credited earnings and the year of retirement. Thus for a person whose earnings increase in a fairly regular manner during the fifteen years prior to retirement and reach a peak in the year before retirement, the average of his best fifteen years gives him an adequacy standard equal to his earnings seven to eight years prior to retirement—adjusted in Sweden only for price-level changes.

Having indicated that the pension-adequacy standard developed in Sweden seeks to maintain into retirement a living standard related to the fifteen best years of earnings, it is important to look at how the system deals with very low and very high earners. Low earners in old-age are provided with a floor of income provided by the *Folkpension* (Chapter 3). The supplementary pension for high earners is limited by the fact that earnings above 7.5 times the base amount cannot be credited toward raising the pension points used in calculating the pension received. Such a ceiling results in the complete inclusion of earnings for persons earning up to about twice the average of Swedish earnings. Based on 1973 average earnings in the United States, this would mean crediting earnings up to about $14,500—in contrast to a United States ceiling of $12,600 in 1974.

Germany

The pension-adequacy philosophy of the German pension system was developed at a time when relatively rapid economic growth coincided with a general feeling of solidarity within the population. This feeling arose as a result of the poverty experienced by almost all Germans during the early postwar years.

An analysis of the adequacy of German pensions may be approached from two perspectives. On the one hand, there is the question of what adequacy was talked about in the construction and augmentation of the system. On the other hand, one can ask how adequate the pension *actually paid* by the system is.

At the beginning it should be stressed that our discussion does not consider minimum pensions. In Germany this part of the income-maintenance problem is taken care of by a highly developed public welfare system—apart from social security. If a pension is lower than the current level of public welfare payments, these payments are available to supplement the pension. These public welfare payments, however, are based on a means test and are calculated by defining a minimum standard of living in real terms.

With respect to the adequacy of the level of old-age pensions, the program was constructed on the basic idea that old people should not live on a living standard below the "general standard" of the nation. This principle underlines the determination of the size of the pension and adjustments of the benefit at and during retirement. It has been shown, however, that the principle has not been perfectly implemented. Various lags between the average wage level, the General Wage Base, and the level of average pensions were built intentionally into the system. Financial and practical reasons led to this development. For example, there were early fears that the nation could not bear the heavy fiscal cost of the system—fears that later developments have shown to be unfounded.

With regard to the size of the pension, it is still an open question whether there now exists or ever existed an explicit philosophy of adequacy. It may be more accurate to argue that the way of calculating the Personal Earnings Base and the "time of inclusion" in the system were based on the principle of providing adequate pensions. Historically the system was developed during a period when a considerable part of German fiscal, economic, and social policy was engaged in providing growth incentives to the economy. The German tax system during this time, for example, cannot be understood without taking this concern into account.

Some experts would argue, therefore, that there was not much discussion of the question whether pensions were adequate or not. For many German economists and government officials the question of how one could reach the point at which the individual does a maximum amount of work in an "achieving society" was a more interesting and more important question.

Having made this important point, it is then possible to recognize that there was one argument of social justice which, in a certain sense, may be arbitrary but which had an important influence on the pension discussion. There existed very early in Germany a pension program of civil servants. This program pays pensions that are about 75 percent of former income. They are, however, subject to taxation, whereas social security pensions are taxed only in certain special cases. The deduction of taxes from the public pensions gives retired civil servants a net pension of about 60 to 65 percent. Prior and during the pension-reform discussions, it was argued by some that the social security system should give old-age pensions of the same size; there seemed to be no reason why a public servant should be given a relatively higher pension than the one given a blue collar worker or a salaried employee. Using the current social security formula, an average pension with 60–65 percent replacement is achieved by the constant of 0.015 (1.5 percent) and forty years of credited service (forty years being assumed to be typical). Though such a calculation in theory produces the desired pension, in practice the desired amount of the pension is not always achieved, because of the different adjustment gaps (see Chapter 4) and an average "inclusion time" lower than the assumed number of years. But even if we ignore the fact that this adequacy estimate is not supported by actual practice, we have to realize that the adequacy level of civil service pensions (upon which, it is sometimes claimed, the benefit levels of the old-age programs are based) have never been explicitly justified.

To give an impression of actual developments in Germany, some statistics for 1970 are presented. It must be noted, however, that the year 1970 tends to exaggerate the effects of the time lags included in the system. In 1970, whereas earnings developments were shaped by economic prosperity and rapid expansion, the pension level was still strongly influenced by the recession years of 1966 and 1967. Although the statistics for 1970 do not provide us with information on the average relation over a period of years between income and wage levels, they may be useful.[2]

A pension level can be calculated in two ways, either by a more theoretical approach, using the General Wage Base and the Adjustment Rate, or by a more pragmatic approach, which looks at the size of the average pension actually paid by the system. It should be stressed, however, that such average pensions are subject to some averaging effect between large and small incomes—an effect that is minimized by the ceiling on the Personal Earnings Base which prevents very large pensions. At the same time there exist many small pensions paid to persons who have recently been included in the system and who have a relatively low time of inclusion. As a result of this statistical problem, the information on average pension size given below must be viewed as only a crude index of the actual situation.

Table 25 gives relevant information on the size of pensions in

2. Of course, a pensioner living in 1970 is not very interested in an average relation of this type, since he has to live on his pension in 1970; the maximum gap between income level and pension level for him is more important than an abstract average.

TABLE 25

The Level of Pensions in the
Federal Republic of Germany, 1970

	DM per Year	Percent Average Earnings	Percent Average Net Earnings
Average wages and salaries[a]	13,632	100.0	129.0
Average net wages and salaries[b]	10,560	77.5	100.0
General wage base[c]	10,318	75.7	97.7
A "normal pension" for workers retiring in 1970 [d]	6191	45.4	58.6
General wage base adjusted for years before 1970 [c]	9780	71.7	92.6
A "normal pension" for workers retiring before 1969	5868	43.0	55.6
Average pension for wage workers retiring at age 65 [e]	4231	31.0	40.1
Average pension for salaried employees retiring a tage 65 [e]	7270	53.3	68.8

[a] Bundesminister für Arbeit und Sozialordnung (1971), p. 229.
[b] Taxes and social security contributions deducted.
[c] Schewe, Nordhorn, and Schenke (1972), p. 72.
[d] Sixty percent of the General Wage Base, equivalent, for example, to a Personal Earnings Base of 100 percent and 40 years of inclusion time.
[e] Schewe, Nordhorn, and Schenke (1972), p. 62.

1970. The most interesting information given is the normal pension for people retiring before 1970. On average, this pension amounts to 55 percent of average net labor income.

As was discussed in Chapter 4, the problem of pension adequacy was not the most important subject of the reform discussion. This may not be true, however, for discussions in the near future. The level of pensions has become an important topic of recent political discussion, which centers on the relation between the general level of income in the economy and actual pension levels.

Belgium

Up to 1974, old-age pensions for the vast majority of pensioners in Belgium were based partly on flat wages and partly on price-adjusted gross earnings. *When the system matures in the year 2018, the old-age pensions will be related exclusively to the workers' average lifetime earnings adjusted for both average price and pro-ductivity changes.*

With regard to the adequacy of the pensions, the Parliament's goal was to replace 75 and 60 percent of average lifetime earnings for couples and unmarried workers respectively. While it is generally agreed that these replacement goals were not arbitrarily chosen, authorities disagree on the exact basis for the selection. Some pension experts say that the replacement rate of 75 percent for couples was chosen by the legislature after estimating that a worker's job expenses (clothing, transport costs, vehicle insurance, etc.) amounted to 25 percent of his gross earnings; since a pensioner no longer had to make these expenditures, he needed only 75 percent of his gross earnings. Others argue that the 75-percent figure was copied from an earlier law establishing the pension program for civil servants.[3]

Canada

In Canada the governments (both federal and provincial) saw their principal role to be one of providing a *floor of protection* for older persons. What evolved was a group of federal programs: the guaranteed income supplement, a universal pension for all Canadians, and an earnings-related national pension for those qualifying through work force participation. Taken together, these public programs provide only minimal levels of income—with the expectation that additional income will be provided through private efforts.

3. The single person's pension was arbitrarily set at 80 percent of the family pension. In addition, the statute accords families a freedom of choice between the family pension, amounting up to 75 percent of one of the spouses' incomes, or two single person's pensions. Families are permitted to choose the most favorable option.

THE REPLACEMENT RATE

To better understand the replacement features of the various pension programs, a computerized simulation model was developed. While an infinite number of simulations would be needed to investigate all the conceivable work histories that will occur for various workers, it is nonetheless possible to identify some typical histories which will cover a wide enough spectrum to give good insight into how the various plans will perform with regard to earnings replacement.

The first step in the construction of such a model involves postulating an aggregate growth pattern for the economy against which individual wage histories can then be evaluated. These "economy data" also provide the necessary aggregates for computing pensions based on formulas that take into account *average* earnings. Average wages in the model are assumed to grow at a steady rate of 3 percent with the general price level rising at 1.5 percent. Alternative calculations are made, however, which assume 5 and 2.5 percent growth rates, respectively.

The assumption that the economic growth rate will remain steady over more than forty years is not entirely realistic, but it is close enough to satisfy our purposes. Over any given period of time we can find some steady growth rate that explains the change from one point in time to the other. Even if the actual change between any two years within the period is different from the overall average, the average rate is a close-enough approximation for understanding some of the more salient features of pension performance within the period. An overall growth figure of 3 or 5 percent is not unreasonable for advanced industrial countries. Indeed, it is probably a bit on the conservative side.

Next it is necessary to specify a hypothetical lifetime earnings history for a worker. In previous studies the usual practice was to assume a hypothetical worker with earnings each year of his work history equal to average earnings for all workers in each respective year.[4]

We believe that this is not a typical earnings pattern, even for

---

4. See, for example, Horlick (1970) and Rittig and Nichols (1974).

PROVIDING ADEQUATE RETIREMENT INCOME

the so-called average worker.[5] A more typical pattern of earnings for workers throughout their work career is one in which the rate of growth in the early years is relatively high—the rate of increase in productivity being highest in the early stages when workers are first acquiring the skills used on the job and moving up "job ladders." In later years when the skills are mastered, the increase in worker productivity typically becomes less dependent upon improved skills and more dependent upon changes in technology. As a result the rate of wage increase will tend to approximate the average. Toward the end of a worker's career, productivity does not necessarily decrease, but workers have often reached the top wage levels, and their individual rate of wage increase will tend to be below the overall average. Thus in order to assess the replacement potential of the various pension programs, a typical case is looked at where the earnings history of the worker starts out above the average in terms of wage rate increase but continually declines, ending his career with wage increases below the average.

Table 26 shows a hypothetical work history for a Swedish worker, assuming that the worker enters the labor force in 1960, works forty years, and retires in the year 2000. The table gives the annual percentage increase in the worker's earnings, his absolute increase, each year's actual earnings, the resulting "pension points," the current year base amount, and the projected average earnings for all workers.

The "earnings level" values were chosen for this worker so that they would produce an earnings history for this worker such that *his average lifetime earnings are equal to the average of "average earnings" for all workers over the same period.*[6] Thus while the individual worker's earnings begin below the average of all workers' earnings in 1960 and also end below average earnings in 1999, the two averages for the total period are equal. Table 26 illustrates the earnings history of what might be called an average worker.

The illustrative case of the "average" worker gives us a useful bench mark for evaluating the replacement potential of the pension

---

5. See Becker (1964) for an analysis and data supporting the view that old workers' earnings typically do not decline as indicated by cross-sectional statistics.

6. See Appendix B for a more complete explanation of the model.

TABLE 26

Earnings History of an Average Swedish Worker

Year	Rate of Earnings Increase	Amount of Total Earnings (kr.)	Pension Points	Average Wages of All Workers
1960		16,347	2.892	20,000
1961	6.0%	17,327	3.084	20,666
1962	5.8	18,340	3.275	21,186
1963	5.7	19,382	3.453	21,851
1964	5.5	20,453	3.613	22,540
1965	5.4	21,551	3.766	23,149
1966	5.2	22,674	3.958	23,800
1967	5.1	23,820	4.155	24,408
1968	4.9	24,985	4.313	25,149
1969	4.7	26,169	4.485	25,954
1970	4.6	27,367	4.638	26,708
1971	4.4	28,577	4.807	27,409
1972	4.3	29,795	4.960	28,120
1973	4.1	31,018	5.137	28,941
1974	3.9	32,242	5.296	29,865
1975	3.8	33,464	5.409	30,728
1976	3.6	34,679	5.516	31,519
1977	3.5	35,883	5.613	32,615
1978	3.3	37,073	5.746	33,482
1979	3.2	38,243	5.880	34,378
1980	3.0	39,390	5.992	35,451
1981	2.8	40,510	6.070	36,384
1982	2.7	41,597	6.177	37,373
1983	2.5	42,647	6.244	38,348
1984	2.4	43,657	6.337	39,574
1985	2.2	44,622	6.402	40,641
1986	2.1	45,537	6.468	42,025
1987	1.9	46,400	6.500	43,360
1988	1.7	47,205	6.500	44,834
1989	1.6	47,950	6.500	46,100
1990	1.4	48,631	6.500	47,633
1991	1.3	49,245	6.500	48,851
1992	1.1	49,788	6.500	50,510
1993	0.9	50,259	6.469	52,217
1994	0.8	50,656	6.417	53,627
1995	0.6	50,975	6.348	55,121
1996	0.5	51,216	6.245	57,008
1997	0.3	51,377	6.176	58,977
1998	0.2	51,457	6.071	60,696
1999	0.0	51,457	5.986	62,765
Average 1960–1999		37,099		37,099

program. It is important to remember, however, that an *average* hides the wide variation in both the actual pensions paid and the amount of replacement for workers with earnings above and below the average. To investigate the variations due to these differences in earnings, we systematically vary the earnings level. We generate a set of pension and replacement rates for workers with earnings *patterns* (increasing by a higher percentage rate in the earlier years, etc.) similar to the average worker but with various earnings *levels* above and below the average. For example, we generate a worker's earnings history which results in lifetime average earnings equal to 90 percent of the "average worker," while still varying the rates of earnings increase from year to year according to the "above average," "average," and "below average" assumptions described above.

Finally, we investigate the differences in earnings replacement which occur if we alter the basic assumptions regarding earnings increases at different stages of the life cycle.

Thus five basic simulations are run for the average worker and for workers with lifetime earnings that are a specified percentage of the average worker's lifetime earnings:

A. The earnings pattern for the average worker discussed above.

B. The earnings pattern for a worker whose earnings are equal in each year to the earnings of all workers and hence increase continuously at the same rate as average earnings.

C. The earnings pattern for a worker in a job where the percentage increase in earnings grows larger as the worker grows older (the reverse of A). As in the case of earnings pattern A, earnings pattern C is constrained to satisfy the rule that the average lifetime earnings of a particular worker must equal the average earnings of all workers over the same period.

D. An earnings pattern similar to A but in an economy where average earnings increase at a rate of 5 percent annually instead of the 3 percent assumed for patterns A, B, and C.

E. An earnings pattern similar to B but in an economy where average earnings increase at a rate of 5 percent annually instead of the 3 percent assumed for patterns A, B, and C.

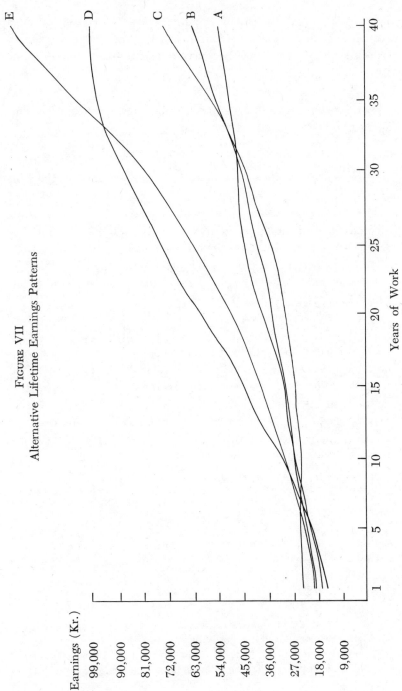

FIGURE VII
Alternative Lifetime Earnings Patterns

Figure VII illustrates these five patterns using Swedish earnings levels. The nature of the assumptions will become clearer as we look at the specific pension programs in various countries.

Sweden

In Sweden the supplementary pension formula explicitly embodies a replacement rate. The formula

PENSION $= .60 \times$ CURRENT BASE AMOUNT $\times$ AVERAGE PENSION POINTS

calls for replacing 60 percent of the average earnings in the best fifteen years of gainful employment, adjusted for price level changes. In addition, each older person receives the same basic or *Folkpension*, and therefore each worker has additional earnings replacement from this pension—the ratio of which varies with his level of earnings. In total, therefore, both pensions together provide a replacement rate that is a combination of the replacement rates embodied in the two different pensions.

Using the earnings history generated by the simulation model (see Table 2), the social security pensions of an average worker are calculated using the procedures specified in the current law and assuming average earnings of 20,000 Kr. in the initial year of the simulation. For the average worker retiring in the year 2000, this results in the pensions and replacement rates shown in Table 27. We see that for this hypothetical worker the total pension received at retirement would be 35,320 Kr. If we now compare this pen-

TABLE 27

Pension and Replacement Rates for the
Average Worker in Sweden, 2000 [a]

Type of Pension	Pension Amount	Replacement
Basic pension	6730 [b]	13%
Supplementary pension	28,590	56
Total pension	35,320	69

[a] Year of hypothetical worker's retirement. See Appendix B for detailed explanation of model used for these calculations.
[b] Amount for unmarried individual. Each person of a couple gets a basic pension, which increases the amount of family earnings replaced by the pensions.

sion with the earnings received in the year prior to retirement, we see that the pension system replaces 69 percent of earnings in this last year of work. Alternatively, the system replaces almost 72 percent of the average annual earnings during the fifteen best earning years.

Table 28 shows the replacement rate for the average worker ("earnings level" equals 1.00 in the first column of the table), but it also gives the replacement rates for workers whose average lifetime earnings are lower and higher than those of the average worker's earnings by some specified percentage. For example, the first case ("earnings level" equals 0.10) represents a worker whose *lifetime* average earnings equal 10 percent of the average of "average earnings for all workers" over the same period. Thus, with average earnings for all workers between 1960 and 1999 estimated to be 37,099 Kr., this case is an example of a worker with lifetime average earnings of only 3710 Kr. Though a worker with such low earnings is not very likely (except for part-time or part-year workers), it and the other very low earnings cases are included to show the entire range of replacement rates implied by the Swedish social security pension system.

Table 28 shows the dominant replacement role played by the *Folkpension* at very low earnings levels, the gradual decline in its importance as the earnings level increases, and the major role of the supplementary pension at the upper end of the earnings scale. Table 28 also shows the effect of the earnings ceiling which by law limits pension points to a 6.5 maximum. The last column gives the maximum pension points received in the fifteen years of best earnings and therefore signals at what earnings level workers' replacement rates are affected by the earnings ceiling (i.e., the pension points maximum). As a result of this ceiling, replacement begins to drop to very low levels for pensioners with exceptionally high preretirement earnings.

The earnings pattern assumed for the average worker was chosen as our best guess of what the lifetime earnings pattern of a typical worker looks like. As discussed above, it assumes that earnings increase most rapidly in the early years of work and that the increases become smaller as the person grows older. In addition it is assumed that money earnings always increase, if only by a small amount in the later years.

TABLE 28

Illustrative Replacement Rates at Various Earnings Levels

Earnings Level [a]	Replacement Rate of			
	Basic and Supplemental	Basic Only	Supplemental Only	Maximum Pension Point [b]
0.10	131%	131	0	—
0.20	86	65	21	0.51
0.30	79	44	35	1.27
0.40	75	33	42	2.02
0.50	73	26	47	2.78
0.60	72	22	50	3.54
0.70	71	19	52	4.29
0.80	70	16	54	5.05
0.90	69	15	54	5.80
1.00	69	13	56	6.50
1.10	63	12	51	6.50
1.20	58	11	47	6.50
1.30	54	10	44	6.50
1.40	50	9	41	6.50
1.50	47	9	38	6.50
1.60	44	8	36	6.50
1.70	41	8	33	6.50
1.80	39	7	32	6.50
1.90	37	7	30	6.50
2.00	35	7	28	6.50

[a] Expressed as a percentage of the earnings level of the average worker.
[b] This column lists the highest pension point received throughout the 15 years of best earnings.

Of course lifetime earnings patterns can vary greatly among individual workers depending on sex, industry, occupation, state of health, and the occurrence of disability or job obsolescence. As indicated in Chapter 3, Swedish unions argued for basing pensions on the best fifteen years rather than on the last year or the last five years of earnings, because they believed that, unlike government and white collar workers, many blue collar workers did not reach their peak earnings just prior to retirement. By using a "best fifteen" standard, the Swedish system avoids giving workers whose earnings have dropped substantially just prior to retirement a pension based on these lower earnings; for such workers a two-thirds replacement of the "best fifteen" years results in an even higher replacement of the lower earnings in the last years. Thus there is no drop in attainable living standards for these workers.

For workers with steadily increasing earnings, however, the "best fifteen years" standard creates a problem. For example, Swedish white collar employees very often have their highest earnings during the years just prior to retirement and want pensions based on these higher earnings and the associated higher living standard. The old-age pension program gives them a pension which roughly corresponds to their mean earnings over the last fifteen years. The result is a pension whose replacement of "last year" earnings is much lower than for the "average worker" discussed previously.

We can illustrate the nature of the problem by calculating pensions and the resulting replacement rates for the different cases described in the preceding section and shown in Figure VII.

TABLE 29

Replacement Characteristics of the Swedish Old Age
Pension Program

Type of Earnings Pattern[a]	Replacement Rate of			
	Total Pension		Basic Pension	Supplementary Pension
	Best 15	*Last Year*	*Last Year*	*Last Year*
Case A Average Worker	72	69	13	56
Case B	69	57	11	46
Case C	65	46	9	37
Case D	59	55	10	45
Case E	55	40	7	33

[a] Case A: The earnings pattern for the average worker, as defined in the prior section.

Case B: The earnings pattern for a worker whose earnings are equal in each year to the earnings of all workers, hence increase continuously at the same rate as average earnings.

Case C: The earnings pattern for a worker where the percentage increase in earnings grows larger as the worker grows older.

Case D: An earnings pattern similar to A but in an economy where average earnings increase at a rate of 5 percent annually instead of the 3 percent assumed for patterns A, B, and C.

Case E: An earnings pattern similar to B but in an economy where average earnings increase at a rate of 5 percent annually instead of the 3 percent assumed for patterns A, B, and C.

Table 29 gives the results. The projected pensions for all cases are very close to the announced goal proclaimed for the Swedish system to provide old-age pensions which amount "to approximately two-thirds of the average annual earnings of the beneficiary during his or her fifteen best earning years" (The National Social Insurance Board, 1971). The replacement varies from 72 percent of the best fifteen years (earnings pattern A) to 55 percent (earnings pattern E).

However, there is much greater variation in replacement based on the last year of earnings. Whereas there is only a small drop for workers with earnings patterns similar to A, there is a sharp drop for the cases where earnings increase a great deal in the later years of work. With earnings growing, along with the economy, at 3 percent, the replacement rate is 69 percent of the best fifteen years but only 57 percent of the last years' earnings. With a 5 percent growth rate the drop is even more dramatic—from 55 percent to 40 percent.

As we indicated in Chapter 3, this characteristic of the Swedish public pension program has important implications for the development of private pensions in the country. Swedish unions, apparently making assumptions similar to our Case B, estimated that the average value of the two national pensions would be about 55 percent of final earnings[7] (Lagerstöm, 1971). It is interesting to note, however, that workers with an earnings pattern similar to Case A would not need a private pension to achieve a goal of 65 percent final wage replacement; the national pensions alone would be adequate.

Germany
In West Germany, as in Sweden, there is a replacement rate explicit in the pension formula. It depends upon (a) the relation between the General Wage Base and the earnings level just before re-

---

7. We made repeated attempts to find out just what assumptions were used by both the unions and the Social Security Organization in the preparation of their projections, but were never successful.

tirement, (b) the time of inclusion in the program, and (c) the relation between the average Personal Earnings Base for all years a person is covered by the program and the Personal Earnings Base for the last year.[8]

With respect to the time of inclusion, the replacement rate increases for each year of inclusion by 1.5 percent. The average time of inclusion for recent retirees is 35 years, as reported in Chapter 4, and results, for example, in a *gross* replacement rate (i.e., replacement of earnings before deduction of taxes) of about 52 percent and a *net* replacement rate of about 67 percent for male employees. Regarding individuals who have a time of inclusion of, for example, 50 years, the net replacement rate would go up to 97 percent. Thus the influence of the time of inclusion can be easily calculated.

This is not true with regard to the more important influence of the Personal Earnings Base. The size of the replacement rate with respect to the Personal Earnings Base depends on the earnings history of the individual—that is, on the distribution of earnings over the life cycle. If an individual has a constant Personal Earnings Base over the life cycle (i.e., his earnings each year have been a constant proportion of the General Wage Base), the replacement rate will not be influenced by the Personal Earnings Base. But if he has, for example, a Personal Earnings Base on average (and also during his last working year) of 150 percent and if his time of inclusion is forty years, his pension at the time of retirement will be one and one-half times the average of pensions received by all persons included for forty years in the program. His net replacement rate will be 77.4 percent, depending only on the time of inclusion. Alternatively, an individual would get a higher replacement rate if his *average* Personal Earnings Base is higher than the Personal Earnings Bases during the years just prior to retirement. This is a case where the person's lifetime earnings pattern, when related to the relevant General Wage Base, shows decreasing earnings during the years before retirement; in such a case the average Personal Earnings Base may be higher than the Personal Earnings Base of the last year. In the opposite case, the replacement rate is lower if the Personal Earnings Base of the last year lies above the average. For

8. For a discussion of factor a, see above, Chapter 4.

example, an individual who has earnings that are increasing throughout his entire earnings history in relation to the General Wage Base will have a lower replacement rate.

To investigate the actual replacement rate resulting from the interaction of these various factors, we have simulated the German old-age pension program using the same general model and assumptions used to study Sweden in the previous section. Table 30 shows

TABLE 30

Replacement Characteristics of the German Pension Program

Type of Earnings Pattern[b]	Replacement Rate[a]
Case A Average Worker	72
Case B	59
Case C	49
Case D	81
Case E	58

[a] Percentage of final earnings.

[b] Case A: The earnings pattern for the average worker, as defined in this Chapter.

Case B: The earnings pattern for a worker whose earnings are equal in each year to the earnings of all workers, hence increase continuously at the same rate as average earnings.

Case C: The earnings pattern for a worker where the percentage increase in earnings grows larger as the worker grows older.

Case D: An earnings pattern similar to A but in an economy where average earnings increase at a rate of 5 percent annually instead of the 3 percent assumed for patterns A, B, and C.

Case E: An earnings pattern similar to B but in an economy where average earnings increase at a rate of 5 percent annually instead of the 3 percent assumed for patterns A, B, and C.

the hypothetical replacement rates for the various cases. The replacement rate for our so-called average worker (Case A) is relatively high—72 percent of the last year's earnings. To understand why the replacement rate is so much higher for Case A than Case B, even though the Personal Earnings Bases are identical,[9] one need

9. The model generates wage patterns in both cases, so that average lifetime earnings of the individual worker equal average earnings for all workers over the period.

TABLE 31

Earnings at Different Points in the Work History
of Two Hypothetical Workers

Career Pattern	Earnings			Lifetime Average
	Initial	Midcareer	Final	
Case A	5077 DM	12,234	15,981	11,522
Case B	6113	11,040	19,358	11,522
Case C	7347	9886	23,122	11,522

only look at the differences in the earnings pattern. Table 31 shows the beginning, midcareer, and final earnings for each case. While midcareer earnings for the average worker are greater than those for Case B (as a result of assuming earnings increases greater than the assumed national average), the average worker's final earnings are significantly lower than the Case B pattern, as a result of lower assumed rates of earnings increase in the later years. Thus, while the two workers receive pensions equal in dollar amount, the replacement rate as measured by the proportion the pension represents of earnings just prior to retirement (in this case, final earnings) is very different. With the Case C earnings pattern the replacement rate is even lower as a result of the higher than average wage increases assumed to occur during the latter part of the work history.

Belgium[10]

Replacement rates in Belgium were much lower than in either Sweden or Germany prior to the 1974 change in the index used to adjust lifetime earnings used in the Belgian pension calculation. This situation changed dramatically with the introduction of the price-plus-productivity adjustment. Table 32 presents the replacement rates for the five different earnings patterns, using the pension regulations in effect before and after 1974. Once again, as with Germany, the pension amounts (not shown in the table) are identical for Case A, B, and C. What varies to cause the difference in replacement is the size of final earnings.

---

10. An alternative analysis of Belgium replacement rates is presented in Carrin (1971).

TABLE 32

Replacement Characteristics of the Belgium Pension Program

Type of Earnings Pattern[b]	Replacement Rate[a]	
	1973 Regulations	1974 Regulations
Case A Average Worker	.56	.73
Case B	.46	.60
Case C	.38	.50
Case D	.53	.84
Case E	.39	.60

[a] Percentage of final earnings.

[b] Case A: The earnings pattern for the average worker, as defined in section B of this Chapter.

Case B: The earnings pattern for a worker whose earnings are equal in each year to the earnings of all workers, hence increase continuously at the same rate as average earnings.

Case C: The earnings pattern for a worker where the percentage increase in earnings grows larger as the worker grows older.

Case D: An earnings pattern similar to A but in an economy where average earnings increase at a rate of 5 percent annually instead of the 3 percent assumed for patterns A, B, and C.

Case E: An earnings pattern similar to B but in an economy where average earnings increase at a rate of 5 percent annually instead of the 3 percent assumed for patterns A, B, and C.

Prior to 1974 the old-age pension formula was based on lifetime earnings adjusted only for price changes occurring in the ensuing years. Table 8 shows that this would produce a replacement rate of 56 percent of final earnings for our average worker and much lower replacement for the other hypothetical earnings patterns. It contrasts with a 69 percent replacement rate for the average worker in Sweden and a 72 percent replacement in Germany. With the introduction of a mechanism to adjust for productivity changes in addition to price changes, however, the replacement rates of the program become comparable with those in the other two countries, rising for the average worker from 56 percent to 73 percent. Finally, it should be noted that all replacement rates would be even higher if the worker were married; the pension formula changes from 60 percent of average lifetime earnings (adjusted) for single pensioners to 75 percent for married pensioners.

Canada

The description of the Canadian Pension Plan (CPP) provided in Chapter 6 makes three facts clear. First, the plan attempts to provide retirement income in some relation to the average earnings of workers over their entire work history. Second, an attempt is made to ensure that the ceiling on pensionable income moves with the average earnings of the economy and is approximately equal to that average. Third, the plan attempts to ensure that the lifetime earnings used in calculating retirement income are adjusted to reflect at current prices what they purchased at the time they were actually earned. How well the CPP performs with regard to these three concerns depends upon the interaction of three factors over time: changes in the price level, general productivity, and the differential growth rate of individual earnings with respect to the overall performance of the economy.

Table 33 shows the economy data used for some of the Canadian simulations (those assuming 5 percent growth). The simulation begins in 1975 (after the current transitional period). The table contains three columns. The first lists average earnings in the economy. The second lists the changes in the pension "earnings index," calculated in accordance with the procedure described in Chapter 6. Since average earnings are assumed to grow at 5 percent in the illustrated economy, it follows that the earnings index will exhibit a similar growth pattern. Therefore, the third column, which shows the YMPE for the economy, also grows at 5 percent.

Where growth is steady, the earnings index is adequate to keep the ceiling on pensionable earnings in line with the growth in average earnings. In cases where the growth rate is less steady, the two can move at different rates. But even where divergence does occur, it will affect the ceiling only slowly because of the use of an eight-year moving average in computing the index. If the growth rate begins to accelerate, the ceiling will lag with this procedure. If the rate slackens, the ceiling will, for a time, run ahead of average earnings.

For any particular worker whose earnings advance with the aggregate average, the approximate size of his pension is easy to determine. For example, assume that a worker enters the labor force at the average earnings level and then receives wage increases

TABLE 33

Average Earnings and Maximum Pensionable Earnings in the
Canadian Economy, Assuming Five Percent Growth

Year	Average Earnings	Earnings Index	YMPE [a]	Year	Average Earnings	Earnings Index	YMPE [a]
1975	$7800	0.00	$7800	1996	$21,730	2.79	$21,700
1976	8190	1.05	8100	1997	22,817	2.92	22,700
1977	8600	1.10	8500	1998	23,958	3.07	23,900
1978	9029	1.16	9000	1999	25,156	3.23	25,100
1979	9481	1.22	9500	2000	26,414	3.39	26,400
1980	9955	1.28	9900	2001	27,734	3.56	27,700
1981	10,453	1.34	10,400	2002	29,121	3.73	29,000
1982	10,975	1.41	10,900	2003	30,577	3.92	30,500
1983	11,524	1.48	11,500	2004	32,106	4.12	32,100
1984	12,100	1.55	12,000	2005	33,711	4.32	33,600
1985	12,705	1.63	12,700	2006	35,397	4.54	35,400
1986	13,341	1.71	13,300	2007	37,167	4.76	37,100
1987	14,008	1.80	14,000	2008	39,025	5.00	39,000
1988	14,708	1.89	14,700	2009	40,976	5.25	40,900
1989	15,443	1.98	15,400	2010	43,025	5.52	43,000
1990	16,216	2.08	16,200	2011	45,176	5.79	45,100
1991	17,026	2.18	17,000	2012	47,435	6.08	47,400
1992	17,878	2.29	17,800	2013	49,807	6.39	49,800
1993	18,772	2.41	18,700	2014	52,297	6.70	52,200
1994	19,710	2.53	19,700	2015	54,912	7.04	54,900
1995	20,696	2.65	20,600	2016	57,658	7.39	57,600

[a] Years Maximum Pensionable Earnings.

similar to the rate of growth of the average. That worker, with
earnings *at the ceiling*, would receive a pension at the end of working career just equal to 25 percent of "pensionable earnings." A
worker beginning at any level *lower than the ceiling* and also receiving earnings increments equal in percentage terms to the overall
increment will likewise receive 25 percent of "pensionable earnings." With workers beginning at more than average earnings and
above the ceiling (and remaining above the average), the pension
will be less than 25 percent.

To illustrate the variety of replacement rates possible with
different earnings levels and patterns, we again simulated for Canada

the five wage patterns discussed above (Table 34). The patterns just discussed above are Cases B and E, and, as expected, the CPP replacement rates are about 25 percent of final earnings.

The "average worker" earnings pattern produces a slightly higher amount of replacement. According to the provisions of the CPP there are a minimum of forty-seven years in an individual's work career, the time between the person's 18th and 65th birthdays.

TABLE 34

Replacement Characteristics of the Canadian Old Age
Pension Program

Type of Earnings Pattern[b]	Replacement Rate[a] of		
	CPP	Universal	Both
Case A Average Worker	.29	.10	.39
Case B	.25	.09	.34
Case C	.20	.07	.27
Case D	.31	.08	.39
Case E	.24	.06	.30

[a] Percentage of final earnings.
[b] Same as for Table 32.

The pension is calculated on the basis of any forty years the individual elects to use. In addition, any months worked beyond an individual's 65th birthday can be used to substitute for low earnings periods prior to that birthday. Though the last forty years represent the years of highest total earnings for all the earnings patterns, it is the relationship of earnings in a particular year to the average which determines pensionable earnings. This results from the operation of the adjustment factor which places the relative position of earnings in the year in which they were earned into dollar amounts reflective of purchasing power in the last years. Since the *rates of increase* in earnings were best for the "average worker" in the early years, the relative position of such workers is also best then. Even though earnings in the last year are the highest in absolute amount, the slow rate of increase in the later years results in a deterioration of the average worker's *relative* position.

Canada, like Sweden, has a two-tiered program. Table 34 therefore shows also the replacement rate projected for the universal flat pension and the total of the two. As in the case of Sweden, we can show the total replacement rate at differing earnings levels using the Case A earnings pattern for all calculations. Table 35 shows the

TABLE 35

Canadian Replacement Rates at Various Earnings Levels

Earnings Level [a]	Universal Only	CPP Only	Both
0.10	104%	30%	134%
0.30	35	30	65
0.50	21	30	51
0.70	15	30	45
0.90	12	30	42
1.00	10	29	39
1.10	9	27	36
1.30	8	23	31
1.50·	7	20	27
2.00	5	15	20
2.50	4	12	16
3.00	3	10	13

[a] Expressed as a percent of the earnings level of the average worker.

replacement rates for workers whose "average worker" earnings levels are lower and higher than those of the worker whose lifetime earnings *equal* average earnings for all workers over the same period.

Replacement Rates in the Four Countries

Having discussed the replacement rates resulting from pension reform in the four separate countries, it is appropriate at this

TABLE 36

Replacement Characteristics for the Average Worker of Old Age Pension Programs in Various Countries

Country	Percent of Final Earnings	
	3% Growth Economy	*5% Growth Economy*
Sweden	69	55
Germany	72	81
Belgium	73	84
Canada	39	39

point to make some comparisons. Table 36 shows the replacement rates in each country for the average worker. Germany and Belgium have the highest, with replacement rates increasing in economies growing at a faster pace. Sweden has a rate only slightly lower in a 3-percent economy, but this rate drops dramatically with faster growth. This drop, as noted above, occurs because Swedish pensions are based on the best fifteen years of earnings, while the replacement rate measure used here is the final year of earnings. As the growth rate rises, the gap between final earnings and average earnings over a fifteen-year period widens.

Canada, with an entirely different replacement policy regarding social security pensions, has a very low replacement rate, which does not change for the two assumed growth rates.

Anticipating the discussion in the next chapter, we can compare the hypothetical pension replacement rates in Table 36 with United States replacement rates resulting from the U.S. social security old-age program (using 1973 benefit levels). It is projected, for example, that in 1980 the overwhelming proportion of couples in the United States will have pensions that represent less than half their preretirement average earnings. Moreover, the majority will have less than 40 percent replacement! [11]

ADJUSTMENTS OF PENSIONS FOR INFLATION AND ECONOMIC GROWTH

In looking at the question whether and how old-age pensions are adjusted, it is useful to distinguish four cases:

1. Adjustment of *new* pensions at the time of initial payment for past *inflation* effects on the pension calculation;

2. Adjustment of *new* pensions at the time of initial payment for past *economic growth;*

3. Adjustment of pensions during retirement for *inflation;*

4. Adjustment of pensions during retirement for *economic growth.*

In this section we review how these adjustments are handled in the four countries.

---

11. See below, Chapter 8, Table 45.

Sweden

Sweden, like all other countries, has been subject to the problems of inflation which have occurred in greater or less degree throughout its recent history. This inflation created a continuous problem for the Swedish aged—dependent during most of the twentieth century in large part upon government transfer payments (welfare, housing supplements, social security, etc.). Legislated payments by the Parliament were constantly being eroded by general increases in prices. Payments under the National Pension Act of 1913, for example, which when originally passed provided only small supplementary payments, became increasingly unacceptable as a result of inflation—even though the benefits were periodically increased and various supplements were added.

The World War II period generated additional inflationary pressures and added public pressure for reform of income-maintenance programs to deal with this and other problems. "In the 1946 pension debate the Liberal leader Ohlin had urged that pension rates be tied to a cost of living index, a view which the government and *Riksbank* in particular rejected as an admission of future inability to master inflation. In responding to the Liberal attack, Social Minister Möller did pledge that the government would adjust pensions to any future price rises" (Heclo, 1971).

In 1949 a special committee composed largely of civil servants developed an index-adjustment plan, which was introduced in 1950. This legislation called for automatically adjusting all pension benefits upward (or downward) every time the measure of the general price level (a "consumer price index") changed by 3 percent. Thus, if the consumer price index rose from 100 to 103, a 3 percent increase was to be immediately implemented, without further legislative action, on the level of pensions paid both to new recipients and to recipients already receiving benefits.

At the same time the price index reform was instituted, recognition was given to the need to improve the real value of pensions:

> It was also decided to make periodic, but not automatic or index-tied adjustments in the real value of the pension according to the rise in the real value of national income. In other words, Parliament declared its policy and intent to increase the

real value of the basic pensions every two years or so, in proportion to the rise in real national income that had ocurred [*sic*] in the interim. For example, if real national income had risen by 10 percent over a 2-year period, a standard supplement to the index-protected pensions should be made of about 10 percent over and above the index adjustment. The intent of this arrangement was that pensioners, along with others in the community, share rather than be left behind in the rising standard of living which an expanding economy affords. (Uhr, 1966)

A succession of index and other increases did occur. For example, "in 1953 pensions were raised in the same proportion by which industrial workers' wages had risen from 1946–52" (Heclo, 1971). As a result, original pensions under the 1946 Act (1000 Kr. for single persons and 1600 for couples) by 1957 had increased 120 percent. During the same period the consumer price index rose only 65 percent—indicating a significant rise in the real value of the pensions.

With the passage of the pension reform act in 1959, no change was made in the basic adjustment principles embodied in the 1950 law. Both new and old pensions were to be automatically adjusted for changing prices, but adjustments for economic growth were to be carried out on an ad hoc basis. We will first look at both price and real adjustment processes for basic pensions and then look at the situation with regard to supplementary pensions.

The 1959 law specified that the automatic adjustment of the basic pension (the *Folkpension*) was to continue for changes in the general price level. Since the pension is calculated as a percentage of the base amount (see Chapter 3), pensions are changed when the base amount changes. As discussed above, the base amount was initially set at 4000 Kr. a year in 1957 prices and is automatically adjusted (on a monthly basis) every time the consumer price index varies by at least 3 percent.

In contrast, the 1959 law did not provide a mechanism for automatically adjusting the real value of the basic pension on a continuous basis to take account of economic growth. However, "Parliament agreed on a basic pension target to be achieved during the decade ahead, i.e., by 1968. It was decided that these basic pensions should be increased in a succession of steps"—reaching by July

1968 the goal set by Parliament a decade earlier of 90 percent (single) and 140 percent (couple) of the base amount (Uhr, 1966).[12]

The result of these changes in the basic pension benefit formula, over and above the price adjustments, was to increase the real value of the pensions. The real adjustments of the basic pension did not end, however, with the implementation of the 1968 scheduled increase. In 1969 the Parliament legislated another schedule. The basic pension for those qualifying for the supplement will be increased 3 percent each year until the real value of the pension has been increased a total of 30 percent by 1978; the multiplicative factor in calculating the pension for these people will be $.9 + .3 = 1.2$ for single persons and $1.4 + 0.3 + 0.3 = 2.0$ for couples.[13]

If we now shift from looking at the basic pension adjustment process to those connected with the supplementary pension, we see that again the principle of automatic price level and no automatic growth adjustment prevails. To ensure that supplementary pension benefits are automatically price adjusted at the time of initial receipt and in the years that follow, a unique system of adjustment was developed and embodied in the 1959 reform legislation. As described in Chapter 3, the person's actual earnings throughout his working career are not used to calculate the supplementary pension. Instead these earnings are converted into "pension points" by relating earnings to the base amount. The average pension points for the best 15 years are then, as part of the pension calculation, multiplied times the current base amount which has been adjusted

---

12. According to information obtained from interviews with Swedish officials, the selection of the 0.9 and 1.4 factors was based primarily on cost considerations. The initial recommendations had been to set the basic pension for a single person between 2500 and 3000 Kr. Actuarial projections indicated, however, that the system "could afford" a higher basic pension. A basic pension of 3600 Kr. for single persons seemed feasible and was therefore selected. Given this desired result, the 4000 *base amount* and the 0.9 multiplicative factor were chosen.

13. The pension supplement is subject to a pension test. If the pensioner receives more than a certain amount of retirement or widow's pension (or both) under the supplementary pension program, the supplement is reduced by the excess amount.

for price changes over the intervening period between the years when pension credits were earned and the years when pensions were actually received.

This adjustment method avoids a very fundamental problem associated with earnings-related pension systems. Unless adjustments are made for price level changes using the Swedish or some alternative method, the resulting pensions are likely to be based upon earnings levels which correspond to much higher current earnings levels in real terms. If the aim of the pension system is to provide sufficient income to maintain some degree of a prior living standard into old-age, some adjustment must be made in the measures used to account for price-level changes. Otherwise benefits tend to be inadequate and inequities develop in the system. For example, in the Swedish system persons with their best earnings concentrated just prior to old age would get a better pension than those with best earnings concentrated around middle-age, despite the fact that their average best earnings (in real terms) may have been equal.

Like the basic pension, Swedish supplementary pensions are not subject to any formal and automatic adjustment for economic growth, neither at the time of initial receipt nor subsequently. There is some adjustment implicit in the system as a result of the fact that benefits are based on the person's best fifteen years and not on his whole work history. These best earnings tend to be the earnings in the later part of a person's work history—earnings which reflect not only the increased seniority, experience, etc. of the worker but also the general increasing productivity of all workers over time as a result of economic growth factors. Of course, the amount of this adjustment depends on the earnings pattern of the individual. Persons whose earnings peak many years before retirement and subsequently fall off will be at a disadvantage, benefiting less from this implicit adjustment factor.

Once supplementary pension benefits begin, there is no further automatic adjustment throughout old age to reflect general economic growth and to maintain parity with the rising living standards of the working population. At the time of the pension reform, discussion of this question took place, but a decision was made against such an adjustment. There was sympathy for some sort of adjustment based upon a wage index, but many feared its costs, given the difficulty of projecting them into the future. It was argued that with the major and liberal changes already embodied in the reform proposal, it was best to make certain that the system could survive during both the good and bad times of the future. An additional and rather forceful argument made against a growth adjustment was that the pensions could always be changed on an ad hoc basis if there developed a general agreement that pensions were too low or that revised actuarial projections indicated that the initial estimates were too conservative.

Thus far no ad hoc adjustments of supplementary pensions have occurred. In June 1970, however, a committee was appointed by the Government to analyze a number of pension questions, including the possibility of adapting pensions to the changes of wages and salaries levels.

Germany

In Chapter 4 we described in detail the method used to calculate German pensions at the time of retirement. This calculation is based upon lifetime earnings; all such earnings, however, are converted to a ratio by dividing a particular worker's earnings by the average earnings of all workers in the same year. Multiplying the average of these ratios for a particular worker times the General Wage Base in the year he retires provides a built-in adjustment to take into account the general rise in wages due to inflation and real growth which have occurred during the pensioner's work history.

This automatic adjustment process is restricted to the calculation of pensions at the time of retirement. At the time pension reform was being debated there were fears that the economy would be harmed by inflationary pressures encouraged by automatic adjustment of pensions during retirement. To deal with the question, a special institution, the Social Advisory Council, was created, its main job being to make recommendations concerning such adjustments. Based upon these recommendations, the Government proposes pension changes, and the Bundestag is given final authority in deciding for or against any recommended adjustments.

In practice this rather complicated system of semiautomatic adjustments did not operate exactly as planned. For all years after

1958 the Social Advisory Council simply recommended that *pensions be adjusted during retirement by the percentage change in the General Wage Base during the previous year*. The Government, as well as the Parliament, then followed the recommendation without exception. Thus the adjustment has been for all practical purposes automatic (disregarding a time lag during implementation).[14]

It might be hypothesized that the Social Advisory Council decided on a policy of automatic adjustment very early in its history and set out to show that such a policy was possible. Before drawing that conclusion, however, one must ask whether the Council really did have a choice in the matter. Since the Council included different interest groups, the recommendations of the type made for such increases had the best chance of being accepted by a majority of the Council. Therefore it must be stressed that the political composition of the Council in large part predetermined that either automatic increases would be recommended or that a stalemate would occur in the Council's discussion.

While the Social Advisory Council has not fulfilled its original role, it has performed another very useful function. To a very significant extent the Council has contributed to the growing and broad acceptance of the pension program which has developed over the years. Many of the modifications instituted after the pension reform in 1957 were first discussed and recommended by the Social Advisory Council. Since all the different interest groups were represented in the Council, many of the needed changes were facilitated by the very thorough and scientific discussions occurring within the Council. Therefore, even if the Council has not fulfilled its initial objective, its contribution to the development of German old-age pensions is of great importance.

---

14. Dr. Ida Merriam, in a prepublication review of this book, has made an important point with which we agree: "The fact that they (the Social Advisory Council) have up to now decided that adjustment on the basis of the general wage base was appropriate does not mean that they are not providing the safeguards of ad hoc adjustment that were intended. Given a sharp and continuing downturn in the German economy, it is entirely possible that the Social Advisory Council would have some other recommendation to make."

Belgium

To take account at retirement of the price and productivity increases that have occurred during a worker's career, each worker's gross earnings are automatically adjusted as follows: gross earnings for each year are multiplied by a price coefficient and a productivity coefficient which are equal to the value of the price and productivity indexes in the year that the pension is calculated divided by the index values for the original year of work.

The adjustment is as follows:

$$E_A = \frac{1}{Y} \sum_{i=1955}^{1972} E_i r_i w_i \qquad (3)$$

where

E_A = average lifetime earnings, adjusted

E_i = gross earnings in year i,

Y = the number of years worked after 1955,

r_i = the price adjustment coefficient, and

w_i = the productivity adjustment coefficient.

Before 1960 the various Belgian social security programs used a variety of mechanisms to adjust pensions *during* retirement. This diversity was eliminated in 1960 by a law that created a uniform adjustment procedure for the entire social security system. The law specified that an increase (decrease) in pensions of 2.5 percent would occur automatically if there was a rise (decrease) in the retail price index number of 2.75 index points. It was further specified that these adjustments would begin two months after the end of any period of two months in which the retail price index reached a number that justified an adjustment. On January 1, 1968, the original retail price index was replaced by a consumer price index, the latter being more likely to reflect price changes for a broader range of consumer goods than was the case with the retail index.[15]

The law was changed in 1971. Pensions were to be increased 2 percent when the average of the consumer price index for two consecutive months reached the next *spilindex cijfer* (pivot index number). The timing of the adjustment was similar to that specified

---

15. To convert the old retail price index to the consumer price index, one multiplies the former by 1.2988. The latter figure was determined by the *Nationale Arbeidsraad* (National Council of Labor).

in the 1960 law. The newer adjustment mechanism, however, had the advantage that increases in pensions were strictly comparable to changes in the consumer price index (Van Haurwaert, 1972).

Starting January 1, 1974, old-age pensions for all "worker" retirees are adjusted during retirement for changes in both prices and the real wages of the employed population. As a result of this change, the economic status of these elderly relative to the working population will be maintained. It is important to emphasize that this new adjustment procedure (unlike the new pension formula discussed in Chapter 5) applies to persons retiring before and after 1973. Thus all Belgians except the self-employed will benefit from the new procedure.

Canada

Since its establishment the Canadian universal pension has been periodically increased on an ad hoc basis. In addition, with the establishment of the CPP in 1966 an automatic inflation adjustment mechanism was legislated. Up to 1972 this annual adjustment was subject to a maximum 2 percent increase in any one year; in that year the ceiling was removed, and the pension is now annually adjusted to compensate for actual increases in the price level.

At retirement the CPP is based upon average lifetime earnings (age 18 to 65), but seven years of lowest earnings are dropped from the calculation. As discussed in Chapter 6, the pensionable earnings for each of the years used is then automatically adjusted by a conversion factor that changes the past purchasing power of these earnings into dollar amounts which generally reflect the prices and standard of living at the time of retirement.

Like the universal pension, CPP pensions are automatically adjusted in retirement based on changes in the consumer price index. The 2-percent adjustment ceiling, however, remains in effect.[16]

---

16. In 1973 the Quebec Plan changed its ceiling from 2 to 3 percent.

Chapter 8

REFORM FOR THE UNITED STATES

THE last five chapters discussed old-age pension programs in four Western European countries. In this chapter we shift focus to look at pension developments and policies in the United States. Again, however, the emphasis is on the adequacy of pensions and possible reforms to promote greater adequacy. In Chapter 2 we presented and discussed four specific questions that, we maintain, are basic to analyzing the adequacy of any pension program (public or private). In addition we discussed two general issues (financing and the pension mix) of importance in establishing general pension policies. In Chapter 7 we discussed the four questions in connection with the four countries studied. In this chapter we again look at these four questions (and also the two general issues) but with the focus on possible pension reform in the United States.

NEEDED IMPROVEMENTS

Although there have been hundreds of changes in the social security laws of the United States since the original legislation, we think it is accurate to state that the major guiding principles underlying the system have not basically changed since its inception. Former Commissioner of Social Security Robert M. Ball (1967) has cited the introduction to the Social Security Advisory Council Report of 1965 as being "the most succinct of recent statements summarizing the principles and purposes of social security." In part that introduction states:[1]

---

1. For readers not familiar with the provisions of the social security law in the United States, Appendix A provides a brief summary of the various provisions.

The Council strongly endorses the social insurance approach as the best way to provide, in a way that applies to all, that family income will continue when earnings stop or are greatly reduced because of retirement, total disability or death. It is a method of *preventing* destitution and poverty rather than relieving those conditions after they occur. And it is a method that operates through the individual efforts of the worker and his employer, and thus is in total harmony with general economic incentives to work and save. It can be made practically universal in application, and it is designed so as to work in ongoing partnership with voluntary insurance, individual savings, and private pension plans.

Under the social security program the right to benefits grows out of work; the individual earns protection as he earns his living, and, up to the maximum amount of earnings covered under the program, the more he earns the greater is his protection. Since, unlike relief or assistance, social security benefits are paid without regard to the beneficiary's savings and resources, people can and do build upon their basic social security protection and they are rewarded for their planning and thrift by a higher standard of living than the benefits alone can provide.

The fact that the program is contributory—that employees and self-employed workers make contributions in the form of ear-marked social security taxes to help finance the benefits—protects the rights and dignity of the recipient and at the same time helps to guard the program against unwarranted liberalization. The covered worker can expect, because he has made social security contributions out of his earnings during his working lifetime, that social security benefits will be paid in the spirit of an earned right, without undue restrictions and in a manner which safeguards his freedom of action and his privacy. Moreover, the tie between benefits and contributions fosters responsibility in financial planning; the worker knows that improved benefits mean higher contributions. In social insurance the decision on how to finance improvements is always an integral part of the decision on whether they are to be made.

(Advisory Council on Social Security, 1965)

Over the years there has certainly been a large amount of criticism of the social security system by those *supporting* such legislation. This criticism, generally accepting the principles expressed in the 1965 advisory council statement, has focused primarily on the need for expanded coverage and liberalization of benefits in order (in the words of the Advisory Council) "to prevent destitution and poverty." In recent years, however, criticisms of the system have begun to shift to some of the basic principles previously taken for granted:

1. Serving as a *basic floor* of income protection;

2. Financing exclusively and uniformly by employer and employee contributions;

3. Providing "social adequacy" without a means test.

In this book we do not concentrate our attention on the financing or social adequacy questions.[2] Instead, we wish to challenge the principle that social security old-age pensions should provide a floor of protection—this floor being defined generally as a level of benefits sufficiently high *to prevent destitution and poverty.*

Robert J. Myers has summarized the issue as follows:

> It can fairly be said that the social security system has widespread, almost universal, acceptance by the American people . . . The real differences of opinion arise in respect to the future course of social security and its relative importance in the economic-security picture . . . We have often heard it said— perhaps ad nauseum—that the social security program should provide only "as a floor of protection" in the economic security area. This, however, is not a precise concept, and one cannot say exactly just how low or how high the floor should be. In fact, one eminent student of social security . . . has suggested that, desirably, the floor should have a luxurious carpet laid on it through government action. One might well raise the question as to why this expansion is necessary . . . There might also be asked why should not such supplementation be done through private action?   (Myers, 1970)

Myers labels advocates of a greater role for social security in aged-income maintenance "expansionists" and designates as "moderates" those persons who "believe that the present system is reasonably adequate." With regard to the floor that social security is to provide,

---

2. The reader is reminded that the Swedish, German, and Canadian aged income-maintenance programs attempt to make a relatively clear separation between income redistribution and the earnings-related programs. In all three countries this explicit separation was one of the objectives or planned characteristics of the original pension-reform legislation.

Myers summarizes the moderate viewpoint as one which seeks a governmental program that would provide benefits which would be "sufficient so that, with assets and real estate normally accumulated, the vast majority of beneficiaries will be able to have at least a reasonable subsistence." Here, then, is the issue. Is social security —as Myers, the Social Security Advisory Council, and many others have argued—merely to provide benefits to ensure that retirees can at least subsist at an "above poverty" level, or are the people of the United States ready to establish collectively a much higher standard?

The Preretirement Standard

From one perspective one might argue that the question is already answered. As indicated in Chapter 1, the income levels of many elderly are beyond subsistence—mainly because of the improved coverage and benefit levels of the current social security pension program. According to Ball (1972), "changes in Social Security enacted in 1972 have so significantly improved and modernized our Social Security Program that we can say in truth that we have a *new* Social Security program—one that provides a new level of security to working people of all ages and to their families." And as wages rise along with the social security contribution ceiling, retirees of the future will be eligible for old-age benefits far beyond the subsistence level. Thus, to be meaningful, the argument of the moderates must be translated into an advocacy of a social security system status quo—with any further pension improvements to take place in the private sector.

One argument against increasing the level of social security benefits that has been made frequently in the past and is still made, probably with less frequency today, is that such increases conflict with the individualistic traditions of our society and discourage people from taking responsibility for making adequate provision for their old age.[3] Faulkner (1963), for example, states that "little change is likely in the long-held conviction of business that OASDI benefits must be held to minimum subsistence levels in order not to depress personal thrift, discourage capital accumulation and investment, and inhibit productivity."

---

3. See Lubove (1968) for historical perspectives on this point.

Derek C. Bok has given what we consider to be a perceptive and inimitable answer to this type of argument:

> There is . . . something disingenuous in the desire to use social security policy to help maintain the self-reliance of the worker. Inheritances, tranquilizers, and a vast array of other products and institutions will arguably affect individual initiative and responsibility in socially undesirable ways. Advertising, salesmanship, and easy credit devices may have much more corrosive effects than a government pension on the willingness to save. Nor is there any apparent reason why social security benefits should have any greater effect on individual responsibility than private pension plans negotiated by large unions and employers. Yet those who are troubled over the effects of social security have expressed little or no concern over these other forces. In short, it is quite arbitrary to seize upon the social security program to promote individual responsibility. If such traits are to be fostered as a matter of public policy, it would be far better to attack institutions that are more clearly detrimental and to impose penalties on the improvident that are less drastic and irremediable than consignment to a penurious old age.
>
> (Bok, 1967)

In recent years there has been less talk about eliminating poverty among the elderly (since this goal seems close to achievement *for the bulk* of the aged). Now many people argue that benefits should be related to some kind of retirement budget based on observed needs and lifestyles of the elderly. For example, the "Income Section" of the 1971 White House Conference on Aging recommended:

> The immediate goal for older people is that they should have total cash income in accordance with the "American standard of living." We therefore recommend the adoption *now,* as the minimum standard of income adequacy, of the intermediate budget for an elderly couple prepared by the Bureau of Labor Statistics . . . For single individuals the minimum annual total income should be sufficient to maintain the same standard of living as for couples (not less than 75 percent of the couple's budget). For the elderly handicapped with higher living expenses, the budget should be appropriately adjusted.
>
> (White House Conference on Aging, 1971)

The Bureau of Labor Statistics (BLS) budgets are for retired couples who are "self-supporting, living independently in their own home, in reasonably good health, and able to take care of themselves" (United States Bureau of Labor Statistics, 1966). The generalized conception of the living standard is translated into a list of commodities and services that can be priced. In the autumn of 1972 the "intermediate level" budget was priced by BLS at $4967 (United States Bureau of Labor Statistics, 1973).

As was indicated in Chapter 1, the establishment of such a budget standard (or even a variety of budgets) for various groups or categories of the aged can never (and are not intended to) adequately reflect the even greater variety of economic circumstances of these aged families prior to retirement. The budgets do "not show how an 'average' retired couple actually spends its money, nor does it show how a couple should spend its money . . . In general, however, the representative list of goods and services comprising the standard reflects the collective judgment of families as to what is necessary and desirable" (United States Bureau of Labor Statistics, 1966). Thus the Nixon Administration responded to the adequacy of income recommendations of the 1971 White House Conference delegates:

> The Administration does not concur in the recommendations of the delegates to the Conference that the "intermediate" budget developed by the Bureau of Labor Statistics become the national goal in this area . . . While these [budget] studies are interesting and useful in their own right, they provide no basis for knowing whether any particular level of income is "adequate" under varying sets of circumstances.
>
> (U.S. Subcommittee on Aging, Committee on Labor and Public Welfare, 1973)

Also, though it is easy to adjust these budgets for price changes, it is much more difficult to adjust them so that they reflect the changing levels of living in the economy; such adjustments contain a high degree of arbitrariness.

We have discussed throughout this book an alternative way (other than poverty indexes or budget levels) of specifying for policy purposes the operational income maintenance goals of various pension programs—that is *to specify the proportion of prior earnings that are to be guaranteed to the worker upon retirment through a pension program(s)*. The pension systems of the countries studied in this book illustrate the application of this income maintenance principle.

The Replacement Rate

Aside from recommendations for helping the aged by improving social security (which often take the form of requesting 5, 10, 20, or 50 percent benefit increases), there has been very little discussion in the United States of just what the level of old-age benefits should be—except from the "moderates," who seek to retain the status quo.[4] For example, if we look at the most recent Advisory Council on Social Security recommendations, we find no discussion of this question. In a section of their report entitled "Criteria for Future Benefit Increases," the Council states that "future congressional consideration of social security cash benefit levels should include consideration of improved benefit levels based on criteria related to (1) the adequacy of benefit amounts for regularly employed low-paid workers and (2) the relationship of benefit levels in general to the levels of living of current workers." Having stated those criteria, the Council reaffirms the goal stated by previous councils of setting benefit levels for low earnings at a level that will keep beneficiaries out of poverty (while avoiding high payments to sporadically covered workers). Having discussed this question extensively, the Council deals with the issue of *general* benefit increases in one short, vague paragraph:

> The Council recognizes that if social security benefits are increased to keep up only with increases in the cost of living, the levels of living of people on the benefit rolls will gradually decline relative to families of people still working. To assure that this situation will not continue over a long period of time, the Council believes that the Congress in its future deliberations should take into account increases from time to time that are higher than increases in the cost of living.

The Advisory Council provides us with no specific guidelines or goals for the setting of present or future benefit levels.

Over the years the principal architect of social security reform

---

4. Of course, the recommendation of the 1971 White House Conference on Aging, quoted above, is relevant, but we have no written record of the arguments pro and con on the conference recommendation.

has been the House Ways and Means Committee of the Congress. In 1967 that committee issued a report that specified the earnings-replacement objective used to explain the benefit levels specified in the social security amendments of 1967:

> The bill embodies the principle that the retirement benefit of a man age 65 and his wife should represent at least 50 percent of his average wages under the social security system . . . In establishing the benefit levels, it was necessary for your committee to consider not only benefit levels but also earnings levels and other factors. It was the committee's judgment that when all factors were taken in conjunction, the benefit for a couple which is based on the maximum credited earnings ought to be approximately 50 percent of the average earnings of the worker, with an appropriate increase in the percentage as the earnings fell below the maximum, until benefits reached what in the light of existing conditions seemed to be an appropriate minimum benefit.
>
> (U.S. House Committee on Ways and Means, 1967b)

A pension formula which seeks to replace 50 percent of *lifetime* earnings, however, usually replaces a much lower percentage of earnings *just prior to retirement*. Later in this chapter we show that the actual social security pension replacement rates for couples retiring between 1960 and 1980 (estimated by a simulation model) tend to be much lower than the Committee's goal. If pensions are compared with the average of earnings five years prior to retirement, one finds that a majority of couples will receive at least 50 percent replacement only in the earnings groups below $4000. In general couples will receive much lower than 50 percent replacement. For example, only 6 percent of the couples with average pre-retirement earnings between $8000 and $8999 will receive as much as 50 percent.

In our opinion a pension program that replaces such a low proportion of prior earnings is not even an "adequate floor of protection." Given our previous discussions of the limitations of private pensions and the difficulties individuals have in providing for themselves through personal savings, we believe the Ways and Means Committee's 50-percent standard is inadequate as long *as it is based upon unadjusted lifetime earnings*. It makes little sense to base pensions on a lifetime-earnings average which by the very nature of the averaging process results in a standard that reflects a living standard experienced decades before retirement. One would expect families to have become accustomed to the higher living standard typically associated with the later years before retirement and would not expect the act of retirement to change dramatically their living expectations. Thus it is certainly not unreasonable to base individual and collective retirement pension plans on a goal of preventing any major decline in lifestyle as a result of retirement; in fact, the "golden years" of retirement are often glamourized as the years when an individual is finally free of work constraints and able to enjoy life more. But we know that this is wishful thinking for many retired persons in the United States and other countries.

Pension reform in the four countries studied and reported on above was aimed at doing something significant about the unsatisfactory economic situation of the aged in each country. In Germany, Sweden, and Belgium the objective of "maintaining living standards during retirement" was an important consideration in designing the new pension program. In Canada the major emphasis was on developing a tiered income maintenance system where the programs in each tier were more adequate and equitable than the programs existing before the reform.

It is our belief that these pension programs illustrate the general direction the United States should take in the further development of its old-age pension program. By making such a statement we do not mean that the United States mix of private and public pensions should be similar to, say, that of West Germany, where there is almost total reliance on public pensions. Rather, we believe this country should formulate new policies to improve both private and public pensions in the United States—starting not with a poverty standard of adequacy but rather using a measure that recognizes the desirability and reasonableness of maintaining living standards in retirement. *Specifically we propose the adoption of a standard that will provide inflation-protected benefits equal to a specified percentage of preretirement average earnings (with minimum and maximum benefit levels).*

Given the problems associated with private pensions (discussed in a later section), especially the problems of extending coverage and adjusting benefits in retirement for inflation, we think that most of the earnings replacement should be carried out through the social security system.

Assuming that 65–80 percent replacement of preretirement earnings before taxes is required to maintain one's living standard in retirement, we feel that the minimum guarantee through social security should be about 55 percent. If they so chose, individuals would then be able to provide with relative ease through private pensions and/or personal saving the rest of the retirement income required to maintain their living standard. Or they could choose to do nothing and live at a lower level in retirement. And individuals who were unable to supplement their social security or were subject to an unexpected financial loss or were misinformed (had unrealistic expectations) about their private pension, etc., would not as a result suffer as sharp a drop in income when retiring as many now do.

With regard to selecting the specific percentage of replacement and the definition of the average preretirement earnings to be used, there are numerous possibilities and no obvious best answers. The recommendation above of 55 percent replacement is to some extent arbitrary and difficult to justify as opposed to, say, 50 percent or 60 percent. Any of these three replacement rates meets the criteria of (a) providing "most" of the earnings replacement through social security, (b) providing some choice to the individual regarding the ultimate replacement (i.e., whether he wishes to provide additional retirement income through personal savings and/or private pensions), and (c) recognizing the existence and continuing role in the United States of private pensions.

Furthermore, it is not necessary that one replacement rate be designated for the entire range of preretirement earnings. If we look at the history of social security in the United States we see that:

> it was assumed from the first that the relation of benefits to past wages should not be constant at all levels, but, rather, that the scale of benefits should be graduated in a manner to favor the lower-paid worker. It was considered sound social insurance philosophy, as opposed to that of private insurance, to give clear emphasis to adequacy as balanced against equity in paying higher proportional benefits where these were needed to provide the bare essentials of living, tapering off as benefits rose

above this level. This philosophy has apparently reflected the predispositions of the American people, since it has seldom, if ever, been challenged.   (Brown, 1972)

If it is thought desirable to continue this philosophy, it is possible to vary the replacement by earnings level. It will be remembered that this is achieved in Sweden and Canada by combining a flat pension with the earnings-related program. But, of course, such a result could be obtained in other ways—for example, a formula or replacement rate schedule which *directly* incorporated weighting or a flat spouse benefit.

Adjustment at Retirement

The measure of preretirement earnings to be replaced is also somewhat arbitrary. As we indicated previously, a wide variety of measures are currently used by various countries. In fact, there is almost no duplication in the measures used among developed countries surveyed and summarized in Table 12 (page 52). Nor does there seem to be any tendency to favor one of the three types of measures over the other two—the *last* year's measure versus the *lifetime* earning's measure versus the *best* year's measure.

We do not favor the last year's measure because of the inequity that is generated among workers with different earnings patterns at the end of their careers. This measure is too subject to the vicissitudes of work-force experience, most of which is outside the control of the worker himself. Such a measure, we expect, is bound to generate antagonisms between, for example, workers whose earnings fall off before retirement and those whose earnings keep rising until retirement.

The best year's measure has the great virtue of simplicity and would be very easy for persons to understand and remember. Many countries combine the *best* and *last* years measures; the Soviet Union, for example, uses the "best five of the last ten years" as the preretirement measure. There is at least one major problem associated with the best year's measure, however. There is great incentive to manipulate or control earnings so that the best years are unusually good, and one of the reasons Sweden chose to use fifteen years for their pension calculation was to avoid this problem. But as we indicated in Chapter 3, this then interfered with the Swedish objective of providing pensions based on the living standard just prior to retirement for workers with steadily increasing wages.[5] In addition to Sweden and Russia, variations of the best years' measure are used by Italy, Poland, and Yugoslavia.

In this country, former Commissioner of Social Security Robert M. Ball suggested in 1966 that one possible alternative to the present earnings measure of the United States was to take the best five of the last fifteen years of earnings (Ball, 1966). Pechman, Aaron, and Taussig (1968) in addition to supporting the Ball alternative recommended using the best five and the best ten years.[6] More recently, Ball has stated that he hoped attention would be given to the "redesign of the [social security] system so that the benefits are related to what people have recently been earning—like a high five or a high ten year average—so that when beneficiaries come on the rolls, their benefits are up to date in relation to current earnings, not only the individual's own earnings, but also the general earnings level that continuously rises in this country" (Ball, 1969).

As we have seen from our study of Germany, Belgium, and Canada—one need not use a last or best year's measure in order to bring benefits up to date in relation to past price and real growth developments. These countries all use average lifetime earnings as the preretirement standard but adjust these earnings. Prior to 1974 the earnings in Belgium were adjusted only for price-level changes occurring during the intervening period between the receipt of earnings and the year of retirement; currently in all three countries, the earnings are adjusted in addition for the subsequent rise in real earnings.

The lifetime earnings measure overcomes the problem of the other two measures, which are apt to measure atypical years (either too high or too low) for many workers. But the adjustment processes in Germany, Belgium, and Canada are relatively complicated

---

5. As we indicated in Chapter 3, the Swedish solution to this problem was to compensate for the resulting lower pensions through private pension plans.

6. Pechman, Aaron, and Taussig's position on this matter is unclear, since they recommend the Ball alternative in one part of the book (page 98), the best five years (page 219) in another part, and the best ten in still another (page 226).

and are difficult for professionals and nonprofessionals alike to understand.[7] Whether such complicated mechanisms are necessary seems to depend on the extent to which one seeks equity among workers with different earnings patterns and the extent to which the best earnings measure creates such equities.

Our preference is to use a combination of the last and best years measures and to at least adjust the earnings by a price index. While the choice is somewhat arbitrary, *we recommend that pensions be related to earnings in the last fifteen years of work.* Given the age of eligibility specified in the current social security law, this would base the pensions on the period from age 50 to age 64 for a person who did not retire early. From this period *we recommend selecting the best ten years for benefit purposes;* a smaller number of years seems unwise because of manipulation and the atypical years problems discussed above.

Finally, it is important to note that the current social security old-age pension program in the United States could easily be modified along the lines suggested above. *The old-age pension program in the United States, designed as an insurance program for the replacement of earnings loss due to retirement, has always related benefits to prior earnings and implicitly specifies a rate of earnings replacement by specification of the benefit calculation formula.* In general, all that is required to implement the new adequacy standard is (a) a more widespread recognition of the earnings replacement implications of the program, (b) a more detailed study of the replacement rates achieved by the present regulations of the program, and, most importantly, (c) a collective decision regarding changes required to improve the earnings replacement potential of the program for all or various categories of beneficiaries.

The establishment of more adequate collective public pensions based upon this adequacy standard need not discourage individual initiative or eliminate private pensions. Instead, it can give individuals a more secure foundation upon which to base their personal

---

7. In one country we were told by those involved in drafting the pension legislation that the pension calculation mechanics were purposely complicated to make the program seem more conservative and therefore to allay the fears of certain legislators. In fact, the changes had little real impact on the actual pensions paid.

saving decisions and encourage private pensions to expand and more adequately deal with the "special problems," unique needs, or varying retirement preferences of different groups of workers. In all four countries we studied—three of which provide the bulk of retirement security through public pensions—private savings and private pensions continue to grow.

Adjustment during Retirement

Once a pension has been calculated, some countries do not adjust it by any automatic process, preferring periodic ad hoc changes. Increasingly, however, countries have adopted automatic or semi-automatic adjustment mechanisms. All four foreign countries we studied adjust automatically for price changes; in addition, three of the countries—Belgium, Germany, and Canada—make productivity (or real) pension adjustments, using an earnings index.[8]

As in Sweden, the uncertainty of the cost to the system of an earnings-index adjustment seems to be a major reason why many countries are reluctant to adopt such a mechanism. In addition, the adequacy of the benefit at the time of retirement is a priority policy consideration for most countries, given assumed financing capacity.

The United States now has a provision in the social security law which automatically adjusts pension during retirement for general increases in the price level. The adjustment mechanism finally became law in 1972 after many years of debate over whether such a provision would discourage significant (and "needed") improvement in the general level of social security pensions adjusted for price changes.

In 1963 it was proposed that retirees be provided some share in economic growth through the establishment of a social credit scheme (Kreps and Spengler, 1963). Since then there has been relatively little discussion of this issue and few advocates of an automatic adjustment mechanism using, for example, an earnings index.

As indicated previously, support for such a reform depends on the relative desirability of competing public expenditures and most especially on the adequacy of retirement pension benefits *at* retire-

---

8. Canada's earnings-index adjustment does not begin until 1976.

ment. Certainly the lack of discussion of this issue in the United States has been in large part a result of public debate and action that was focused on the poverty of the aged and the very low levels of pensions both at and during retirement.

While we feel that it is desirable to incorporate eventually some sort of growth adjustment mechanism into the social security program, we also feel that the principal focus of any major reform of benefit level in the near future should be on achieving a higher level of benefit adequacy at retirement.

SIMULATIONS OF THE GERMAN AND SWEDISH PROGRAMS

What will the distribution of old-age pension income look like for retired Americans in 1980? How different would their pensions be if the United States had a pension program similar to the one in the Federal Republic of Germany or Sweden? What proportion of an American worker's preretirement earnings would be provided at retirement by a German or Swedish-type pension program? How would these pensions compare with those to be received under the current program of the United States?

This section, focusing on the above questions, presents the results of a detailed simulation analysis of the pension mechanisms used in two of the four foreign systems studied.[9] The object of the analysis (and the resulting projections) is not so much to predict what the *actual* future pensions of the retired aged will be in the United States; rather, it is an attempt to compare similarities and differences in the pension levels, replacement rates, and distributional effects of the three different types of pension mechanisms. By contrasting the current old-age pension program in the United States with two significantly different programs, we can gain insight into the desirability of the reforms proposed in the previous section and various implications of such action.

To find out how different the pensions would be for the American elderly (using different old-age pension programs), a representative sample of people in the United States who were between the

---

9. Financial limitations prevented simulation analysis of the Canadian and Belgium old-age pension programs.

ages of 45 and 60 in the year 1960 is used as the basic simulation population. Various work and demographic experiences of this pre-retirement population are simulated and the population is "aged" twenty years. At the end of the simulation everyone still alive is age 65 or older and pensions of retired persons are based on the work and earnings histories generated. The next section describes the methodology in more detail, and the succeeding sections present and discuss the resulting projections.

The Simulation Methodology

In recent years simulation techniques have become increasingly popular in many diverse fields: business, the natural sciences, military logistics, and the social sciences (to name a few).[10] Simulation is one of many methodological techniques used to simplify a complex net of relationships for purposes of analysis. Stochastic simulation (the type used for this study) allows for the element of chance in addition to asserting specified relationships among variables. Although individuals, for example, exhibit sweeping variety with regard to demographic characteristics and economic activity, it is often possible when considering large numbers of people to identify a few important characteristics in order to predict with some confidence the outcomes for particular groups.

The simulation technique permits working at the microeconomic level. The economic/demographic activity of individuals in the sample is simulated on a person-by-person basis. By working at this very low level of aggregation, summary tabulations of pensions can be broken down in a wide variety of ways to highlight particular variables of special interest.[11] An earlier version of the stochastic simulation model used here has been described extensively in a prior study (Schulz, 1968). The simulation process, however, is briefly summarized below:

The basic data for the simulation are from a sample of the United States population in 1960. This sample, called the "one-in-a-thousand sample," is on a set of tapes produced by the United States

---

10. See, for example, Orcutt, et al. (1974), Krupp (1972), Mc-Clung, et al. (1971), and Naylor (1969).

11. See Schulz (1968) for a discussion of the advantages and disadvantages of simulation.

Bureau of the Census and contains separate records of characteristics of a 0.1 percent sample of the population as recorded in the 1960 census.[12] Each record contains forty coded characteristics of an individual, including certain demographic, work-force, income, and family characteristics information. From this sample are taken (a) all married couples where the husband is between 45 and 60 years of age (inclusive), and (b) all unmarried individuals where the individual is between 45 and 60 (inclusive). These persons constitute the basic population that is "aged" into retirement.

In order to project the pension income of the retired aged, it is necessary to construct a "life process" model which will permit simulation of activities that have an important influence on pensions. These activities can be divided into the following three categories: (a) demographic, (b) work force and earnings, and (c) pension status.

For example, not everyone in 1960 between 45 and 60 can be expected to live at least twenty years. Hence the first life-process activity considered in the model is death. A probability of death for each particular year is specified for individuals based on their sex, race, and age. A random drawing from the associated probability distribution is used to determine whether an individual will die or live that year. Similarly, probabilities are specified for other possible occurrences built into the model: labor force exit and entry, job change, social security pension coverage of state and local government employees, retirement, and unemployment.

Each possible "occurrence" specified in the model is treated in a manner similar to the live-die occurrence—each person being considered in turn. By sequential handling of the various occurrences, it is possible to make the consideration of any one occurrence dependent upon occurrences that were handled before it. For example, one possible occurrence for a person in the work force is a change of job. The consideration of this occurrence in the computer for a particular individual is made conditional on the outcome of the "leave work force" occurrence considered before it. If the individual "left" the work force, obviously there is no need to consider whether he has changed jobs.

---

12. Details about the sample are given in United States Bureau of the Census (undated).

Once one year's simulation is completed, the individual, if he survives, is aged another year and the process immediately repeated. This continues until the year 1980 is reached (that is, completion of twenty "passes" in the computer). Another individual is then considered, and the whole simulation process repeated. After all individuals have been processed, the resulting sample population represents most of the future aged population, since the surviving individuals of the original age 45 to 60 population are now 65 to 85 years of age.

During the simulation, earnings histories are kept for each individual. Individuals in the simulation who work full-time during a particular year and do not change jobs are given an employment income equal to their "wage level." [13] Females who work part time receive earnings equal to 50 percent of their wage level.

Individuals (full or part time) in the simulation who change jobs in any particular year are subject to a reduction of earning because of possible time lost between jobs. In the simulation, a random number is generated each time a worker changes jobs. The probabilities of losing (a) no time, (b) 1 to 4 weeks, (c) 5 to 10 weeks, (d) 11 to 26 weeks, or (e) more than 26 weeks are estimated from Bureau of Labor Statistics data.

By means of the earnings histories generated by the simulation process, the old-age pensions are calculated in accordance with the legislative provisions of the social security programs of the United States, Germany, and Sweden. In calculating the pensions for the United States program, the following assumptions and exceptions were made:

1. In the simulation it is assumed that all men in eligible occupations or industries qualify for OASDI pensions *in terms of*

---

13. The wages and salary incomes of persons in the work force in 1959 are part of the information reported for persons in the 1/1000 census sample. This information is used as a basis for assigning wage levels to these individuals. For persons not in the work force in 1959, wage assignments are made on the basis of race, age group, education, and regional location for males, and race, age group, and education for females. Although the potential wages of these persons are probably not independent of their work-force status, assuming so introduces bias in a liberal direction.

time; women, however, are tested for pension eligibility based upon their simulation and presimulation work histories.

2. "Creditable" earnings for pension calculation purposes are assumed to be similar to the West German system (two times the average national earnings of the three previous years) and are assumed not to be limited by the lower ceiling schedule of the current United States law.[14]

3. The histories for earnings before the year 1959 are based upon the individuals' recorded wages for 1959—deflated by the historical growth of average wages and a normally distributed random variate (Schulz, 1972).

4. The benefit levels of the United States social security pensions are based upon the levels enacted by the Congress in 1972. It was assumed that these levels would rise at an average rate of 3 percent per year between 1972 and 1980 as a result of the automatic inflation adjustment feature of the program (and any ad hoc increases).

The German Simulation

What would the distribution of social security old-age pensions look like in 1980 if the basic structure of the German pension program had been in effect in the United States since about 1940?[15] Table 37 summarizes the simulation estimations for units aged 65 or more who are *totally retired.*

---

14. The aim of this assumption is to make the comparisons more meaningful by not excluding higher pensions which would be produced by the United States OASDI formula. Projections using ceilings that approximate the present United States law are available in Schulz (1968).

15. The simulation model was developed and run before the 1972 changes in the German old-age pension (see above, Chapter 4) became final. The model therefore does not include the German flexible retirement option and the minimum pension. Likewise, it was not possible to incorporate into the United States simulations all the changes resulting from the enactment of the H.R. 1 (now Public Law 92-603) in late 1972. The United States system used for the simulations is best characterized as the old-age pension program in 1972 (before the new changes went into effect in 1973) but with benefit levels as specified by H.R. 1. Relevant changes not incorporated are (a) a change in the computation of benefits for men, (b) a special minimum benefit for low-income, long-term workers, (c) the automatic adjustment of the taxable earnings ceiling (see assumption 2 in the text above), and (d) higher benefits for those who work past age 65.

TABLE 37

Projected Old Age Pension Income from a German-Type
Social Security System, 1980
(percentages)

Income	Couples[a]	Single Men[b]	Widowed Women	Women Never Married
Total percentage	100 [d]	100	100	100
Less than $3000	18	34	33	83
$3000–3999	6	6	6	5
$4000–4999	6	8	9	4
$5000–5999	9	8	9	2
$6000–6999	13	14	10	2
$7000–7999	10	8	9	1
$8000–8999	10	6	7	1
$9000–9999	8	6	5	1
$10,000–11,999	14	9	6	–[c]
$12,000 or more	7	2	6	0

[a] If wife is retired, pension is sum of husband and wife's pension; if wife is not retired, husband's pension only is used; if husband is not retired, the unit is excluded from calculation.
[b] Never married or widowed men.
[c] Less than 0.5 percent.
[d] Columns may not sum to 100 because of rounding.

Looking at Table 37, one is immediately struck by the very high pensions that would be paid by this type of program. In every category except that for women who never married, most pensions paid are two to three times higher than social security benefits currently paid in the United States. In the case of couples, 70 percent of the units are projected to have benefits of $5000 or more; 20 percent are projected to have social security benefits exceeding $10,000. The distribution for single men and widowed women indicates a lower proportion of relatively high pensions, but even among these units, there are about half with pensions equal to or greater than $5000.

As was explained previously, the German social security old-age pension program did not have a minimum benefit provision prior to 1972; poverty problems were dealt with entirely by a sepa-

rate program administered primarily by state and local governmental units. This resulted in very small pensions being paid to persons
with only a few years of work-force participation. Therefore, it is
not surprising to find some very low pension recipients in Table
37.[16] For example, 18 percent of the couples and 34, 33, and 83
percent of single men, widowed women, and women who never
married (respectively) are projected to have social security benefits
under $3000. The large proportion of "never married" women with-
out benefits or with very low benefits is explained by the fact that
many have little or no work history. One must remember that the
West German program pays pensions whose amounts are directly
related to the number of years worked.

We can compare these projected social security pensions for
the population of the United States (based upon the West German
program) with projected benefits of the current United States program.[17] Table 38 presents a comparison of the projected 1980 old-
age pension distributions for couples, single men, and widowed
women. The table gives a comparison of the relatively static United
States pension program with its lower earnings-replacement goals
versus a pension program with higher replacement goals and adjustment features which take into account the dynamic factors of
both price level changes and real economic growth in calculating
benefits *at the time of retirement*.[18]

Replacement Rates. Table 39 presents the pension-earnings
ratio distributions for the various demographic groups. It is important to note that in addition to the fact that the ratios were calculated using an average of the last five years of earnings in the

---

16. Even if the new minimum provision had been incorporated
into the simulation model (which was not the case), there would still be
some recipients of very small pensions, given that only long-term workers
are eligible for the new minimum.

17. Based on legislation in effect January 1, 1973.

18. The German system also adjusts benefits *after* retirement for
price and growth changes. In the simulation only price adjustments were
made for the period after initial retirement to compare the two programs
with regard to replacement rates *at* retirement. Ideally, additional comparisons should have been made which incorporated the German adjustment *during* retirement features. Cost considerations prevented these
additional simulation runs.

TABLE 38

Projected Old Age Pensions for U.S. Social Security Recipients,[a] Based upon the U.S. and West German Systems, 1980 [b]
(percentages)

Income	Couples[c]		Single Men[c]		Widowed Women	
	U.S.	*German*	*U.S.*	*German*	*U.S.*	*German*
Total percentage	100[e]	100	100	100	100	100
Less than $3000	35	18	75	34	78	33
$3000–3999	7	6	22	6	20	6
$4000–4999	22	6	3	8	2	9
$5000–5999	12	9	0	8	0	9
$6000–6999	4	13	0	14	0	10
$7000–7999	–[d]	10	0	8	0	9
$8000–8999	0	10	0	6	0	7
$9000–9999	0	8	0	6	0	5
$10,000–11,999	0	14	0	9	0	6
$12,000 or more	0	7	0	2	0	6

[a] Excluded are persons not eligible for social security old-age benefits and, because of methodological problems, persons who were retired before or during 1960.

[b] The distributions for women never married were also made, but the result is not presented in this table. See Table 37 for the German distribution.

[c] See footnotes a and b of Table 37.

[d] Less than 0.5 percent.

[e] Columns may not sum to 100 because of rounding.

denominator, the pension used in the numerator is the simulated pension received by each individual in the first year of retirement (between 1960 and 1979) and not the pension in the final year of the simulation (which would be higher because of the 3 percent annual inflation increase assumed in the study).

In evaluating the results presented in Table 39, we can use two benchmark measures: (a) the proportion of units with a pension-earnings ratio below 0.50 and (b) the proportion of units with a ratio above 0.60. These benchmarks are used because "in the United States, some social planners currently speak of an assured flow of income of probably 50 percent of the earnings of recent years—

TABLE 39

Projected Ratio at Retirement of Old Age Pension Income
to Preretirement Earnings,[a] Based upon a German-Type System
(percentages)

Ratio	Couples[c]	Single Men[c]	Widowed Women[d]	Women Never Married
Total percentage	100[e]	100	100	100
Less than 0.20 [b]	2	0	18	11
0.20 to 0.29	3	2	8	18
0.30 to 0.39	5	2	11	18
0.40 to 0.49	9	4	14	13
0.50 to 0.59	19	11	16	11
0.60 to 0.69	26	26	14	5
0.70 to 0.79	24	35	13	4
0.80 to 0.89	8	14	4	3
0.90 to 0.99	3	5	1	2
1.0 or more	3	3	1	16

[a] Average of five years prior to retirement.
[b] Includes persons receiving no pension but with some earnings in the relevant years.
[c] See footnotes a and b of Table 37.
[d] Ratio based upon dead husband's earnings (if appropriate) and own earnings (if any).
[e] Columns may not sum to 100 because of rounding.

not the lifetime earnings—for a single worker and 66⅔–70 percent for a couple" (Horlick, 1970).[19]

In the case of couples, nearly two thirds (64 percent) are projected as having a ratio of 0.60 or higher when German-type mechanisms were in effect. Only 19 percent receive pensions amounting to less than 50 percent of their earnings, and, as we shall show below, most of these couples have very high earnings above the German social security earnings ceiling. The proportion of single units

19. See also Chapter 2, above, for discussion of why a ratio of this magnitude might be sufficient to maintain a couple's living standard in retirement. As reported in Chapter 2, Henle (1972) estimates a required replacement rate of 80 percent for persons with lower preretirement income levels and 70 percent for those with higher.

with a ratio of 0.60 or more varies from a high of 83 percent for single men to a low of 30 percent for women who never married—with female widows also being low with 33 percent.

TABLE 40

Projected Ratio at Retirement of Couples' Old Age Pension Income to Preretirement Earnings[a] by Preretirement Earnings Group, Based upon a German-Type System

Earnings group	Ratio				
	0.49 or less	0.50–0.69	0.70–0.99	1.00 or more	Total Percent[c]
Less than $1000	0	24	27	49	100
$ 1000 to 1999	23	36	31	10	100
$ 2000 to 2999	20	34	40	6	100
$ 3000 to 3999	20	31	45	4	100
$ 4000 to 4999	12	40	47	1	100
$ 5000 to 5999	8	40	48	4	100
$ 6000 to 6999	7	39	52	3	100
$ 7000 to 7999	7	36	55	1	100
$ 8000 to 8999	9	46	44	1	100
$ 9000 to 9999	11	56	32	1	100
$10,000 to 11,999	17	59	24	—[b]	100
$12,000 to 13,999	13	66	22	0	100
$14,000 to 15,999	21	71	8	0	100
$16,000 or more	67	33	0	0	100

[a] Average of five years prior to retirement.
[b] Less than 0.5 percent.
[c] Percentages may not sum to 100 because of rounding.

Table 40 is a tabulation of the pension-earnings ratios for couples by various preretirement earnings groups. The table shows clearly that the very high and very low ratios tend to be concentrated among the lowest and highest earners, respectively. A more interesting finding is that the replacement ratio is 70 percent or better for a majority (or close to a majority) of couples in every income group between $2000 and $8999. Clearly a German-type program with a pension formula identical to the one existing in West Germany today would revolutionize the public pension levels of American recipients.

Of course, any earnings-related pension program can provide very high benefits with the appropriate formula specification. What is unusual and, we would argue, desirable about the German program (and certain other European pension programs) is that its formula explicitly embodies a relative concept or definition of income adequacy by guaranteeing long-term workers a relatively high earnings-replacement rate consistent with historical price level changes and rising real earnings levels *regardless of what those changes might be in the unforeseen future.*

Contrast the pension-earnings ratio resulting from a German-type program with those resulting from the United States old-age pension program. Whereas the German-type program results in relatively few couples with a pension-earnings ratio below 0.50, Table 41 indicates that the United States social security program will re-

TABLE 41

Comparison of Pension-Earnings Ratios
at Time of Retirement for U.S. Couples
(percentages)

Ratio	German-Type	Current U.S.
Total percentage	100	100
Less than 0.20 [a]	2	15
0.20 to 0.29	3	21
0.30 to 0.39	5	26
0.40 to 0.49	9	17
0.50 to 0.59	19	8
0.60 to 0.69	26	5
0.70 to 0.79	24	2
0.80 to 0.89	8	2
0.90 to 0.99	3	1
1.0 or more	3	4

[a] Includes persons receiving no pension but with some earnings in the relevant years.

sult in nearly 80 percent of the same couples receiving a social security pension at retirement which will be less than 50 percent of the average earnings of their last five years.

Factors Influencing German Replacement Rates. In order to

understand the projections of replacement rates using a German-type program, it is important to keep in mind certain characteristics of the German program and the simulations. This is especially important in understanding why many persons receive pensions which depart significantly from the "two-thirds replacement" goal of the German system—replacing a very high or very low proportion of preretirement earnings. Some of the more important factors are discussed below.

If we want to understand why some pension replacement levels are low, probably the most important factor is the one previously mentioned: the social security earnings ceiling. The German ceiling on "insurable earnings" in any particular year is equal to twice the average of national average earnings for the prior three years. In Germany the *monthly* ceiling was 1850 DM (approximately $650) in 1971. As shown in Table 40, this ceiling provision has the effect in the simulation of dramatically reducing the pension replacement rate for very high earners.

Another factor reducing the replacement rate is the fact that the ratios of a worker's earnings to average national earnings are averaged for the worker's entire work history.[20] But earnings used in the calculation of the replacement rate are only for the last five years. Thus the two-thirds replacement factor in the German pension formula for a typical worker with steadily increasing earnings (.015 times 45 years of coverage) is based on lower average earnings than the average earnings used to calculate the replacement rates in Table 40. Hence, the actual replacement rate is lower than 65 percent in this illustrative case (and also commensurately lower for other earnings levels).

In addition to the factors discussed above, there is one aspect of the simulation procedures which reduces the replacement rates for certain couples. In general the couples' pension-earnings ratio is calculated by dividing the total earnings of both the husband and the wife (if any) by their total average wages *if the wife was retired when the husband retired.* If the wife was not retired, only the husband's earnings and pension were considered. However, if a wife worked just prior to retirement but did not work long enough

---

20. In the simulation this is for a maximum of twenty years (see the section below, "Varying the Wage History").

to attain pension eligibility, her earnings were added into total earnings, reducing the combined replacement rate for the couple.

On the other hand, *high* replacement rates are possible if a person works an exceptionally long period of time. Table 42 shows the

TABLE 42

Number of Years Worked before Retirement
(percentages)

Years	Men	Unmarried Women	Married Women
0–4	0	9	39
5–9	0	3	15
10–14	0	7	18
15–19	0	8	15
20–24	–[a]	7	6
25–29	–[a]	4	4
30–34	2	4	2
35–39	7	8	1
40–44	14	14	–[a]
45–49	35	17	0
50–54	34	15	0
55 or more	8	4	0

[a] Less than 1 percent.

distribution of "years worked" generated in the simulation for
United States men, unmarried women, and married women. The
table shows that given the assumptions of the simulation and the
"probabilities of retirement at various ages" used, the simulation
projects a significant number of persons with fifty or more years of
work experience. We do not know how realistic this work-years
distribution is for people born in the United States between
1915 and 1930, since we do not know of any actual statistics for
the United States work force with which we could compare them.
Certainly, given longer schooling and earlier retirement, we would
not expect many retirees of future generations to accumulate more
than forty-five creditable years. (In the next section, however, we
investigate the effects of eliminating the work-length feature of the
German program.)

Another way high replacement can result in the simulation is if a worker becomes unemployed during the last five years of work. Such unemployment reduces the average earnings of the last years (very greatly where unemployment is long-term or frequent). Since the pension itself is based on lifetime earnings, the effect of this unemployment on the pension level is not as great—sometimes resulting in a high replacement rate.

Eliminating the Work-Length Provision. A special simulation run was made to determine the effect on replacement rates if the work-length provisions of the German program were eliminated. In this simulation, the German formula was modified, replacing the "constant (.015) times the number of years of credited work" by the constant .65. Thus the formula was changed to give eligible workers 65 percent of earnings (as measured by the ratio averaging mechanism) regardless of years worked. To be eligible for a pension, however, the worker had to meet the eligibility requirement of the current United States social security program.

Table 43 compares the two different simulations run. Without the work-length provision the tails on both ends of the distribution are reduced. But the biggest shift occurs at the upper end, with sharp drops in the number of workers receiving 70 to 89 percent replacement. As one would expect, the bulk of workers receive pensions which achieve replacement close to the specified level of two thirds. In fact, 77 percent of the couples receive replacements between 50 and 79 percent.

Varying the Wage History. The West German method of calculating a pension involves comparing the worker's creditable earnings to average national earnings (for a three-year period). This comparison, according to the current law, must be made for every year worked throughout the entire lifetime of work. The average of these comparison ratios is inserted into the formula used to calculate the pension to be paid.

Since the simulation extended over the 1960 to 1979 period and began with a sample of the United States population between the ages of 45 and 60, to calculate the German pension it was necessary to reconstruct the earnings histories of workers before 1959 (see Schulz, 1972). It was not possible, in most cases, to reconstruct the entire work history; instead, the basic simulation projections were

TABLE 43

Effect of the Work-Length Provision
on Replacement Rates for Couples

Ratio	German-Type System[a]	
	with work length provision[b]	without work length provision
Total percentage	100 [d]	100
Less than 0.20 [c]	2	1
0.20 to 0.29	3	3
0.30 to 0.39	5	4
0.40 to 0.49	9	8
0.50 to 0.59	19	22
0.60 to 0.69	26	46
0.70 to 0.79	24	9
0.80 to 0.89	8	2
0.90 to 0.99	3	1
1.0 or more	3	5

[a] Average of earnings for five years prior to retirement used as measure of preretirement earnings.
[b] The formula constant used is 0.015.
[c] Includes persons receiving no pension but with some earnings in the relevant years.
[d] Columns do not sum to 100 because of rounding.

calculated upon the simulated earnings histories for the twenty years prior to the year of retirement of each worker. However, two alternative sets of calculations were made, one based upon the "ten year period prior to retirement" work history, and the other based on the years of work between 1940 and the year of retirement.

The latter measure (unlike the others) results in basing workers' pensions on differing numbers of years worked (depending on the year of retirement) and has the effect of raising the average length of work history used for pension calculation purposes.[21] Thus, this set of projections, from a work-history standpoint, is closer to the actual German system but suffers from the serious

21. Workers retiring during the first year of simulation (1960) would have their pension calculated on the twenty years of prior work history. In contrast, workers retiring in the last year of the simulation (1979) could have up to thirty-nine years of work history.

limitation of lack of comparability among the various individual pension calculations.

Table 44 compares the pension distributions projected using the three different wage histories. The projections based on ten- and twenty-year histories are almost identical. The third projection differs very slightly.

TABLE 44

Comparison of the 1980 Old Age Pension Distributions
for Couples Using Different Wage Histories
(percentages)

Income	Wage History		
	Last 10 Years	Last 20 Years	Last 20–39 Years[a]
Total percentage	100	100	100
Less than $3000	18	18	20
$3000–$4999	13	12	12
$5000–$6999	24	22	16
$7000–$8999	18	20	21
$9000 or more	28	29	31

[a] The wage history varies according to the year of retirement; see text discussion.

Varying the Formula Constant. As previously explained, old-age pensions paid in the Federal Republic of Germany vary according to the number of years worked in creditable employment. This is accomplished by multiplying in the pension formula the total number of years worked by the constant 0.015. The value of this constant is related to the proportion of earnings replacement desired by the German Government. Thus a worker with forty years of work experience gets a pension equal to 60 percent (40 years × .015) of the earnings of workers currently employed who are of equivalent status. Equivalent status refers to a worker with current earnings that bear the same relationship to average national earnings as did the retired worker's prior earnings to prior average national earnings (on average). Workers with years of work credit greater than forty years get a pension with higher earnings replacement (and vice versa).

In the simulation runs, two German-type pensions were calculated for each pensioner—one using the West German constant of 0.015, the other using a lower constant of 0.0111. The latter constant results in a pension equal to 50 percent earnings replacement for a worker with forty-five years of work credit (as contrasted with about 67 percent using a constant of 0.015).

TABLE 45

Comparison of Couples' Pension Earnings[a] Ratios
Using Alternative Constants
(percentages)

Ratio	German-Type System with a		U.S. OASDI
	0.015 Constant	0.0111 Constant	
Total percentage	100	100	100
Less than 0.20 [b]	2	4	15
0.20 to 0.29	3	6	21
0.30 to 0.39	5	15	26
0.40 to 0.49	9	32	17
0.50 to 0.59	19	32	8
0.60 to 0.69	26	8	5
0.70 to 0.79	24	2	2
0.80 to 0.89	8	—[c]	2
0.90 to 0.99	3	—[c]	1
1.0 or more	3	1	4

[a] Average of earnings for five years prior to retirement used as a measure of preretirement earnings.
[b] Includes persons receiving no pension but with some earnings in the relevant years.
[c] Less than 0.5 percent.

Table 45 illustrates the differences in pension-earnings ratios which arise from using the lower constant. The differences, as would be expected, are quite large. Only 11 percent (compared to 64 percent) of the couples are projected to have a pension-earnings ratio of 0.60 or more when the lower constant is used. Again, however, there is a significant difference between the ratios resulting from the United States program and the German one with a lower constant. Using the 0.50 ratio as a possible policy goal for the "basic floor of protection" to be provided by social security, we find 64 percent of the couples with ratios between 0.40 and 0.59 using the German-type systems with the 0.0111 constant. In contrast, only 25 percent of the couples have ratios in that range under the projected current United States system.

Swedish Program Simulations

The Swedish old-age pension program has policy objectives very similar to those of the Federal Republic of Germany. As described in Chapter 3, the pension mechanism used to implement these objectives is, however, very different. Using the simulation model, we can investigate (as we did in the case of Germany) some of the implications if the United States were to adopt a program using mechanisms like those in Sweden. Also, we can contrast the projected United States pensions using a Swedish-type old-age pension program with pensions generated by a German-type and the current United States program.

Table 46 shows the projected distribution of social security old-

TABLE 46

Projected U.S. Old Age Pension Income from a Swedish-Type
Social Security System, 1980
(percentages)

Income	Couples[a]	Single Men[b]	Widowed Women	Women Never Married
Total percentage	100 [d]	100	100	100
Less than $3000	17	36	69	69
$ 3000–3999	10	11	14	18
$ 4000–4999	11	10	7	6
$ 5000–5999	13	15	4	3
$ 6000–6999	14	11	2	1
$ 7000–7999	10	6	1	1
$ 8000–8999	9	6	1	1
$ 9000–9999	6	5	1	–[c]
$10,000–11,999	8	2	1	–[c]
$12,000 or more	2	0	–[c]	0

[a] If wife is retired, pension is the sum of husband and wife's pension; if wife is not retired, husband's pension only is used; if husband is not retired, the unit is excluded from calculation.
[b] Never married or widowed men.
[c] Less than 0.5 percent.
[d] Columns may not sum to 100 because of rounding.

age pensions for various groups of American aged resulting from the use of a Swedish-type pension mechanism. Table 47 then con-

TABLE 47

Projected U.S. Old Age Pensions,[a]
Based upon U.S., German, and Swedish-Type Systems, 1980
(percentages)

Income	Couples			Widowed Women		
	U.S.	German[d]	Swedish	U.S.	German	Swedish
Total percentage	100 [b]	100	100	100	100	100
Less than $3000	35	18	17	78	33	69
$ 3000–3999	7	6	10	20	6	14
$ 4000–4999	22	6	11	2	9	7
$ 5000–5999	12	9	13	0	9	4
$ 6000–6999	4	13	14	0	10	2
$ 7000–7999	–[c]	10	10	0	9	1
$ 8000–8999	0	10	9	0	7	1
$ 9000–9999	0	8	6	0	5	1
$10,000–11,999	0	14	8	0	6	1
$12,000 or more	0	7	2	0	6	–[c]

[a] Excluded are persons not eligible for social security old-age benefits and, because of methodological problems, persons who were retired before or during 1960.
[b] The column may not sum to 100 because of rounding.
[c] Less than 0.5 percent.
[d] The constant used in the German pension formula is 0.015.

trasts for couples and widowed women these pensions with the ones projected using the current United States and, alternately, a German-type mechanism. For couples the "Swedish" pensions, like the "German" pensions, result in significantly higher pensions for couples when compared to the projected United States pensions. Although the Swedish and German distributions are generally similar, there are differences at the two tails: 30 percent (German) versus 38 percent (Swedish) with pensions below $5000 and 29 percent (German) versus 16 percent (Swedish) with pensions above $9000.

Tables 48 and 49 show the projected replacement rates of the Swedish pensions and again contrast them with the German and United States rates. Again the German and Swedish are similar and provide much higher replacement than the current United States

TABLE 48

Projected Ratio at Retirement of
Old Age Pension Income to Preretirement Earnings,[a]
Based upon a Swedish-Type System
(percentages)

Ratio	Couples	Single Men[c]	Widowed Women[d]	Women Never Married
Total percentage	100 [e]	100	100	100
Less than 0.20 [b]	3	2	44	—[f]
0.20 to 0.29	3	2	23	3
0.30 to 0.39	8	4	14	9
0.40 to 0.49	21	20	6	13
0.50 to 0.59	22	16	7	12
0.60 to 0.69	20	23	4	10
0.70 to 0.79	10	17	1	10
0.80 to 0.89	6	8	—[f]	7
0.90 to 0.99	3	3	—[f]	4
1.0 or more	5	7	2	32

[a] Average of five years prior to retirement.
[b] Includes persons receiving no pension but with some earnings in the relevant years.
[c] See notes a and b of Table 37.
[d] The ratio is based upon dead husband's earnings (if appropriate) and own earnings (if any).
[e] Columns may not sum to 100 because of rounding.
[f] Less than 0.5 percent.

program. There are two major differences, however, between the German and Swedish distributions: a much larger proportion of Swedish pensions falls into the 40–49 percent replacement category, and a larger proportion of German pensions falls into the 70–79 percent category.

The generally higher German benefits are in part due to the "years of work" factor in the German pension formula and the large number of workers with long work histories.

The Costs of Alternative Mechanisms

The simulation also allows us to compare the relative costs of the alternative pension programs. This is done by aggregating the

TABLE 49

Comparison of Pension Earnings Ratios
at Time of Retirement for U.S. Couples
(percentages)

Ratio	Current U.S.	German-Type	Swedish-Type
Total percentage	100	100	100
Less than 0.20 [a]	15	2	3
0.20 to 0.29	21	3	3
0.30 to 0.39	26	5	8
0.40 to 0.49	17	9	21
0.50 to 0.59	8	19	22
0.60 to 0.69	5	26	20
0.70 to 0.79	2	24	10
0.80 to 0.89	2	8	6
0.90 to 0.99	1	3	3
1.0 or more	4	3	5

[a] Includes persons receiving no pension but with some earnings in the relevant years.

individual pensions for each program and calculating ratios between them. Using the current United States cost as a basis for comparison, the relative costs of alternatives are as follows:

1. German-type system with .015 constants is 75 percent more.

2. German-type system with .0111 constant is 31 percent more.

3. Swedish-type system is 51 percent more.

These comparisons illustrate clearly that financing adequate old-age pensions is a major undertaking. The estimates serve to remind us that significant changes in public pensions will be costly and emphasize the importance of carefully rethinking our financing techniques.

WHAT MIX OF PENSIONS IN THE UNITED STATES?

In the United States, economist Milton Friedman has been the most consistent contemporary academic advocate of complete abolition of public pensions. But although Friedman himself has bemoaned the low "level" of writings discussing the relative advantages of private versus public pensions, his own writings are filled with political/philosophical bias and contribute little to the needed analysis.[22] While never directly advocating private pensions, Friedman calls for the end of public pensions:

> Social Security combines a highly regressive tax with largely indiscriminate benefits and, in overall effect, probably redistributes income from lower to higher income persons. I believe that it serves no essential social function. Existing commitments make it impossible to eliminate it overnight, but it should be unwound and terminated as soon as possible. (Friedman, 1971)

Like Friedman's criticism most of the other major objections to public old-age pensions center on equity questions connected with the current social security program's financing and benefit structure. Nelson McClung, for example, in justifying the need for private pensions as a supplement to social security bases his argument on the small amount of "individual equity" embodied in the operation of the latter:

> There is a place for employee pension plans and, in particular, private pension plans. The objective of pension plans should be to replace income in retirement. Those who are poor in retirement because they have always been poor, should be taken care of under other programs which explicitly redistribute income . . . Pension plans should adhere strictly to the principle of individual equity. Social security has demonstrated that it is not capable of doing this . . .   (McClung, 1969)

Such inequities do not necessarily justify abolition of public pension programs in the United States in favor of private pensions; they may merely justify reform. If one looks at existing private pension programs in the United States, one finds all kinds of problems; elsewhere Schulz has argued that private pensions in the United States are riddled with inequities (United States Senate Special Committee on Aging, 1970b).

Scholars in the pension field are familiar with the controversy over emphasis upon individual equity versus social adequacy. Pri-

---

22. "As I have gone through the literature, I have been shocked at the level of the arguments that have been used to sell social security not only by politicians, or by special-interest groups, but more especially by self-righteous academics" (Friedman, 1971).

258 PROVIDING ADEQUATE RETIREMENT INCOME

vate insurance is supposed to be based upon the concept of individual equity, and social insurance is supposed to take into account (and, according to some, emphasize) "social adequacy." [23] But what is the justification for the poor vesting, the lack of portability, the absence of adequate survivors' benefits, and the lack of reinsurance provisions which characterize private pensions? In the words of one American pension expert and actuary, Thomas H. Paine, "the initial job of most pension plans when first established is *to concentrate on retirement income for the older worker,* hence the importance of past service benefits" [emphasis added] (United States Senate Special Committee on Aging, 1970a).

Thus private pensions have tried to supplement the social adequacy function of social security by past service credits. Unfortunately, the result has been to reduce the individual equity of such plans. According to the Staff of the American Enterprise Institute (1968):

> . . . there is general agreement that grants of past service pensions do constitute the crux, in the main, of the problems with which the proposals on pension vesting, funding, and reinsurance seek to deal . . . If past service credits are not granted, vesting costs are materially reduced. Consequently, available pension resources can be allocated to earlier vesting of the individual pension rights.

Congress—by refusing to deal quickly and realistically with the severe income problems of people retiring during the past three decades (and before), either through the social security system or, as some have proposed, through a negative income tax system—is partly responsible for the many seriously inequitable private pension plans that exist today. By not providing social security benefits high enough to keep retirees at least out of poverty, Congress has encouraged (probably forced) workers, unions, and concerned employers to seek alternative ways of dealing with the economic problems facing workers *approaching* retirement. The private pension plans, when first established, have tended to emphasize the provision of those retirement benefits more favorable to older workers (for example, past retirement credits versus vesting). No one would

---

23. See, for example, Myers (1965).

argue with the assertion that older workers are the "first" to experience the serious retirement income inadequacies of earlier years when there were no or poor private pensions. The issue is whether the problem can be more equitably and adequately dealt with by private or public action. We would argue that if large groups of older workers or aged persons have serious economic problems due to events beyond their control, the best way to deal with those problems is on a collective level through financing mechanisms that can more equitably distribute the costs of such programs over the entire population and/or place the cost on those who have the best ability to pay.

Alternative Criteria for Assessing Pensions

Boulding has argued that one valid criteria for choosing between private versus public programs is whether there are significant economies of scale in their operation. "If there are these economies—that is, if the cost of administering the insurance declines with every increase in the amount of insurance written—then a state monopoly will almost inevitably be cheaper than a number of competing private companies . . . We may venture a hypothesis that where the operations of insurance are fairly routine, the case for state or national monopoly is stronger than where the operations involve great difficulties of definition of rights" (Boulding, 1958).

The United States private pension industry has become huge, with the market value of its assets increasing by 1972 to about $150 billion. Insurance companies, unions, corporations, and banks (in various combinations) administer these funds. Although there has been no study of the comparative costs of these private pension plans versus social security, it is hard to imagine that the current conglomeration of thousands of private plans, many covering as few as several hundred workers, can have lower administrative costs.[24]

---

24. In fiscal year 1973, for example, only 2.3 percent of social security dollars spent were for administrative costs. The issue of comparative costs is complicated by the fact that social security financing in the United States is on a pay-as-you-go basis, while private pension funds generate costs as a result of the investment activities carried out, usually, on behalf of the employer and also the general economy.

Another important argument in favor of public pensions is their ability, in contrast to private plans, to deal with the need to adjust pensions for inflation and economic growth. The problem of inflation has plagued pension programs since their inception. All countries have had to struggle with this problem, continually adjusting pension programs and benefits to offset increases in price levels. Inflation has varied from the catastrophic rate, for example, in early Germany (which completely wiped out the monetary value of that country's social security reserves and benefits) to the relatively mild price increases, for example, in the United States during the 1958–68 period.[25]

Gradually most industrialized countries (including the United States in 1972) have introduced some sort of automatic benefit adjustment mechanisms into the social security system to deal more effectively with the inflation problem (Table 14, Chapter 2).[26] In contrast, private pension plans, with the exception of a few variable annuity plans, virtually ignore the problem.[27] This results, first, because of employers' unwillingness to make financial commitments based on guesses about future price levels. It is much easier for government to deal with the inflation problem—given its inherent taxing powers and its ability to minimize the size of the monetary fund necessary to guarantee the financial soundness of the pension program. And the actual history of social security systems in various countries dealing with inflation supports that conclusion. In addition, public pension programs have shown an ability to devise equitable ways of permitting retired persons to share systematically in the real economic growth of the country.

A third factor for assessing public and private pensions is the ease and extent to which workers can be covered. Here again public pensions have a decided advantage. It has proved to be a relatively easy matter in all countries to extend social security coverage to large segments of the labor force. Coverage of agricultural workers and the self-employed has presented problems—especially in developing countries—but in general, extension of coverage has been

---

25. Over this period the consumer price index rose about 18 percent, averaging less than 2 percent per year.

26. See Norwood (1972).

27. See U.S. Labor-Management Services Administration (1973).

quite comprehensive. In the United States, for example, coverage of the gainfully employed is now virtually universal.

In contrast, extension of private pension coverage presents serious problems. It becomes especially difficult to extend coverage among small employee groups because of:

1. The high costs per employee of establishing and maintaining a plan;
2. The lack of pressure from employees or unions;
3. The high turnover of small businesses;
4. The fact that small business firms are often relatively young;
5. The fact that small employers tend to view pensions as personal costs;
6. The personality of small business owners who tend to emphasize individual self-reliance in financial matters.

As a result of these and other factors, a sizable proportion of the work force may remain uncovered (Schulz, 1970).

In fact, this is the case in the United States. Estimates of private pension coverage are subject to a wide margin of error.[28] Recent estimates for the United States have varied from 35 percent (United States General Subcommittee on Labor, 1972) to close to 50 percent (Kolodrubetz, 1972b). The best study thus far available is for "full-time employees" only and reports 47 percent coverage—with coverage for men being 52 percent and coverage for women being much lower at 36 percent (Landay and Kolodrubetz, 1973). In all cases, however, the coverage estimated is far short of total coverage. And—in contrast to the high coverage growth periods of the forties, fifties, and sixties—the rate of increase in the proportion of United States workers covered by private pensions appears to have declined significantly in recent years.

Arguments Favoring Private Pensions

Given these arguments in favor of public pensions, what can be said supportive of expanding private pensions? The three major arguments often voiced in favor of private pensions are:[29]

---

28. See the discussion in Kolodrubetz (1973a), p. 28.

29. These and other issues are discussed by Schulz more fully in United States Senate Special Committee on Aging (1970b).

1. *Private pensions are a product of the free choice of workers in negotiation with management and are more compatible with the ideas of freedom than compulsory public pensions.*

The philosophical arguments made today against *expanding* social security are very similar to the arguments originally voiced in the thirties against the *establishment* of a social security system:

> Social insurance [in the thirties] was condemned as an alien importation, if not a foreign conspiracy. Commercial insurance representatives perfected this stratagem in their campaign against compulsory health insurance. Proposed health insurance legislation, which provided for government contributions to local funds, even outdistanced the "state socialism" of Germany and propelled the nation toward "Marxian socialism." Such proposals were symptomatic of a "reckless advocacy of hopeless panaceas of social and political reforms." Democracy, "the perpetuity of our . . . fundamental conceptions of personal and political liberty," was at stake. Social insurance was perhaps the most dangerous form of radicalism. More subtle than anarchism or nihilism, it duped Americans, by means of a "cleverly disguised propaganda," into accepting a "needless enlargement of the sphere of the state." The path to "internationalism and racial decay," social insurance heralded the decline of private enterprise and private life, "lived in accordance with rational ideas and legitimate desires, free from undue restraint and interference."   (Lubove, 1968)

If we look at the reality, we see that freedom of choice nearly always plays a very minor role. For the vast majority of workers who are now or will be covered by private plans there was not, is not now, and is not likely to be any choice. Almost all private pension schemes are compulsory. Regarding the details of the plan, workers must register their individual preferences through union representatives (if they are unionized) or be content with the pension benefits which management gives them.

Surveys of the provisions of various plans show that existing private pension plans contain few if any options. Workers usually cannot choose, for example, between pensions protected against inflation versus nonprotected pensions, optional employee contributions versus only employer contributions, or earlier versus later vesting.[30] Nor do workers usually have any control over how the pension funds are to be invested.

2. *While social security must remain very uniform in its coverage provision for various individuals, private pension plans are flexible and can be tailor-made to meet differing situations and conditions.*

Though it is true that private pension plans encompass a smaller number and fewer types of workers than social security, one should not overlook the heterogeneity of workers included in a great many private pensions. Workers with widely different occupations in the same firm or from different types and sizes of firms are often included under the same pension plan. Or, as in the case of the Teamsters Union plan, workers from entirely different industries are covered. Such diversity of coverage makes it difficult to design a plan that will serve the specific needs of all workers covered.

It is true that private plans permit a certain amount of adaptation to the special circumstances of particular groups of employees, but one would find it difficult to justify with this reason the wide disparity in private pension provisions currently existing. It seems clear that much of the disparity exists today as a result not of the special circumstances of employees, but because of the conflicts between employers and employees over the purposes of private pensions.[31]

Thus a private plan that provides for early retirement with adequate income in an occupation where physical deterioration on the job occurs at an early age is an example of such flexibility. But a plan that has high service and age requirements for vesting, as a result of a desire to provide past service credits to the more senior employees, is no doubt responding to the power position of the older employees (in the company or union) at the expense of the younger employees.

---

30. See, for example, United States Bureau of Labor Statistics (1969).

31. See the discussion on this point in United States Senate Special Committee on Aging (1970b).

3. *Private pension plans are vital to assure the saving necessary to provide sufficient investment in a growing economy.*

Table 50 shows the magnitude of business saving relative to nonresidential fixed investment during the last decade. The data indicate a fundamental fact: in the key growth sector of *corporate* production, the overwhelming majority of funds needed to finance new investment comes from the *internal* funds of these corporations. As Galbraith has observed, "The decisions on what will be saved are made in the main by a few hundred large corporations." [32]

TABLE 50

Business Saving and Investment, 1958–1971
(billions of dollars)

Year	Gross Business Saving[a]	Total Nonresidential Fixed Investment
1958	49.4	41.6
1959	56.8	45.1
1960	56.8	48.4
1961	58.7	47.0
1962	66.3	51.7
1963	68.8	54.3
1964	76.2	61.1
1965	84.7	71.3
1966	91.3	81.6
1967	93.0	83.3
1968	95.4	88.8
1969	97.0	98.5
1970	97.3	100.9
1971	109.9	105.8
1972	123.8	120.4

[a] Undistributed corporate profits, corporate inventory adjustments, capital consumption allowances, and wage accruals less disbursements.
Source: United States Council of Economic Advisors (1973), tables B–13 and C–20.

There is no evidence to indicate that there has been a great insufficiency of saving in our economy relative to investment pro-

32. Galbraith (1967).

pensities. Instead, we have had to worry periodically about an excess of total private saving over private investment—causing lower government saving (i.e., bigger deficits) through automatic and/or discretionary fiscal policy.

A comprehensive study of the economic aspects of pensions by the National Bureau of Economic Research has concluded:[33]

> Our research has supported the proposition that pension saving is a net addition to personal saving. Less clearly established, perhaps, is the extension of this conclusion to state that it is a net addition to total national saving. The impact on saving by business and Government is not clear, but it seems doubtful that it is materially affected.
>
> There is also some evidence that this major impact has already been felt. If it is desirable to sustain the growth of saving in the economy, some other economic policies may be more fruitful in the future . . .   (Murray, 1968)

Finally, it should be noted that generation of savings is not limited to private pensions. Public social security reserve funds, as illustrated by the Swedish example, can also be a mechanism for the mobilization of savings.[34] In fact, such an option may be particularly attractive in developing countries where private pensions are virtually nonexistent (Schulz, 1970).

A Minor Role for Private Pensions

If we look at the pension systems currently existing in various countries, we see that there is a tendency to rely heavily on public pensions or a private/public combination *with extensive regulation* of the private sector. Table 51 summarizes for fourteen countries the existence of regulating private-pension legislation in the key areas of mandatory vesting, mandatory coverage, pension insurance, and minimum benefits. The fourteen countries are divided into two groups—six countries that rely heavily on public pensions and eight countries (including the United States) that do not.

---

33. For an alternative viewpoint—with which we do not agree because it is based on research which was done over a decade ago and which has suffered from methodological limitations—see Holland (1972).

34. For an extensive discussion of this question, see Kassalow (1968).

TABLE 51

General Characteristics of Private Pension Plans
in Selected Countries, 1972 [a]

	Does National Legislation Require:			
Heavy Reliance on Public Pensions[b]	Mandatory Vesting	Mandatory Coverage	Pension Insurance	Minimum Benefit Standard
Austria	No	No	No	No
Belgium	Yes—5 yrs.[d]	No	No	No
Federal Republic of Germany	No	No	No	No
Italy	No	No	No	No
Norway	Yes—5 yrs.	No	No	No
Sweden	No[c]	No	No[c]	No[c]

Heavy Reliance on Private Pensions[b]	Mandatory Vesting	Mandatory Coverage	Pension Insurance	Minimum Benefit Standard
Canada	Yes—Age 45/10 yrs.	No	No	No
Denmark[e]	Yes—5 yrs.	Yes	No	No
Finland	Yes—4 mo.	Yes	Yes	Yes
France[f]	Yes—immediate	Yes	Yes[g]	No
Great Britain[h] "Contract-out" plans	Yes—immediate	No	No	Yes
Others	No	No	No	No
Netherlands[h]	Yes—5 yrs.	Yes	No	No
Switzerland [i]	No	No	No	No
U.S.A.[h]	No	No	No	No

ᵃ Based primarily on information reported in Kleiler (1971).

ᵇ Countries are categorized on the basis of the amount of earnings replacement provided by the public pension for the average worker.

ᶜ Although Sweden does not have legislation requiring such provisions, two large privately negotiated plans covering most white and blue collar workers provide for immediate vesting, pension insurance, and a minimum benefit standard.

ᵈ Insured pension plans only. This requirement is not specified in a statute but was promulgated in a circular issued by the insurance supervisory authorities in 1942.

ᵉ Danish pensions (Danish Labor Market Supplementary Pension) are administered by a self-owning institution developed by nationwide bargaining and applied to nearly all employees. This national private pension plan operates under major government supervision.

ᶠ Categorizing France as relying heavily on private plans is somewhat arbitrary. The line between social security and supplementary pensions is unclear because of large-scale coordination and regulation by the government.

ᵍ The assessment method of financing is used, and a government decree extended compulsory participation in order to create large plans that would guarantee continuity of contributions.

ʰ Major legislation in this area pending.

ⁱ In December 1972 Switzerland approved in a national referendum a constitutional amendment that requires (by 1975) employers to establish private pensions providing old-age, survivors, and disability insurance with immediate vesting and portability.

Inspection of Table 51 shows that there is much greater regulation in countries that do not rely heavily on public pensions. All the countries in this group except the United States have some form of mandatory vesting standard, and half the countries have a mandatory coverage provision. Furthermore, at the time this was written the two countries without major regulatory legislation in this area (Great Britain and the United States) were in the process of considering the adoption of such. In contrast, very little private-pension legislation has been passed in countries relying on public pensions.

In countries that rely heavily on private pensions and, as a matter of national policy, attempt to guarantee high earnings replacement, the tendency is for the private and public pensions programs to be closely coordinated by a large number of legislative and administrative mechanisms. France is a good example of this phenomenon. In France the distinction between social security and private pension programs is very difficult to make, considering the elaborate coordinating mechanisms that have been established (Doublet and Hecquet, 1971; Horlick and Skolnik, 1971).

Given the various pros and cons of private pensions described above, it seems clear to us that there is a useful role to be played by private pensions but that *countries should rely primarily on public pensions for the bulk of old-age income security provision.* At a minimum, countries that rely in any substantial way on private pensions should legislate minimum standards of operation which will provide some high degree of assurance that persons covered will eventually receive private pensions at a level which, when combined with public pensions, will provide reasonably adequate retirement income. In the words of Marshall:

> One of the virtues claimed for capitalist private enterprise is that it can take risks, and it earns a considerable part of its substantial rewards by doing so. But a government cannot allow risk-taking in welfare—or only minimally. It cannot leave any important part of its overall responsibilities in the hands of private agencies unless it takes steps to limit risk by regulation, supervision, inspection or safety-nets . . .
>
> (T. H. Marshall, 1972)

A COMPREHENSIVE RETIREMENT INCOME SECURITY PROGRAM
FOR THE UNITED STATES

Finally, we would like to incorporate the above recommendations into a comprehensive income-security program for retired people.[35] Although it is surely unrealistic to hope that the Congress will ever pass comprehensive legislation which *simultaneously* deals with all the areas listed below, it would be useful if policymakers and advocates for the elderly had a more comprehensive framework in mind when dealing with the economic problems of growing old.

The Basic Floor

To begin with, there now seems to be a growing acceptance in the United States that income should be raised as soon as possible to an agreed-upon "poverty level" for all Americans not now adequately sharing in the nation's economic abundance. In January 1974 a new "supplemental security" program administered by the Social Security Administration and financed out of general revenues replaced the old programs providing assistance to the poor aged, the blind, and the disabled.[36] The new program builds a floor under all older Americans: $140 per month for single persons and $210 for elderly couples (as of July 1974). In addition to disregarding the first $20 of other income, the program permits exemption of the first $65 of earned income, plus one half of earnings above $65. Such a basic floor of economic security becomes the initial building block of the aged's retirement security. It is the foundation of a commitment from the nation to the most unfortunate to provide them with the basic essentials of life, regardless of the misfortunes that have brought the poor to their distressed situation. Even with this uniform floor there remains a continuing need for state and

---

35. Not all the recommendations presented here are based upon our prior analysis of foreign pension programs. Our analysis of these programs was purposely restricted to a limited number of factors. We felt it appropriate, however, to end this book with a more general statement of our views.

36. This discussion of the Supplemental Security Program should not be interpreted as support of this particular type of welfare reform over others that have been proposed.

local programs to take account of regional variations and other special circumstances.

Adequate Old Age Pension Benefits

Social security is a universally approved program and a time-tested and efficient system of providing further basic income protection to the retired elderly. It is very important that there be appropriate distinctions between a welfare program that necessarily requires a needs test and the present social insurance system, in which benefits are a matter of right, based on past contributions. Although the minimum-income guarantee should be provided through the *welfare system,* the primary means of assuring adequate retirement income should be through the social security system. All American workers currently covered and financially able to contribute during their working years to this national pension system should be required to do so. The system has already proven its superiority and popularity in providing major retirement security.[37] Private pensions and personal saving are necessary components to most individuals' retirement programs, but only a national pension system can deal effectively with the retirement need for

1. Universal and equitable protection;
2. Protection against the problems of economic instability—inflation and recessions;
3. Growing pension benefits as the nation's productivity, hence total per-capita output, increases.

Just as there is widespread citizen and professional support for social security, there is also general agreement that current benefits are too low. There is a need for a new adequacy goal for social security. We propose the adoption of an adequacy of income standard for social security old-age benefits which would provide inflation-protected benefits equal to at least 55 percent of the individual's or family's (if married) preretirement average earnings during the

37. Justifiable or necessary exceptions to this may be (a) government workers, given the political attachment to their separate pension programs, (b) the poor, who should be effectively freed from most tax burdens for equity reasons, and (c) various special groups for religious reasons.

best ten of the last fifteen years prior to retirement (with specified minimum and maximum benefit levels).[38]

Implementation of this level of benefits would require a large increase in pension revenues. It is probably necessary, therefore, that

1. there be a phase-in schedule for increased benefits and revenues over a period of five to ten years;

2. in order to keep the contribution rates paid by individuals as low as possible and minimize the inequities of regressive taxation, *general revenue financing should be used to meet current benefit payment obligations to individuals who have contributed amounts below their expected actuarial benefits.* Current beneficiaries, on average, will receive much greater benefit amounts than the contribution they paid into the system. Current workers should not be required to meet these obligations through a proportional/regressive tax system.

Improved Pension Supplements

Participation in the first two parts of the "Income Security Program" (welfare and social security) are compulsory; individuals are required to pay taxes to support the welfare system and to make contributions for future social security retirement benefits. It is questionable whether it is desirable to extend compulsion beyond these two programs.

However, if individuals desire to have sufficient income in retirement so that their standard of living will be close to or equal to their preretirement standard, they must supplement their preparation through social security with other action. A high percentage of the work force currently supplements social security pensions through private pensions set up at the place of employment. These private plans vary tremendously in their provisions, and presumably their major asset is to be responsive to the varying needs of different types of workers. At the same time there is increasing acceptance of legislated minimum standards for private pension operation.

But what about individuals not covered by private pensions? Many of them would choose, if they were available, to take ad-

---

38. With this higher level of pensions, spouse benefits could probably be eliminated—improving the equity of the financing system. We have not discussed the question of equity for women in social security programs. For information on practices in five countries see Haskins and Bixby (1973).

vantage of private pension plans with their tax-free employer-contribution provisions and the financial benefits typically arising out of "group investment." It seems only equitable that a comprehensive retirement security program expand the retirement preparation opportunities of this group. To this end, it is recommended that workers not covered by a private pension plan be given the voluntary choice of joining either (a) a "supplementary social security program" [39] or (b) participating in a self-financed retirement plan with contributions not taxable until realized as retirement income.[40]

Encouragement of Personal Saving

Of course, everyone is free to save for retirement. But why save if there is a good chance, as in the past, that inflation will wipe out the value of the savings? Currently, all methods of seeking inflation protection for personal retirement savings have serious drawbacks, not the least of which is that they require a degree of economic and financial sophistication which most people lack; hence, people hesitate to take advantage of, or remain ignorant of, the opportunities. In addition, various methods of protection against inflation

---

39. Although we have not studied all the possibilities carefully and are not prepared, therefore, to strongly recommend one over the other, our ordered preferences are for one of the following: (a) a program that is an "add-on" to the present OASI programs, where current employer/ employee contributions could be increased by joint agreement between the management and employees of a particular firm, (b) a program similar to that proposed in 1971 by the Conservative Government in Great Britain (Secretary of State, 1971), which is a funded scheme run on the lines of a private pension by an independent Board of Management, or (c) a limited number of private, competitive, cooperative, insured institutions to be licensed and regulated by the Securities and Exchange Commission (Nader and Blackwell, 1973).

40. As part of a private-pension reform package, the Nixon Administration proposed in 1972–73 that wage and salary earners be permitted to set up their own individual retirement plans with tax-deferral provisions. See American Enterprise Institute (undated). At the time of this writing (March 1974), the United States Congress had passed private-pension standards legislation which also would liberalize self-employed plans (commonly called Keogh plans) and would allow workers uncovered by private pensions to put aside some of their salary and take a deduction for the entire amount.

suffer from varying degrees of nonliquidity and risk, minimum required amounts of money, high transaction fees and/or commissions, and lack of general availability.

For many years, the late Senator McNamara, as Chairman of the Senate Special Committee on Aging, advocated that the United States Government sell to individuals "retirement bonds" or "constant purchasing power bonds," the value of which would be guaranteed against the erosions of inflation (United States Senate Special Committee on Aging, 1961). Many noted economists (James Tobin, Milton Friedman, Henry Wallich, and Guy Arvidsson) have also advocated the introduction of such bonds. More recently, the Senate Special Committee on Aging's Task Force on the Economics of Aging noted in their report that such bonds "merit serious consideration as a potential method of increasing voluntary retirement savings" (United States Senate Special Committee on Aging, 1969).

Health Cost Protection

No matter how well one prepares financially for retirement, there always remain fears regarding the large potential drain on financial sources as a result of serious illness and growing physical incapacity. As old-age approaches, the incidence of illness increases and the probability of serious or long-term illness rises sharply. Present Medicare/Medicaid and private health insurance help significantly to reduce the insecurity arising from this problem; but there is general agreement that much more must be done if we are to meet adequately the problems of retirement insecurity arising from the threat of major illness. There is a need for the enactment of a national health plan that would guarantee the availability of comprehensive, quality health care to all Americans.

Current proposals for national health plans do not, however, make adequate provision for long-term care and do not authorize sufficient supportive services or the personal care that would enable many to avoid institutionalization. This omission has serious implications for the aged—creating great insecurity and hardship.[41]

There is a need to develop financial support for long-term care and supportive services programs. Such programs would help to allay

---

41. See, for example, Robert Morris (1973).

two of the greatest fears held by many older persons: the possibility of being financially wiped out and subject to pauperistic medical care and services, and the fear of premature institutionalization. In the hope of avoiding the stigma and the degradation of such an occurrence, many older persons, afraid to use their retirement savings for necessary current expenditures, lock in these funds. A meaningful program of long-term care and supportive services is a vital part of a comprehensive income-security program for the retired.

The Right to Work

One need not be against retirement to advocate that public policy give older workers opportunities to work under decent conditions. But the fears and the economic ignorance of the 1930's still remain with us today. Many people still believe that opening job opportunities to the elderly necessarily reduces the jobs available to younger workers. This is a false economic doctrine. If there is one lesson to be learned from the "new economics," it is that the Government, through appropriate monetary and fiscal policy, can stimulate the economic expansion necessary to create jobs for all Americans, young and old, who want to work and who have the necessary skills.

No longer is there any justification for forcing older workers out of the work force, nor is there any justification for discouraging them from supplementing their retirement income by part-time employment. *Instead, business, unions, and government should be actively engaged in creating part-time employment opportunities for older persons.*

Liberalizing the social security retirement test has been condemned by many experts as a scheme to help people with high incomes at the expense of those with little income. This, of course, is true if one is talking about complete elimination of the test. It is certainly not true if the retirement test is liberalized to encourage and allow people with low or moderate incomes to work part time in retirement because of economic or psychological need.[42] As recommended by the 1971 White House Conference on Aging:

---

42. See Schulz (1971) for a fuller discussion of this point.

The social security retirement test should be liberalized to allow persons to receive old-age benefits without reduction up to the point where the total of social security plus earnings equals at least $5,000 per year. In no case should benefits be reduced for persons earning under $1,680.

THE CHALLENGE REPEATED

As we stated at the beginning of this book, it is time that a broad review of our retirement income maintenance system was undertaken and serious thought given to the requirements of providing adequate retirement incomes for *the future aged.* A study by Schulz (1968) of the economic status of the retired aged in 1980 showed that given past trends in the improvement of United States old-age pension benefits, poverty and low income among the aged would be significantly reduced but would not be completely eliminated; the latest available data confirm that projection. Furthermore, the relative economic status of the aged will remain very poor and perhaps deteriorate if major changes are not soon forthcoming. Moreover, present trends indicate that we must be prepared to deal with the economic implication for the aged of (a) retirement at earlier ages, (b) longer life, and (c) changing retirement life-style expectations.

As we have argued above, to a large extent pension-benefit levels in the past and the increases in these levels have been stimulated not so much with the purposeful intent of tapping a greater part of the nation's rising national product for old people but rather as a secondary result of attempts to deal with the severe and potentially explosive hardship problems facing many older people. In consequence, these past efforts have been aimed primarily at raising the economic status of the aged to some minimum standard or subsistence level in the face of rising prices.

It is time now to develop pension mechanisms that will allow the retired aged to share in the growing productivity and output of the nation—to share the "harvested fruits." What this requires is the development of various means to permit an orderly, equitable but *substantial* transfer of income from the working to the retired population in order to improve the latter's relative economic status.

The national dialogue and debate over the desirability of such a change is just beginning. More people must be made aware of the need for "dynamic pensions" today for the ever-changing needs of the tomorrows.

Appendix A

SUMMARY OF U.S. OLD AGE, INVALIDITY, AND DEATH PROGRAMS [*]

THE national old-age, survivors, disability, and health insurance (OASDHI) program, popularly referred to as social security and administered by the federal government, is the largest and most important of the social insurance programs in the United States. The cash benefit provisions of the program are designed to replace partially the income that is lost when a worker retires, becomes severely disabled, or dies. The program also provides partial protection against the high cost of health care during old age and disability. The program's aim is to prevent destitution and poverty rather than to relieve those conditions after they occur.

At the beginning of 1972, about 113 million people were insured for cash benefits. Sixty-eight million were permanently insured; that is, they had worked long enough under the program to qualify for retirement benefits even if they do no more covered work. About 91 percent of the nation's elderly are either getting monthly cash benefits or will be eligible for their benefits when they or their spouses stop working; 95 percent of young children and their mothers can count on monthly survivor insurance benefits if the family breadwinner dies; and about 80 percent of people aged 21–64 have protection in the event of the breadwinner's long-term disability (either as insured workers or as dependents of insured workers). More than 28 million people—one out of eight persons in the country—are receiving cash benefits at a monthly rate of about $3.9 billion (as of December 1972). OASDHI benefits were virtually the only source of retirement income in 1967 for more than one half of the aged

---

[*] Excerpted from U.S. Social Security Administration (1973), Part II.

married couples getting benefits and nearly two thirds of the non-married aged beneficiaries. When all types of income are taken into account, OASDHI benefits made up almost all the income of about one fourth of the married beneficiaries and two fifths of the nonmarried aged.

By the sixth year of Medicare (January 1972), about 21.0 million aged persons were enrolled in the hospital insurance (HI) program and 20.1 million aged persons had elected to avail them-selves of the supplementary medical insurance (SMI) program. Benefit payments during fiscal year 1972 amounted to $8.4 billion; $6.1 billion under HI and $2.3 billion under SMI. There were about three hospital admissions for every 10 persons enrolled and one skilled nursing facility admission for each thirteen hospital admis-sions. About four fifths of the enrolled SMI population used SMI services and more than 7 out of 10 persons in this group used suf-ficient services to be eligible for reimbursement. Moreover, Medicare payments for hospital care and physicians' care are estimated to account for more than two thirds of all expenditures for such serv-ices provided to the aged.

The Social Security Act of 1935 covered employees in non-agricultural industry and commerce only. Since 1935, coverage has been extended to additional employment, so that today the old-age, survivors, disability, and health insurance program approaches uni-versal coverage. During a typical week, more than nine out of ten persons who work in paid employment or self-employment are covered or eligible for coverage under the program, compared with fewer than six out of ten when the program began in 1937. Except for special provisions applicable only to a few kinds of work, coverage is on a compulsory basis. Unlike some of the social security systems of other countries, the United States program covers all kinds of workers, whether they are wage earners, salaried, self-em-ployed, farmhands, or farm operators, and includes workers with high earnings. The wide applicability and compulsory nature of the program are essential to its effectiveness in preventing dependency and want and in assuring the American worker and his family of continuous protection during all phases of his working career.

Nearly all work performed by citizens and noncitizens, regard-less of age or sex, is covered if performed within the United States (defined for social security purposes to include American Samoa, Guam, Puerto Rico, and the Virgin Islands).

In addition, the program covers work performed outside the United States by American citizens who are (1) employed by an American employer, (2) employed by a foreign subsidiary of an American corporation electing coverage for its employees, or (3) self-employed, under certain circumstances. Employment on American vessels or aircraft outside the United States is usually covered, irrespective of the worker's citizenship.

The majority of workers excluded from coverage under the program by the Social Security Act fall into three major categories: (1) those covered under federal civilian staff retirement systems, (2) household workers and farm workers who do not earn enough or work long enough to meet certain minimum requirements (workers in industry and commerce are covered regardless of regularity of employment or amount of earnings), and (3) persons with very low net earnings from self-employment (generally less than $400 a year). The remaining few excluded from coverage by law are in a variety of very small employment groups. An example is certain nonresident, nonimmigrant aliens temporarily in the United States to carry out the services for which they are admitted, such as teaching, studying, or conducting research. Certain family employment is also excluded, such as employment of a child under 21 by his parent or employment of a wife by her husband.

Employees of state and local governments are covered under agreements between the states and the Secretary of Health, Education, and Welfare. Each state decides what groups of eligible employees will be covered, subject to provisions in the federal law which assure retirement system members a voice in any decisions to cover them under OASDHI. Coverage of employment by states and their political subdivisions is not made compulsory because of federal-state problems that would be raised by any federal law levying a tax on the governmental functions of states and localities. At present, about two thirds of all state and local employees have been brought under coverage.

Special arrangements were also adopted in making coverage available to employees of nonprofit organizations operated exclusively for religious, charitable, scientific, literary, or educational purposes. Such organizations are traditionally exempt from taxation. To get coverage for its employees such an organization must waive its exemption from social security taxes. When this is done, all current employees who elect coverage and all employees hired or reemployed in the future are covered. Almost all employees of nonprofit organizations who are eligible for coverage are now covered.

The professional services of ministers, members of religious orders who have not taken a vow of poverty, and Christian Science practitioners are covered automatically under the provisions applicable to the self-employed unless within a limited period exemption is claimed on grounds of conscience or religious principles. Religious orders whose members have taken a vow of poverty may make an irrevocable election to cover their members as employees.

Beginning with 1957 the basic pay of military servicemen has been covered under the regular contributory provisions of the law. In addition, gratuitous (noncontributory) wage credits of $300 a quarter are provided to take account of remuneration received in kind—such as quarters, meals, and medical services. The social security trust funds are reimbursed from federal general revenues for the additional cost of benefits payable because of the noncontributory wage credits.

Noncontributory wage credits of $160 a month are also provided veterans, with certain restrictions, for each month of active military service from September 1940 through December 1956. In general, these wage credits may not be used if another federal periodic retirement or survivor benefit (other than a benefit from the Veterans Administration) is being paid based on the same period of service. However, servicemen who continue in military service after 1956 are given credit for service during the period 1951–56 even if the service is used for purposes of benefits paid by the uniformed services.

Benefits are paid as a statutory right, without regard to need and no matter how much property or nonwork income the individual may have.

To qualify for cash benefit payments for himself and his dependents or survivors, a worker must have demonstrated his attachment to the labor force by a specified amount of work in covered employment or self-employment. The amount of covered work required is, generally speaking, related to how long a person could be expected to have worked under the program. In the long run, a person must have worked at least ten years in covered jobs to qualify for retirement benefits. Of course, many workers now retired and getting benefits could not be expected to have worked ten years in covered employment because their jobs were not covered until they were near retirement age. Therefore, whenever the law was amended to bring major groups under the program for the first time, provision was made so that workers who were near retirement age when their jobs were brought under the program could become insured within a reasonably short time.

The period of time a person must have spent in covered work to be insured for benefits is measured in "quarters of coverage." A person paid $50 or more in covered nonfarm wages in a calendar quarter is credited with a quarter of coverage. A person paid $100 or more of covered farm wages in a year is credited with a quarter of coverage for each full $100 of such wages ($400 or more of such wages result in four quarters of coverage). Self-employment income of $400 or more in a year results in four quarters of coverage for the year (net earnings from self-employment of less than $400 in a year are not covered). A person is credited with four quarters of coverage for any year in which his total earnings (wages and self-employment income) reach the maximum amount of annual earnings subject to contributions and counted toward benefits ($12,000 in 1974).

For most types of benefits, the worker must be "fully insured." In general, a fully insured person is one who has at least as many quarters of coverage (acquired at any time after 1936) as the number of years elapsing between age 21 and 62 or date of death or disability, whichever occurs first. For those who reached age 21 before 1951, the requirement is one quarter of coverage for each year between 1950 and retirement age, disability, or death. A worker with 40 quarters of coverage is fully insured for life and needs no further employment to qualify for retirement or survivor benefits.

A minimum of six quarters of coverage is required except that workers who reached retirement age or died before 1957 may acquire a "transitional insured status" with three to five quarters of coverage and receive special payments. Special payments may also be payable to a wife or widow on the basis of her husband's record under this provision if she reached age 72 before 1969.

Under amendments passed in 1966, certain people attaining age 72 before 1968 who had no coverage at all, or fewer than three quarters of coverage, were made eligible for similar special payments under another transitional provision. These special payments are suspended for any month for which the individual receives a cash payment under a federally aided public assistance program. In addition, they are reduced by the amount of any periodic benefit that a person is eligible to receive from a government pension system (excluding workmen's compensation and veterans' service-connected compensation). A person attaining age 72 after 1967 needs three quarters of coverage for each year after 1966 and up to the year he reaches age 72 to be eligible for the special benefits. These transitional provisions do not apply to persons reaching age 72 after 1971 since their quarters-of-coverage requirements for fully insured status are the same as or less than those under the transitional provisions.

If a worker dies before acquiring a fully insured status, survivor benefits may be paid to his young widow with children if he is "currently insured." An individual is currently insured if he has acquired six quarters of coverage within the 13-calendar-quarter period ending with the quarter in which he died.

To be insured for disability benefits, a worker must be fully insured and he must meet a test of substantial recent covered work. The latter involves having worked in covered employment for at least 5 of the 10 years before the onset of disability. Somewhat more liberal insured status requirements apply to workers who are disabled before age 31, or who are blind.

The law provides in general that a beneficiary who has substantial earnings from work will have some or all cash benefits withheld, depending on the amount of his annual earnings. Benefits will also be withheld from a person getting dependent's benefits if the worker on whose account he is eligible for benefits has substantial income from work. This provision, which is generally called the retirement test, is included in the law to assure that monthly benefits will be paid to a worker only when he has substantially retired and to his dependents and survivors only when they do not have substantial earnings from work. This is in line with the basic purpose of monthly benefits under the program—to replace some of the earnings from work that are lost by a worker and his family when he retires in old age, becomes disabled, or dies.

The retirement test has been liberalized several times by the Congress to keep pace with higher earnings levels and increased benefits. In the future the amount a beneficiary can earn without having benefits reduced will be increased automatically—in proportion to the rise in average earnings—whenever OASDHI cash benefits are increased automatically. At present (1974) a beneficiary whose earnings do not exceed $2,100 a year can get benefits for all twelve months of the year. For earnings above $2,100, one dollar in benefits is withheld for each two dollars of earnings. Benefits are payable, however, regardless of annual earnings, for any month in which the beneficiary earns $175 or less in wages and does not render substantial services in self-employment. Benefits are also payable to beneficiaries beginning with the month when they reach age 72 regardless of their earnings. The age 72 provision recognizes that some people go on working and paying contributions to the end of their lives and might otherwise never get any monthly benefit.

Under the special retirement test that applies to beneficiaries who work outside the United States in noncovered employment, a beneficiary is presumed retired in, and benefits are payable in full for, any month in which he works six or fewer days; he gets no benefits for any month in which he works seven or more days.

Monthly retirement benefits are payable at age 62 to a retired insured person and to the wife or dependent husband of a retired worker. Benefits are payable to the wife of a retired worker at any age if she has in her care a child under 18 or disabled who is entitled to benefits on the earnings record of her husband. Child's benefits are paid to the retired worker's unmarried child under age 18 or from age 18 through 21 if he is a full-time student. They are also paid regardless of age if the child has been disabled since before age 22.

Monthly survivor benefits are payable to a widow or dependent widower at age 60, or, if disabled, at age 50; to a widow at any age if she has in her care a child under 18 or disabled who is entitled to benefits on the earnings record of her husband; to unmarried children under age 18, from age 18 through 21 if in school, and at any age if child has been disabled since before age 22; and to a dependent parent at age 62. A lump-sum benefit is also payable on the death of an insured worker to help meet the special expenses connected with his last illness or death.

Under certain circumstances, benefits may also be paid to the divorced wife of a retired, deceased, or disabled worker and to the remarried widow or widower of a deceased worker. Generally speaking though, dependent and survivor benefits are terminated when the dependency situation ends, for example, by the marriage of a child beneficiary or by remarriage of an adult.

Most benefits payable to aged beneficiaries before age 65 are actuarially reduced to take into account the longer period over which the benefits will be paid. This reduction continues throughout the period of entitlement. The major unreduced benefits payable are those to wives and widows with children in their care and to dependent parents (who may start receiving benefits at age 62).

A person (e.g., a wife or dependent husband) who is eligible for a benefit based on his own earnings and who also may be eligible for a benefit as a dependent will draw his own benefit, plus any excess of the other benefit over his own, in effect, the larger of the two.

Benefit protection under the program, both for a worker and his dependents and survivors, is related to the average monthly earnings that the insured worker had from covered employment. The amount of the worker's average monthly earnings is affected by the worker's level of earnings and, over the long run, the covered employment. From the beginning of the program, there has been an upper limit on the amount of annual earnings taxable and creditable toward OASDHI benefits. (The limit is $10,800 in 1973, $12,000 in 1974, and will be automatically adjusted thereafter to reflect increasing wage levels.)

In recognition of the fact that low-paid workers have less margin for reduction in their incomes at retirement than do higher-paid workers, OASDHI benefits are based on a formula that is weighted to provide the worker with low earnings a relatively greater percentage of average monthly earnings than is provided the higher-paid worker. Also, in the interest of social adequacy, dependents' and survivors' protection is provided without additional cost to the worker with dependents.

For most workers, monthly earnings are averaged over a period of years beginning with 1951, or age 22 if later, up to the year of disability, death, or retirement—age 62–65 for men, depending on year of birth, and age 62 for women. For all men born after 1912, age 62 will be used. Generally, the five years of lowest earnings are disregarded when the average is computed; years of high earnings after reaching retirement age can be substituted for earlier years of low earnings.

In the relatively few cases when the combination of a worker's average monthly earnings before 1951 plus his subsequent earnings produces a larger benefit than his average earnings after 1950, the year 1937 is used as the starting date for the computation instead of 1951.

After the worker's average monthly earnings have been figured, the monthly benefit amount payable at age 65 or at disablement— the primary insurance amount—is then obtained from a table in the law. The minimum primary insurance amount is $84.50 a month. The 1972 amendments provide a special minimum for those who worked for many years at low earnings, where the special minimum is higher than the benefit under the regular computation provisions. This special minimum is equal to $8.50 multiplied by the number of years of covered employment in excess of 10 years, up to a maximum of 30 years ($170 a month).

After 1974, all monthly benefits (except the special minimum) will be tied to the cost of living, as measured by the Consumer Price Index of the Bureau of Labor Statistics, and be increased (but not more than once a year) by the same percentage that the index increases if it rises 3 percent or more from the time of last adjustment in benefits. The increase in benefits will be automatic unless Congress has enacted an ad hoc general increase or one becomes effective in the calendar year before the automatic increase would otherwise go into effect.

The contribution and benefit base—the maximum amount of a worker's annual earnings on which he pays contributions and that is creditable for benefits—will also be subject to future automatic increases. These increases can go into effect only in a year in which benefits are automatically increased. The base increases will assure that the program continues to provide benefit protection which does not erode as wage levels increase and will help to finance the automatic increases in benefits to reflect increasing prices.

The maximum possible monthly benefit for a man retiring at age 65 in 1973 is $266.10 ($276.40 for a woman). These figures will increase in the future, both as a result of the higher earnings creditable under the automatically adjusted contribution and benefit base, and as a result of automatic increases in benefits to reflect increases in the cost of living.

The monthly benefit for dependents and survivors is calculated as a percentage of the insured person's primary insurance amount. Total family benefits are limited by a fixed maximum amount varying between 150 percent and 188 percent of the worker's primary insurance amount, as appears in a table in the law. The family maximum in 1973 ranged from $126.80 a month to $646.70 a month, the latter being payable to a family of three or more on the basis of average monthly earnings of $825. Average earnings this high were possible in 1973 where the worker was young when he died. As with the maximum possible retirement benefit, the highest family maximum will increase in the future under the automatic adjustment provisions.

For those who choose to delay their retirement, an additional one percent is added to their old-age benefits for each year after 1970 (one twelfth of one percent for each month) that they do not get benefits between ages 65 and 72 because of earnings. This increase does not apply to those receiving the special minimum nor to those receiving dependents' or survivors' benefits.

Appendix B

THE SIMULATION MODEL

WAGE or salary changes generally reflect both changes in the level of average prices (inflation or deflation) and changes in productivity. For the simulations presented in Chapter 7, a model was developed to generate and project national average wages in the four countries studied. Before discussing a sample economy, a number of concepts used in the model need to be explained:

1. *Time Period and Base Year.* Economic time series, such as national annual wage levels and price and growth indices, are generated for a time period beginning at the first and ending at the last simulated year. EBEG and EEND are used to denote these years.

All time series in the model are simulated relative to a base year. It is desirable from the viewpoint of simplicity to have the base year be the first year of the simulation economy. From a mathematical point of view this simplification is not necessary; however, we believe that it facilitates understanding of the model.

2. *Price Index.* Price changes are reflected in a simulated price index. This index is a time series in ascending annual sequence between the years EBEG and EEND. Its value at the base year is one.

3. *Price Ratio.* The ratio of successive annual price indices reflects relative changes from year to year. This price ratio, RPRI, is a time series, defined as follows:

(1) $\text{RPRI}(Y) = \text{XPRI}(Y - 1)/\text{XPRI}(Y)$, for
       $\text{EBEG} < Y <= \text{EEND}$ by 1.

4. *Productivity Index.* Similar to the price index, the productivity index reflects changes in productivity. XPRO is used to denote this time series, with a value of one assigned for the initial year.

5. *Productivity Ratio.* Similar to the price ratio, the produc-

tivity ratio, RPRO, reflects annual relative changes in productivity. The following relation holds:

(2) RPRO(Y) = XPRO(Y − 1)/XPRO(Y), for
      EBEG < Y < = EEND by 1.

6. *Base Wage and National Annual Wage Level.* The base wage is a parameter that determines the national annual wage level (or average) at the beginning year. Its numerical value is set at the beginning of the simulation and is a reflection of the prevailing annual national average wage of the country under study at the year EBEG. If we use WBEG for the beginning wage and W for the time series of wages, the following relation holds:

(3) W(EBEG) = WBEG.

It is assumed that the wage level reflects productivity as well as price changes. Therefore, the following relation is used to simulate a wage index series and the annual average wage series:

(4) XW(Y) = XPRI(Y) × XPRO(Y) for all Y, and

(5) W(Y) = WBEG × XW(Y), for all Y.

Since each year's index is the product of the rates of change for all preceding years (see expressions 1 and 2), the product of the price and productivity indices was used instead of an additive combination. The rate of change of W is the product of the rates of change of these two indices:

(6) RW(Y) = RPRI(Y) × RPRO(Y) for
      EBEG < Y < = EEND, or alternately

(7) RW(Y) = W(Y − 1)/W(Y) for
      EBEG < Y < = EEND.

7. *Simulation of Price and Productivity Ratios.* Only two series, RPRI and RPRO, need be simulated; all other series can be calculated on the relations discussed above. The population means of these two series are AMPRPRI and AMPRPRO, where the symbol sequence AMP stands for the arithmetic mean of a population. In addition to these means, the half-range of a uniform distribution is specified and values of the series are sampled from it. Using HR to denote the half-range, the values of the two ratio series will fall within the following limits:

(8) AMPRPRI − HRRPRI < = RPRI(Y) < =
AMPRPRI + HRRPRI, and

(9) AMPRPRO − HRRPRO < = RPRO(Y) < =
AMPRPRO + HRRPRO.

Within the above ranges, ideally the occurrence of each value is equally likely. On the other hand, given limitations in pseudo-random number generators, uniformity is not always obtained. This shortcoming, however, is not detrimental to the analysis, since these two series, as well as the derived series, are exogenous variables in the combined worker-economy model.

For illustrative purposes, a hypothetical economy generated by the model is shown in Table A-1. The economy begins in 1973 (EBEG = 1973) and ends in 2012 (EEND = 2012). The arithmetic mean of the population of price ratios (AMPRPRI) is 1.025 (i.e., the population mean changes in prices are 2.5 percent). The reader should note that because of sampling variation, the sample arithmetic mean is not necessarily equal to the population mean. In the simulation, the sample mean happens to be slightly larger than the population mean (AMSRPRI = 1.027).

The arithmetic mean of the population of productivity changes (AMPRPRO) is 1.02 (i.e., the mean productivity changes for the population, in a statistical sense, is 2 percent). Again, the sample mean can (but does not have to) equal the population mean.

Variation in annual price or productivity ratios is introduced by drawing samples from a uniformly distributed population of ratios falling within the above specified intervals as defined in expressions 8 and 9 above. A value of .025 (HRRPRI) was chosen for prices, and a value of .02 (HRRPRO) was selected for the productivity ratio series. Price ratios, therefore, are sampled from a population of uniformly distributed values within the limits of 1 and 1.05. Similarly, productivity ratios are sampled from the interval 1.00 and 1.04.

The statistics shown in the last row of Table A-1 need to be explained. The arithmetic mean of a sample (i.e., a statistic) has been calculated for each series. The symbol sequence "AMS" is used to denote this statistic. The reader should note that because of sampling variation, the sample means do not need to agree with population means.

TABLE A-1

A Hypothetical Economy

YEAR	RPRI	XPRI	RPRO	XPRO	RW	XW	W
1973	1.025	1.000	1.020	1.000	1.045	1.000	7500
1974	1.035	1.035	1.015	1.015	1.050	1.050	7876
1975	1.009	1.044	1.007	1.022	1.016	1.067	8003
1976	1.039	1.084	1.032	1.055	1.072	1.143	8576
1977	1.005	1.090	1.002	1.057	1.008	1.152	8640
1978	1.032	1.125	1.010	1.067	1.042	1.201	9005
1979	1.046	1.177	1.038	1.107	1.085	1.303	9773
1980	1.035	1.218	1.019	1.128	1.055	1.375	10310
1981	1.048	1.277	1.015	1.146	1.064	1.462	10968
1982	1.021	1.304	1.040	1.191	1.062	1.553	11644
1983	1.045	1.363	1.022	1.217	1.068	1.658	12437
1984	1.032	1.406	1.013	1.233	1.046	1.734	13005
1985	1.032	1.452	1.005	1.239	1.037	1.799	13490
1986	1.009	1.464	1.028	1.273	1.036	1.864	13981
1987	1.010	1.478	1.003	1.277	1.013	1.888	14157
1988	1.030	1.523	1.009	1.289	1.040	1.963	14721
1989	1.045	1.591	1.030	1.327	1.076	2.112	15837
1990	1.046	1.664	1.015	1.347	1.061	2.241	16809
1991	1.024	1.703	1.021	1.375	1.045	2.342	17564
1992	1.029	1.753	1.031	1.417	1.061	2.484	18628
1993	1.012	1.773	1.037	1.469	1.049	2.605	19539
1994	1.009	1.789	1.025	1.506	1.034	2.694	20208
1995	1.046	1.871	1.021	1.539	1.068	2.879	21591
1996	1.048	1.961	1.021	1.570	1.070	3.079	23094
1997	1.023	2.007	1.011	1.588	1.035	3.187	23904
1998	1.009	2.026	1.002	1.591	1.011	3.223	24170
1999	1.045	2.117	1.028	1.636	1.075	3.463	25975
2000	1.035	2.191	1.035	1.693	1.071	3.711	27829
2001	1.006	2.205	1.034	1.751	1.041	3.863	28970
2002	1.022	2.254	1.011	1.771	1.033	3.991	29935
2003	1.023	2.306	1.038	1.839	1.062	4.240	31797
2004	1.043	2.404	1.008	1.853	1.051	4.456	33418
2005	1.047	2.518	1.024	1.898	1.073	4.780	35852
2006	1.000	2.519	1.034	1.963	1.034	4.945	37087
2007	1.025	2.583	1.026	2.015	1.052	5.203	39022
2008	1.047	2.705	1.012	2.038	1.060	5.514	41352
2009	1.008	2.728	1.033	2.105	1.042	5.743	43069
2010	1.024	2.794	1.011	2.128	1.035	5.946	44596
2011	1.020	2.850	1.010	2.149	1.030	6.125	45935
2012	1.001	2.854	1.001	2.151	1.002	6.139	46042
AMS	1.027	1.830	1.020	1.501	1.048	2.954	22158

It should also be noted that the sample mean of the wage ratio series is slightly larger than the corresponding population mean. The population mean is the product of the population means of the price and productivity series (see expression 6). The value of the population mean is 1.046—compared to the sample mean of 1.048 (the product of the corresponding sample means of the price and productivity ratio series).

The model also simulates personal earnings histories of a particular shape (or distribution) vis-à-vis the national wage level of the particular country being studied.

A number of concepts used to simulate these histories need to be explained:

1. *Career.* The career of an individual is a time period beginning in the year of first earnings and ending in the year of last earnings. The career is assumed to be continuous, meaning that the individual does not take leaves of absence for extended duration. Though earnings are never allowed to become zero in any one year, temporary unemployment as well as job changes can be generated in the simulation.

The beginning of the earnings history, or career, is referred to by CBEG, and the last year is designated CEND. The duration of the career, or the number of earnings years, is CYS. The following relation exists between the three:

(10) $\text{CYS} = \text{CEND} - \text{CBEG} + 1.$

2. *Earnings.* The earnings of an individual are simulated annually. They constitute a time series E, consisting of CYS elements in annually ascending sequence.

3. *Lifetime Earnings Average.* This term designates the arithmetic mean of all earnings over the career. The symbol AMS is used:

(11) $\text{AMSE} = \text{SUM}(\text{E}(\text{Y}))/\text{CYS}$, for
$\text{CBEG} < = \text{Y} < = \text{CEND}$ by 1.

"Lifetime earnings average" is an important concept. It determines the individual's level of earnings but does not determine the shape (or pattern) of earnings throughout the career (i.e., the distribution of personal income over a lifetime).

4. *Earnings Level.* The earnings level, ELEVEL, determines lifetime average earnings as follows:

(12) AMSE = AMSW × ELEVEL, where

(13) AMSW = SUM(W(Y))/CYS, for
CBEG < = Y < = CEND by 1.

In other words, the arithmetic mean of the sample of national wage averages throughout the career (AMSW), multiplied by the earnings level, will determine the individual's lifetime average earnings. Assuming an earnings level of one, lifetime average earnings received will equal sample average national wages over the same period. This does not mean, however, that earnings equal national annual average wages at all times during the career; within this constraint, earnings may differ annually to reflect a personal income distribution of particular shape.

5. *Earnings Ratio.* The earnings ratio, as the term implies, is the ratio of earnings of two successive years. It is a time series of CYS − 1 elements in ascending sequence. If we use RE for this series, the following relation exists:

(14) RE(Y) = E(Y − 1)/E(Y), for
CBEG < = Y < = CEND − 1 by 1.

It should be noted that earnings increase whenever RE is greater than 1, and decrease when RE is less than 1. The earnings ratio is an important concept, since it determines the earnings distribution. The earnings ratio is simulated in this model by means of three parameters: the earnings ratio at the beginning and at the end of the career (REBEG and REEND respectively) and the half range of the earnings ratio, which is used to determine an interval within which uniformly distributed random values are generated.

The annual arithmetic mean of the earnings ratio varies between REBEG and REEND, and satisfies the following relationship:

(15) AMSRE(T) = REBEG − T ×
(REBEG − REEND)/(CYS − 2),
for CBEG − EBEG < T < CEND − EBEG by 1.

The actual value of the earnings ratio, however, is generally not its mean. Instead, it is an equally likely value from the following interval:

(16) AMSRE(Y) − HRRE < = RE(Y) < =
AMSRE(Y) + HRRE, for all Y > CBEG.

6. *Earnings Distribution or Pattern.* Various indicators of the earnings distribution have been constructed. The series EP shows earnings adjusted by the price index in terms of prices prevailing during *the first year of work*, CBEG. It is determined by the relation:

(17) EP(Y) = E(Y) × XPRI(CBEG)/XPRI(Y), for all Y.

An index of the price-adjusted earnings series, XEP, is calculated as follows:

(18) XEP(Y) = EP(Y)/EP(CBEG), for all Y.

The time series EG is used for growth adjustments. This is a particularly important series, for it shows real earnings (i.e., the worker's position relative to the labor force, free of price and productivity effects):

(19) EG(Y) = E(Y) × W(CBEG)/W(Y), for all Y.

An index of this growth-adjusted series, XEG, is calculated in a manner similar to the price-adjusted earnings-index series:

(20) XEG(Y) = EG(Y)/EG(CBEG), for all Y.

BIBLIOGRAPHY, GENERAL

Aaron, Henry J. "Social Security: International Comparisons," in Otto Eckstein, ed., *Studies in the Economics of Income Maintenance* (Washington: Brookings Institution, 1967).

Aaron, Henry J., John A. Brittain, Joseph A. Pechman, Alice Rivlin, Charles Schultze, and Nancy H. Teeters. Letter to the *Washington Post* (October 4, 1972).

AAUP. "Statement of Principles on Academic Retirement and Insurance Plans," *AAUP Bulletin*, 55, No. 3 (1969), 386–89.

Achinger, Hans, Joseph Hoeffner, Hans Muthesius, and Ludwig Neundoerfer. *Rothenfelser Denkschrift—Neuordnung der Sozialen Leistungen.* Denkschrift auf Auregung des Herrn Bundeskanzlers Erstattet (Cologne, Greven Verlag, 1955).

Advisory Council on Social Security, 1965. *The Status of the Social Security Program and Recommendations for Its Improvement* (Washington, D.C.: U.S. Social Security Administration, 1965).

Advisory Council on Social Security, 1971. *Reports of the 1971 Advisory Council on Social Security,* communication from the Secretary of Health, Education, and Welfare, 92nd Congress, 1st session (Washington, D.C.: GPO, 1971).

Allmänna Pensionsfonden (The National Pensions Insurance Fund). *Report for the Year 1972* (1973).

———. *The Swedish National Pension Insurance Fund—A Survey* (undated).

"Antipoverty Policies and Changing Welfare Concepts in Canada," *Social Security Bulletin* (July 1970), 13–20.

Atkinson, A. B. "Income Maintenance and Income Taxation," *Journal of Social Policy,* 1 (1972), 135–48.

———. "National Superannuation: Redistribution and Value for Money," *Bulletin of the Oxford University Institute of Economics and Statistics,* 32 (1970), 171–85.

Auerback, Walter. "Modelleines Sozialplans—eine Skizze," in *Die Krankenversicherung* (1952).

Ball, Robert M. Testimony in U.S. Senate Special Committee on

Aging, *Economics of Aging: Toward a Full Share in Abundance,*
Part 1, Survey Hearing (Washington, D.C.: GPO, 1969).

Ball, Robert M. HEW News Release dated December 29, 1972.

———. "Policy Issues in Social Security," *Social Security Bulletin,*
29 (1966), 7.

———. "Some Reflections on Selected Issues in Social Security," in
U.S. Joint Economic Committee, *Old-Age Income Assurance,*
Part I, General Policy Guidelines, 90th Congress, 1st session
(Washington, D.C.: GPO, December 1967), 48–57.

Barfield, Richard. *The Automobile Worker and Retirement: A Second Look* (Ann Arbor, Michigan: Institute for Social Research,
University of Michigan, 1970).

Barfield, Richard, and James Morgan. *Early Retirement: The Decision and the Experience* (Ann Arbor, Michigan: Braun-Brumfield, 1969).

Becker, Gary S. *Human Capital* (New York: National Bureau of
Economic Research and Columbia University Press, 1964).

Bixby, Lenore E. "Income of People Aged 65 and Older: Overview
from 1968 Survey of the Aged," *Social Security Bulletin,* 33, No.
4 (1970), 3–34.

Bixby, Lenore E., and Virginia Reno. "Second Pensions among
Newly Entitled Workers: Survey of New Beneficiaries," *Social
Security Bulletin,* 34, No. 11 (1971), 3–7.

Bok, Derek C. "Emerging Issues in Social Legislation: Social Security," *Harvard Law Review,* 80 (1967), 717–64.

Boulding, Kenneth. *Principles of Economic Policy* (Englewood
Cliffs, N.J.: Prentice Hall, 1958.

Brittain, John A. "The Real Rate of Interest on Lifetime Contributions toward Retirement under Social Security," in U.S. Joint
Economic Committee. *Old-Age Income Assurance,* Part III. 90th
Congress, 1st session (Washington, D.C.: GPO, December
1967).

———. *The Payroll Tax for Social Security* (Washington: Brookings
Institution, 1972).

Broberg, Rolf. Personal communication to the authors (1973).

Brown, J. Douglas. *An American Philosophy of Social Security*
(Princeton: Princeton University Press, 1972).

Bryden, W. Kenneth. "Old-Age Pensions and Policy Making in Canada," unpublished Ph.D. thesis, University of Toronto (1970).

Bundesminister für Arbeit und Sozialordnung. *Sozialbericht 1971*
(Stuttgart: Ministrey, 1971).

Byrnes, John. Floor statement appearing in the *Congressional Record* (June 30, 1972), p. H6511.

Cagan, Phillip. *The Effect of Pension Plans on Aggregate Saving.*

Occasional Paper No. 95 (New York: National Bureau of Economic Research, 1965).

Campbell, Colin D. "Social Insurance in the United States: A Program in Search of an Explanation," *Journal of Law and Economics*, 12 (1969), 249–65.

Carlson, Valdemar. "Institutional Change in a Welfare State," *The Journal of Risk and Insurance*, 33 (1966), 587–96.

Carrin, Guy. "An Inquiry into the Adequacy of the Belgian Old-Age Pension Schemes for Workers," *Tijdschrift voor Sociale Wetenschappen* (December 1971), 432–39.

Ceccarelli, Jane M., and Alfred M. Skolnik. "Wage-Replacement Rates under the OASDHI Retirement Provisions," *Research and Statistic Note*, No. 18, Office of Research and Statistics, U.S. Social Security Administration (Washington, D.C.: HEW, December 3, 1973).

Centre de Recherche et d'Information Socio-Politiques. *Le Problème des Déshérités en Belgique*, Courrier Hebdomadaire, No. 379 (Brussels: CRISP, May 13, 1967).

Chen, Yung-Ping. *Income*, background paper for the 1971 White House Conference on Aging (Washington, D.C.: GPO, 1971).

———. "Inflation and Productivity in Tax-Benefit Analysis for Social Security," in U.S. Joint Economic Committee, *Old-Age Income Assurance*, Part III, 90th Congress, 1st session (Washington, D.C., GPO, December 1967).

La Cité. "La Situation des Pensionnés" (January 4–7, 1967).

Cohen, Wilbur J. "Toward a National Policy on the Aging," address given to the 25th Conference on Aging of the Institute of Gerontology at the University of Michigan—Wayne State University (September 1972).

Cohen, Wilbur J., and Milton Friedman. *Social Security: Universal or Selective?* Rational Debate Seminars (Washington: American Enterprise Institute, 1972).

Commissie van de Kamer van Volksvertegenwoordigers. *Report*, Parlementaire Documenten, 122 (Brussels, 1923–24).

Cruikshank, Nelson H. *The Stake of Today's Workers in Retirement Security*, U.S. Senate Special Committee on Aging, Committee Print, 91st Congress, 2nd session (Washington, D.C.: GPO, 1970).

Dawson, William H. *Social Insurance in Germany, 1883–1911* (London: Scribner, 1912).

Deleeck, H. *Maatschappelijke Zekerheid en Inkomensherverdeling in België* (Leuven: Standard Uitgeverij, 1966).

Delperee, A. "De Belgische Sociale Zekerheid in de Economie ende Maatschappij," *Belgisch Tijdschrift voor Sociale Zekerheid* (February 1962), 210–21.

Department of National Health and Welfare. *The Canada Pension Plan* (Ottawa: Queen's Printer, 1965).

———. *Disability Benefits, Canada Pension Plan* (Ottawa: Queen's Printer, 1970).

———. *Income Security for Canadians* (Ottawa: Queen's Printer, 1970).

———. *Retirement Pensions, Canada Pension Plan* (Ottawa: Queen's Printer, 1970).

———. *Survivors' Benefits, Canada Pension Plan* (Ottawa: Queen's Printer, 1970).

Department of National Health and Welfare, Social Security Research Division. *The Measurement of Poverty*, memorandum 19 (Ottawa: Queen's Printer, November 1970).

Doerfel, Hans-Juergen. "Moeglich-Keiten zur Schaetzung von Lebensein Kommenverlaeufen aus Queischnittsanalysen" (Darmstadt: dissertation, 1970).

Dominion Bureau of Statistics. *Survey of Pension Plan Coverage, 1965* (Ottawa: Queen's Printer, December 1967).

Doublet, Jacques, and Paul Hecquet. "Actuarial Study of Pension Funds and Non-Statutory Old-Age Insurance Schemes—Their Relations With General Schemes: National Summaries, France," paper presented at the Fifth International Conference of Social Security Actuaries and Statisticians (Berne: mimeo., 1971).

Douse, H. L. "Canadian Pension Plans No Longer a Major Obstacle to the Employment of Older Workers," *Industrial Gerontology*, 3 (October 1969), 1–8.

Eckstein, Otto. "Financing the System of Social Insurance," in William G. Bowen, *The Princeton Symposium on the American System of Social Insurance* (New York: McGraw Hill, 1968).

Epstein, Lenore A. *Income Security Standards in Old-Age*, U.S. Research Report, 3 (Washington: U.S. Social Security Administration, undated).

Epstein, Lenore A., and Janet H. Murray. *The Aged Population of the United States*, Research Report, 19, U.S. Social Security Administration Office of Research and Statistics (Washington, D.C.: GPO, 1967).

"Evolutie van de Ontvangsten en Uitgaven van de Sociale Zekerheid Tussen 1958–1965." *Belgisch Tijdschrift voor Sociale Zekerheid* (September/October 1967), 1227.

Faulkner, E. J. "Social Security and Insurance: Some Relationships in Perspective," *Journal of Insurance*, 30 (1963), 197–218.

Federation of Swedish Industries. *Modern Trends in Swedish Pension Systems* (Stockholm: The Federation, 1968).

Fisher, Paul. "Minimum Old-Age Pensions," *International Labour Review*, 102, No. 1 (1970), 51–78.

————. "Developments and Trends in Social Security throughout the World, 1967–1969," *International Social Security Review,* 24, No. 1 (1971), 3–34.

————. *Old-Age and Sickness Insurance in West Germany in 1965.* Research Report 13, Social Security Administration Office of Research and Statistics (Washington, D.C.: GPO, 1966).

Frank, M. "Invloed van de Sociale Zekerheid op de Inkomensverdeling en de Bevordering van de Productiviteit," *Belgisch Tijdschrift voor Sociale Zekerheid* (April 1964), 627–41.

DeGadt, J. "Het Sociaal Statuut van de Zelfstandigen," in Instituut voor Sociaal Zekerheidsrecht, *De Ontwikkeling van de Belgische Wetgeving van de Sociale Zekerheid, 1965–1970* (Leuven: Het Instituut, 1971).

Galbraith, John K. *The New Industrial State* (New York: New American Library, 1967).

Goldin, Kenneth D. "Social Insurance Finance," *Rivista Di Diritto Finanziario E Scienza Delle Finanze,* 30 (1971), 355–79.

Goldstein, Sidney. "Changing Income and Consumption Patterns of the Aged, 1950–1960," *Journal of Gerontology,* 20, No. 4 (1965), 453–61.

Gordon, Margaret S. *The Economics of Welfare Policies* (New York: Columbia University Press, 1963).

————. "Income Security Programs and the Propensity to Retire," in Richard H. Williams, et al., eds., *Processes of Aging,* Vol. 2 (New York: Atherton Press, 1963).

Gordon, Robert J. "Inflation in Recession and Recovery," in *Brookings' Papers on Economic Activity,* Vol. 1 (1971), 105–66.

Government of Canada. *Working Paper on Social Security in Canada,* 2nd ed. (Ministry of National Health and Welfare, 1973).

Graefin von Bethusy-Huc, Viola. *Das Sozialleistungssystem der Bundesrepublik Deutschland* (Tubingen, 1965).

Greene, Mark R., Charles H. Pyron, Vincent Manion, and Howard Winklevoss. *Early Retirement: Company Policies and Retirees' Experiences* (Washington, D.C.: Administration on Aging, 1969).

Havighurst, R. J., J. M. A. Munnichs, B. Neugarten, and H. Thomae. *Adjustment to Retirement: A Cross-National Study* (Assen: Van Gorcum, 1970).

Heckscher, Eli F. *An Economic History of Sweden* (Cambridge: Harvard University Press, 1963).

Heclo, H. Hugh. "Politics and Social Policy," Ph.D. dissertation, Yale University (New Haven, 1970).

Heidbreder, Elizabeth, W. W. Kolodrubetz, and Alfred Skolnik. "Old-Age Programs," in U.S. Joint Economic Committee, *Old-Age Income Assurance,* Part II (Washington, D.C.: GPO, 1966).

Henle, Peter. "Recent Trends in Retirement Benefits Related to Earnings," *Monthly Labor Review*, 95 (1972), 12–20.

Holland, Daniel M. "Building the Base to Support Retirement," in Tax Foundation, *Financing Retirement: Public and Private*, 23rd National Conference (New York: The Foundation, 1972), pp. 33–38.

Holmquist, I. "Swedish Practice in Adjusting Pensions," paper presented at the International Social Security Association Conference on Social Security Research (mimeo., undated).

Horlick, Max. "The Earnings Replacement Rate of Old-Age Benefits: An International Comparison," *Social Security Bulletin*, 33 (1970), 3–16.

Horlick, Max, and Doris E. Lewis. "Adjustment of Old-Age Pensions in Foreign Programs," *Social Security Bulletin*, 33 (1970), 12–23

Horlick, Max, and Robert Lucas. "Role of the Contribution Ceiling in Social Security Programs: Comparison of Five Countries," *Social Security Bulletin*, 34 (1971), 19–31.

Horlick, Max, and Alfred M. Skolnik. *Private Pension Plans in West Germany and France, Research Report*, 36, U.S. Social Security Administration Office of Research and Statistics (Washington, D.C.: GPO, 1971).

Hoskins, Dalmer, and Lenore Bixby. *Women and Social Security: Law and Policy in Five Countries*, Research Report, 42, U.S. Social Security Administration, Office of Research and Statistics (Washington, D.C.: GPO, 1973).

Information Canada. *The Canada Pension Plan* (Ottawa: Queen's Printer, 1970).

———. *How to Get Your 1972 Guaranteed Income Supplement* (Ottawa: Queen's Printer, 1971).

———. *Your Old-Age Pension* (Ottawa: Queen's Printer, 1971).

Jantz, Kurt. "Schwerpunkte des Weiteren Renten reformgesetzes," *Bundesarbeitsblatt*, 24, No. 3/4 (1973), 131–34.

Kassalow, Everett M., ed. *The Role of Social Security in Economic Development*, Research Report, 27, U.S. Social Security Administration Office of Research and Statistics (Washington, D.C.: GPO, 1968).

Katona, George. *Private Pensions and Individual Saving*, Monograph 40 (Ann Arbor, Michigan: Survey Research Center, 1965).

Kelly, L. A. *Emerging Social Security Issues*, Reprint Series, 12 (Kingston, Ontario: Industrial Relations Center, Queen's University, 1969).

Kervyn, A. "Programmatie en Sociale Zekerheid," *Belgisch Tijdschrift voor Sociale Zekerheid* (May 1964), 735–44.

Kirschen, E. S. "Sociale Zekerheid en Economische Politiek," *Belgisch Tijdschrift voor Sociale Zekerheid* (April 1964), 599–609.

Kleiler, Frank M. *Canadian Regulation of Pension Plans* (Washington, D.C.: Labor-Management Services Administration of U.S. Department of Labor, 1970).

——. *European Regulation of Pension Plans* (Washington, D.C.: Labor-Management Services Administration, U.S. Department of Labor, 1971).

——. *Regulation of Pension Plans in Canada and Europe,* Conference of Actuaries in Public Practice and International Association of Consulting Actuaries (San Francisco: October 1970).

Kolodrubetz, W. *A Methodological Study of Private Pensions,* Social Security Administration Staff Study (Washington, D.C.: Social Security Administration, 1972).

——. "Employer-Benefit Plans, 1971," *Social Security Bulletin,* 36, No. 4 (April 1973), 27–33.

——. "Private Retirement Benefits and Relationship to Earnings: Survey of New Beneficiaries," *Social Security Bulletin,* 36, No. 5 (May 1973), 16–37.

——. "Two Decades of Employee-Benefit Plans, 1950–70: A Review," *Social Security Bulletin,* 35, No. 4 (1972), 10–22.

Kreps, Juanita. Testimony before the Committee, in U.S. Senate Special Committee on Aging, *Economics of Aging: Toward A Full Share in Abundance,* Part II, Concluding Hearings (Washington, D.C.: GPO, 1970).

——. *Lifetime Allocation of Work and Leisure,* Research Report, 22, U.S. Social Security Administration (Washington, D.C.: GPO, 1968).

Kreps, Juanita, and Joseph J. Spengler. "Equity and Social Credit for the Retired," in Kreps, Juanita, *Employment, Income, and Retirement Problems of the Aged* (Durham, N.C.: Duke University Press, 1963), 198–229.

Krupp, Hans-Juergen. "The Use of Simulation Methods in Urban Public Finance," paper presented at the Congress of the Institut International Finances Publiques (New York, 1972).

Lagerström, Lennart. *Social Insurance and Private Occupational Pensions in Sweden* (Stockholm: Svenska Personal-Pensions-kassan, 1971).

Landay, D. M., and W. W. Kolodrubetz. *Coverage and Vesting of Full-Time Employees under Private Retirement Plans: Findings from the April 1972 Survey* (Washington, D.C.: HEW, Labor, and Treasury Depts., 1973).

Lubove, Roy. *The Struggle for Social Security, 1900–1935* (Cambridge, Mass.: Harvard University Press, 1968).

Mackenroth. "Die Reform der Sozialpolitik durch einen Deutschen Sozialplan," *Schriften des Vereins für Sozialpolitik,* New Series, 4 (1952), 39–76.

Marshall, T. H. "Value Problems of Welfare-Capitalism," *Journal of Social Policy,* 1 (1972), 15–32.

McClung, Nelson. "The Economics of Pension Finance," *Journal of Risk and Insurance,* 36 (1969), 425–31.

McClung, Nelson, John Moeller, and Eduardo Siguel. *Transfer Income Program Evaluation,* Urban Institute Paper (Washington: The Urban Institute, 1971).

McConnell, John. "Role of Public and Private Programs in Old-Age Income Assurance," in U.S. Joint Economic Committee, *Old-Age Assurance,* Part 1, 90th Congress, 1st session (Washington, D.C.: GPO, 1968).

Merriam, Ida. "Implications of Technological Change for Income," in Juanita M. Kreps, ed., *Technology, Manpower, and Retirement Policy* (Cleveland: World Publishing Co., 1966).

———. "Income Maintenance: Social Insurance and Public Assistance," in Shirley Jenkins, ed., *Social Security in International Perspective* (New York: Columbia University Press, 1969).

———. Private correspondence with authors (July 1973).

Mertens, J. "De Bestaansmeddelen van de Bejaarden in Belgie," *Belgisch Tijdschrift voor Sociale Zekerheid* (August 1971), 765–876.

Michanek, Ernst. *For and Against the Welfare State: The Swedish Experience* (Stockholm: The Swedish Institute, 1964).

Miller, S. M., and P. A. Roby. *The Future of Inequality* (New York: Basic Books, 1970).

Ministerie van Sociale Voorzorg. *Algemeen Verslag over de Sociale Zekerheid* (Brussels: the Ministry, various years).

———. *Statistisch Yaarboek van de Sociale Zekerheid* (Brussels: the Ministry, 1970).

Molin, Björn. *Tjänstepensionsfrogan: En Studie i Svensk Partipolitik* (Göteborg: Scandinavian University Books, 1965).

Morgan, James, et al. *Income and Welfare in the United States* (New York: McGraw Hill, 1962).

Morgan, John S. "An Emerging System of Income Maintenance: Canada in Transition," in Shirley Jenkins, ed., *Social Security in International Perspective* (New York: Columbia University Press, 1969).

Morris, Robert. "What Do You Do after the Doctor Leaves?" *Harper's Magazine* (January 1973).

Murray, Janet. "Homeownership and Financial Assets: Findings from the 1968 Survey of the Aged," *Social Security Bulletin,* 35 (1972), 3–23.

Murray, Roger F. *Economic Aspects of Pensions: A Summary Report,* National Bureau of Economic Research (New York: Columbia University Press, 1968).

Musgrave, Richard. "The Role of Social Insurance in an Overall Program for Social Welfare," in Bowen, et al., *The American System of Social Insurance* (New York: McGraw Hill, 1968).

Myers, Robert J. *Social Insurance and Allied Government Programs* (Homewood, Illinois: Irwin, 1965).

―――. "Government and Pensions," in American Enterprise Institute for Public Policy Research, *Private Pensions and the Public Interest* (Washington, D.C.: The Institute, 1970), 29–49.

―――. "Social Security's Hidden Hazards," *Wall Street Journal* (July 28, 1972).

Nader, Ralph, and Kate Blackwell. *You and Your Pension* (New York: Grossman, 1973).

National Insurance Board. *The Swedish Social Insurance Scheme, Statistical Data Covering 1968 (1960)–1972*. Edition 6 (Stockholm: The Board, 1971).

Nationale Actie voor Bestaanszekerheid. *De Derde Leeftijd . . . Een Avontuur* (Brussels: Nationale Actie, May 1969).

Naylor, Thomas H., ed. *The Design of Computer Simulation Experiments* (Durham, N.C.: Duke University Press, 1969).

Niemeyer, Werner. "Das Sechzehnte Rentenanpassungsgesetz mit der neuen Rentenniveausicherungsklausel," *Bundesarbeitsblatt*, 24, No. 7/8 (1973), 379–83.

Norwood, Janet L. "Cost-of-Living Escalation of Pensions," *Monthly Labor Review*, 95 (1972), 21–23.

Orcutt, Guy, Steven Caldwell, Harold Guthrie, Gary Hendricks, Gerald Peabody, James Smith, and Richard Wertheimer. *Microanalytic Simulation for Policy Exploration*, Working Paper 5095 (Washington, D.C.: Urban Institute, 1974).

Orshansky, Mollie. "Counting the Poor: Another Look at the Poverty Profile," *Social Security Bulletin*, 28 (1965), 3–29.

―――. Testimony before the Subcommittee on Employment, Manpower, and Poverty of the Committee on Labor and Public Welfare, United States Senate, 92nd Congress, 1st Session (Washington, D.C.: GPO, 1971), pp. 69–74 and 79–80.

Pechman, Joseph A., Henry J. Aaron, and Michael K. Taussig. *Social Security: Perspectives for Reform* (Washington, D.C.: Brookings Institution, 1968).

Prest, A. R. "Some Redistributional Aspects of the National Superannuation Fund," *The Three Banks Review*, 32 (June 1970), 3–22.

Price, Daniel N. "OASDHI Benefits, Prices, and Wages: Effect of 1967 Benefit Increase," *Social Security Bulletin*, 31 (1968), 28–35.

Projector, Dorothy S. "Should the Payroll Tax Finance Higher Benefits Under OASDI? A Review of the Issues," *The Journal of Human Resources*, 4 (1969), 61–75.

Pryor, Frederic L. *Public Expenditures in Communist and Capitalist Nations* (Homewood, Illinois: Irwin, 1968).

Riley, Matilda White, and Anne Foner. *Aging and Society*, Volume 1, *An Inventory of Research Findings* (New York: Russell Sage Foundation, 1968).

Rimlinger, Gaston. *Welfare Policy and Industrialization in Europe, America, and Russia* (New York: Wiley, 1971).

Rittig, Albert, and Nichols, O. R. *Actuarial Note No. 87* (Washington, D.C.: U.S. Soc. Sec. Admin., 1974).

Rosenthal, Albert H. *The Social Programs of Sweden: A Search for Security in a Free Society* (Minneapolis: University of Minnesota Press, 1967).

Samuelson, Paul. "Social Security," *Newsweek* (February 13, 1967), 8.

Schewe, Dieter, Karlhugo Nordhorn, and Klaus Schenke. *Survey of Social Security in the Federal Republic of Germany*, 8th ed. (Bonn: Federal Ministry for Labour and Social Affairs, 1972).

———. *Übersicht über die Soziale Sicherung, 8th ed.* (Bonn: Minister für Arbeit and Sozialordnung, 1970).

Schoetter, P., and G. Spitaels. "Sociale Zekerheid en Openbare Onderstand," *Belgisch Tijdschrift voor Sociale Zekerheid* (May 1966), 499–559.

Schreiber, Wilfred. "Existenzsicherheit in der Industriellen Gesellschaft," in Boettcher, E., ed., *Sozialpolitik und Sozialreform* (Tübingen: J. C. B. Mohr, 1957).

Schultze, Charles, Edward R. Fried, Alice M. Rivlin, and Nancy H. Teeters. *Setting National Priorities: The 1972 Budget* (Washington, D.C.: Brookings Institution, 1971).

Schulz, James H. *The Economic Status of the Retired Aged in 1980: Simulation Projections*. Research Report 24, U.S. Social Security Administration Office of Research and Statistics (Washington, D.C.: GPO, 1968).

———. "Social Insurance as a Source of Saving for Investment in Iran," *Journal of Developing Areas*, 4 (1970), 225–38.

———. Statement in U.S. Senate Special Committee on Aging, *Economics of Aging: Toward a Full Share in Abundance*, Part 10A, *Pension Aspects* (Washington, D.C.: GPO, 1970).

———. "Reform of the Social Security Retirement Test," *Industrial Gerontology* (Winter 1971), 19–24.

———. *Retirement*, background paper for the 1971 White House Conference on Aging (Washington, D.C.: GPO, 1971).

———. "Comparative Simulation Analysis of Social Security Systems," *Annuals of Economic and Social Measurement,* 1/2 (1972), 109–127.

Schulz, James H., and Guy Carrin. "The Role of Savings and Pension Systems in Maintaining Living Standards in Retirement," *Journal of Human Resources,* 7 (1972), 343–65.

Secretary of State, Department of Health and Social Security. *Strategy for Pensions: The Future Development of State and Occupational Provision* (London: Her Majesty's Stationery Office, 1971).

Shanas, Ethel, Peter Townsend, Dorothy Wedderburn, Heening Friis, Poul Milhoj, and Jan Stehouwer. *Old People in Three Industrial Societies* (New York: Atherton Press, 1968).

Sozialdemokratischen Partei Deutschlands. *Sozialplan für Deutschland,* Gutachten Erstattet auf Anregung des SPD—Vorstands Von Auerbach (Berlin: Dietz Verlag, 1957).

Spitaels, G., and D. Klaric. *Le Salaire et la Converture des Besoins Sociaux: Vingt Ans de Securité Sociale en Belgique* (Brussels: Institut de Sociologie de l'Université Libre de Bruxelles, 1968).

Statistics, Canada. *Trusteed Pension Plans Financial Statistics 1970* (Ottawa: Queen's Printer, January 1972).

The Swedish Institute. *Social Benefits in Sweden* (Stockholm: Trygg Hansa, 1972).

Swedish Ministry of Health and Social Affairs. *National Insurance Act—May 25, 1962,* revised English translation (Stockholm: the Ministry, 1971).

Taira, Kaji, and Peter Kilby. "Differences in Social Security Development in Selected Countries," *International Social Security Review,* 22, No. 2 (1969), 139–53.

Thompson, Gayle B. "Income of the Aged Population: 1971 Money Income and Changes for 1967," *Research and Statistics Note,* No. 14-1973, Social Security Administration, Office of Research and Statistics (Washington, D.C.: DHEW, 1973).

Thurow, Lester C. "The Optimum Lifetime Distribution of Consumption Expenditures," *American Economic Review,* 59 (1969), 324–30.

Uhr, Carl G. *Sweden's Social Security System,* Research Report, 14, U.S. Social Security Administration Office of Research and Statistics (Washington, D.C.: GPO, 1966).

United Nations. *Demographic Yearbook 1970* (New York: 1971).

United States Bureau of the Census. "Poverty in the United States 1959 to 1966," *Current Population Reports,* Consumer Income, Series P-60, No. 68 (Washington, D.C.: GPO, 1969).

————. "Characteristics of the Low-Income Population: 1971," *Current Population Reports,* Consumer Income, Series P-60, No. 82 (Washington, D.C.: GPO, July 1972a).

————. "Money Income in 1971 of Families and Persons in the United States," *Current Population Reports,* Consumer Income, Series P-60, No. 83 (Washington, D.C.: GPO, 1972b).

————. "Illustrative Population Projections for the United States: The Demographic Effects of Alternative Paths to Zero Growth," *Current Population Reports,* Population Estimates and Projection, Series P-25, No. 82 (Washington, D.C.: GPO, 1972c).

————. "Money Income in 1972 of Families and Persons in the United States," *Current Population Reports,* Consumer Income, Series P-60, No. 87 (Washington, D.C.: GPO, 1973a).

————. "Characteristics of the Low Income Population: 1972," *Current Population Reports,* Consumer Income, Series P-60, No. 88 (Washington, D.C.: GPO, 1973b).

————. "One-in-a-Thousand Sample Description and Technical Documentation," *U.S. Census of Population and Housing: 1960* (Washington, undated).

United States Bureau of Labor Statistics. *Digest of 100 Selected Pension Plans under Collective Bargaining, Spring 1968,* BLS Bulletin 1597 (Washington, D.C.: GPO, 1969).

————. *Retired Couple's Budget for a Moderate Living Standard,* Bulletin 1570-4 (Washington, D.C.: GPO, 1966).

————. *Revised Equivalence Scale,* Bulletin 1570-2 (Washington, D.C.: GPO, 1968).

————. "Three Budgets for a Retired Couple, Autumn, 1972," news release (August 10, 1973).

United States Committee on Ways and Means. "President's Proposals for Revision in the Social Security System," *Hearings,* Part 1 (Washington, D.C.: GPO, 1967a).

United States Council of Economic Advisors. "Annual Report of the Council of Economic Advisors," in *Economic Report of the President* (Washington, D.C.: GPO, 1973).

United States Department of Health, Education, and Welfare. *Social Security Programs in the United States* (Washington, D.C.: GPO, 1971).

United States House Committee on Ways and Means. *Social Security Amendments of 1967: Report of the Committee on Ways and Means,* House Report No. 544, 90th Congress, 1st session (Washington, D.C.: GPO, 1967b).

United States Joint Economic Committee. *The Distribution of Personal Income,* 88th Congress, 2nd session (Washington, D.C.: GPO, 1964).

United States Labor-Management Services Administration. *Union Status and Benefits of Retirees* (Washington, D.C.: GPO, 1973).

United States Senate Special Committee on Aging. *A Constant Purchasing Power Bond: A Proposal for Protecting Retirement In-*

come, 87th Congress, 1st Session (Washington, D.C.: GPO, 1961).

———. *Economics of Aging: Toward a Full Share in Abundance— Task Force Working Paper,* 91st Congress, 1st session (Washington, D.C.: GPO, 1969).

———. *Economics of Aging: Toward a Full Share in Abundance,* Part 10B—Pension Aspects (Washington, D.C.: GPO, 1970a).

———. *Pension Aspects of the Economics of Aging: Present and Future Roles of Private Pensions,* Committee Print, 91st Congress, 2nd session (Washington, D.C.: GPO, 1970b).

United States Social Security Administration. *Reports of the 1971 Advisory Council on Social Security,* House Document No. 92–80, 92nd Congress, 1st session (Washington, D.C.: GPO, 1971a).

———. *The Research Program of the Social Security Administration,* Report of the 1967 SSA Advisory Committee on Research Development (Washington, D.C.: GPO, 1968).

———. *Social Security Programs throughout the World, 1971,* Research Report 40 (Washington, D.C.: GPO, 1971).

———. *United States Projections for OASDI Cost Estimates,* Actuarial Study No. 62 (Washington, D.C.: GPO, 1971b).

United States Subcommittee on Aging, Committee on Labor and Public Welfare, *Post-White House Conference on Aging Reports, 1973* (Washington, D.C.: GPO, 1973).

———. *History of the Provisions of Old-Age, Survivors, Disability, and Health Insurance 1935–1972,* DHEW Publication (SSA) 73-11510 (Washington, D.C.: DHEW, 1973).

Van Hauwaert, F. "De Aanpassing van het Indexcijfer in het Verband van de Belgische Sociale Zekerheid voor Werknemers," *Belgisch Tijdschrift voor Sociale Zekerheid* (January 1972), 86–104.

Vergauwen, L. "De Ontwikkeling van de Wetgeving over de Pensioenen van de Zelfstandigen," in Instituut voor Sociaal Zekerheidsrecht, *De Ontwikkeling van de Belgische Wetgeving van de Sociale Zekerheid, 1965–1970* (Leuven: Het Instituut, 1971).

Versichelen, M. "Armoede in de Welvaartstaat," *Belgisch Tijdschrift voor Sociale Zekerheid* (September 1970), 1081–1152.

Wang, Gisela C. "Flexible Retirement Feature of German Pension Reform," *Social Security Bulletin,* 36 (1973), 36–41.

Weisbrod, Burton A., and W. Lee Hansen. "An Income–Net Worth Approach to Measuring Economic Welfare," *American Economic Review,* 58 (1968), 1315–29.

Werkgroep voor Alternatiere Economie. *Armoede in België* (Antwerp: Nederlandse Boekhandel, 1972).

White House Conference on Aging, 1971. *A Report to the Delegates from the Conference Sections and Special Concerns Sessions* (Washington: the Conference Staff, 1971).

Zöllner, Detlev. "Relating Social Insurance Benefits to Earnings," *International Social Security Review,* 23 (1970), 224–36.

BIBLIOGRAPHY BY COUNTRIES

INTERNATIONAL

Aaron, Henry J. "Social Security: International Comparisons," in Otto Eckstein, ed., *Studies in the Economics of Income Maintenance* (Washington: Brookings Institution, 1967).

Doublet, Jacques, and Paul Hecquet. "Actuarial Study of Pension Funds and Non-Statutory Old-Age Insurance Schemes: Their Relations With General Schemes: National Summaries, France," paper presented at the Fifth International Conference of Social Security Actuaries and Statisticians (Berne: mimeo., 1971).

Fisher, Paul. "Minimum Old-Age Pensions," *International Labour Review*, 102 (1970), 51–78.

———. "Developments and Trends in Social Security throughout the World, 1967–1969," *International Social Security Review*, 24 (1971), 3–34.

Goldin, Kenneth D. "Social Insurance Finance," *Rivista Di Diritto Finanziario E Scienza Delle Finanze*, 30 (1971), 355–79.

Gordon, Margaret S. *The Economics of Welfare Policies* (New York: Columbia University Press, 1963).

———. "Income Security Programs and the Propensity to Retire," in Richard H. Williams, et al., eds., *Processes of Aging*, Vol. 2 (New York: Atherton Press, 1963).

Havighurst, R. J., J. M. A. Munnichs, B. Neugarten, and H. Thomae. *Adjustment to Rettirement: A Cross-National Study* (Assen: Van Gorcum, 1970).

Horlick, Max. "The Earnings Replacement Rate of Old-Age Benefits: An International Comparison," *Social Security Bulletin*, 33 (1970), 3–16.

Horlick, Max, andDori s E. Lewis. "Adjustment of Old-Age Pensions in Foreign Programs," *Social Security Bulletin*, 33 (1970), 12–23.

Horlick, Max, and Robert Lucas. "Role of the Contribution Ceiling in Social Security Programs: Comparison of Five Countries," *Social Security Bulletin*, 34 (1971), 19–31.

Hoskins, Dalmer, and Lenore Bixby.*Women and Social Security:*

Law and Policy in Five Countries, Research Report 42, U.S. Social Security Administration Office of Research and Statistics (Washington, D.C.: GPO, 1973).

Kassalow, Everett M., ed. *The Role of Social Security in Economic Development*, Research Report 27, U.S. Social Security Administration Office of Research and Statistics (Washington, D.C.: GPO, 1968).

Kleiler, Frank M. *European Regulation of Pension Plans* (Washington, D.C.: Labor-Management Services Administration, United States Department of Labor, 1971).

———. *Regulation of Pension Plans in Canada and Europe*, Conference of Actuaries in Public Practice and International Association of Consulting Actuaries (San Francisco: October 1970).

Pryor, Frederic L. *Public Expenditures in Communist and Capitalist Nations* (Homewood, Illinois: Irwin, 1968).

Rimlinger, Gaston. *Welfare Policy and Industrialization in Europe, America, and Russia* (New York: Wiley, 1971).

Schulz, James H. "Social Insurance as a Sourse of Saving for Investment in Iran," *Journal of Developing Areas*, 4 (1970), 225–38.

Shanas, Ethel, Peter Townsend, Dorothy Wedderburn, Henning Friis, Poul Milhoj, and Jan Stehouwer. *Old People in Three Industrial Societies* (New York: Atherton Press, 1968).

Taira, Kaji, and Peter Kilby. "Differences in Social Security Development in Selected Countries," *International Social Security Review*, 22 (1969), 139–53.

United Nations. *Demographic Yearbook 1970* (New York: 1971).

United States Social Security Administration. *Social Security Programs throughout the World, 1971*, Research Report 40 (Washington, D.C.: 1971).

Zöllner, Detlev. "Relating Social Insurance Benefits to Earnings," *International Social Security Review*, 23 (1970), 224–36.

BELGIUM

Carrin, Guy. "An Inquiry into the Adequacy of the Belgian Old-Age Pension Schemes for Workers," *Tijdschrift voor Sociale Wetenschappen* (December 1971),

Centre de Recherche et d'Information Socio-Politiques. *Le Probleme des Déshérités en Belgique*, Courrier Hebdomadaire, 379 (Brussels: CRISP, May 13, 1967).

La Cité. "La Situation des Pensionnés" (January 4–7 1967).

Commissie van de Kamer van Volksvertegenwoordigers. *Report*, Parlementaire Documenten, 122 (Brussels: 1923–24).

Deleeck, H. *Maatschappelijke Zekerheid en Inkomensherverdeling in België* (Leuven: Standaard Uitgeverij, 1966).

Delperee, A. "De Belgische Sociale Zekerheid in de Economie ende Maatschappij," *Belgisch Tijdschrift voor Sociale Zekerheid* (February 1962), pp. 210–21.

"Evolutie van de Ontvangsten en Uitgaven van de Sociale Zekerheid Tussen 1958–1965." *Belgisch Tijdschrift voor Sociale Zekerheid* (September/October 1967), 1227.

Frank, M. "Invloed van de Sociale Zekerheid op de Inkomensverdeling en de Bevordering van de Productiviteit," *Belgisch Tijdschrift voor Sociale Zekerheid* (April 1964), 627–41.

DeGadt, J. "Het Sociaal Statuut van de Zelfstandigen," in Instituut voor Sociaal Zekerheidsrecht, *De Ontwikkeling van de Belgische Wetgeving van de Sociale Zekerheid, 1965–1970* (Leuven: Het Instituut, 1971).

Kervyn, A. "Programmatie en Sociale Zekerheid," *Belgisch Tijdschrift voor Sociale Zekerheid* (May 1964), 735–44.

Kirschen, E. S. "Sociale Zekerheid en Economische Politiek," *Belgisch Tijdschrift voor Sociale Zekerheid* (April 1964), 599–609.

Mertens, J. "De Bestaansmeddelen van de Bejaarden in Belgie," *Belgisch Tijdschrift voor Sociale Zekerheid* (August 1971), 765–876.

Ministerie van Sociale Voorzorg. *Algemeen Verslag over de Sociale Zekerheid* (Brussels: the Ministry, various years).

———. *Statistisch Yaarboek van de Sociale Zekerheid* (Brussels: the Ministry, 1970).

Nationale Actie voor Bestaanszekerheid. *De Derde Leeftijd . . . Een Avontuur* (Brussels: Nationale Actie, May 1969).

Schoetter, P., and Spitaels, G. "Sociale Zekerheid en Openbare Onderstand," *Belgisch Tijdschrift voor Sociale Zekerheid* (May 1966), 499–559.

Spitaels, G., and D. Klaric. *Le Salaire et la Converture des Besoins Sociaux: Vingt Ans de Securité Sociale en Belgique* (Brussels: Institut de Sociologie de l'Université Libre de Bruxelles, 1968).

Van Hauwaert, F. "De Aanpassing van het Indexcijfer in het Verband van de Belgische Sociale Zekerheid voor Werknemers," *Belgische Tydschrift voor Sociale Zekerheid* (January 1972), 86–104.

Vergauwen, L. "De Ontwikkeling van de Wetgeving over de Pensioenen van de Zelfstandigen," in Instituut voor Sociale Zekerheidsrecht, *De Ontwikkeling van de Belgische Wetgeving van de Sociale Zekerheid, 1965–1970* (Leuven: Het Institut, 1971).

Versichelen, M. "Armoede in de Welvaartstaat," *Belgisch Tijdschrift voor Sociale Zekerheid* (September 1970), 1081–1152.

Werkgroep voor Alternatiere Economie. *Armoede in België* (Antwerp: De Nederlandse Boekhandel, 1972).

CANADA

"Antipoverty Policies and Changing Welfare Concepts in Canada," *Social Security Bulletin* (July 1970), 13–20.

Bryden, W. Kenneth. "Old-Age Pensions and Policy Making in Canada," unpublished Ph.D. thesis, University of Toronto (1970).

Department of National Health and Welfare. *The Canada Pension Plan* (Ottawa: Queen's Printer, 1965).

———. *Disability Benefits, Canada Pension Plan* (Ottawa: Queen's Printer, 1970).

———. *Income Security for Canadians* (Ottawa: Queen's Printer, 1970).

———. *Retirement Pensions, Canada Pension Plan* (Ottawa: Queen's Printer, 1970).

———. *Survivors' Benefits, Canada Pension Plan* (Ottawa: Queen's Printer, 1970).

Department of National Health and Welfare, Social Security Research Division. *The Measurement of Poverty*, memorandum 19 (Ottawa: Queen's Printer, November 1970).

Dominion Bureau of Statistics. *Survey of Pension Plan Coverage, 1965* (Ottawa: Queen's Printer, December 1967).

Douse, H. L. "Canadian Pension Plans No Longer a Major Obstacle to the Employment of Older Workers," *Industrial Gerontology*, 3 (October 1969), 1–8.

Government of Canada. *Working Paper on Social Security in Canada*, 2nd ed. (Ministry of National Health and Welfare, 1973).

Information Canada. *The Canada Pension Plan* (Ottawa: Queen's Printer, 1970).

———. *How to Get Your 1972 Guaranteed Income Supplement* (Ottawa: Queen's Printer, 1971).

———. *Your Old-Age Pension* (Ottawa: Queen's Printer, 1971).

Kelly, L. A. *Emerging Social Security Issues*, Reprint Series, 12 (Kingston: Industrial Relations Center, Queen's University, 1969).

Kleiler, Frank M. *Canadian Regulation of Pension Plans* (Washington, D.C.: Labor-Management Services Administration of U.S. Department of Labor, 1970).

Morgan, John S. "An Emerging System of Income Maintenance: Canada in Transition," in Shirley Jenkins, ed., *Social Security in International Perspective* (New York: Columbia University Press, 1969).

Statistics Canada. *Trusteed Pension Plans Financial Statistics 1970* (Ottawa: Queen's Printer, January 1972).

FEDERAL REPUBLIC OF GERMANY

Achinger, Hans, Joseph Hoeffner, Hans Muthesius, Ludwig Neundoerfer. *Rothenfelser Denkschrift: Neuordnung der Sozialen Leistungen,* Denkschrift auf Auregung des Herrn Bundeskanzlers Erstattet (Cologne: Greven Verlag, 1955).

Auerback, Walter, "Modelleines Sozialplans—eine Skizze," *Die Krankenversicherung* (1952).

Bundesminister für Arbeit und Sozialordnung. *Sozialbericht 1971* (Stuttgart: The Ministry, 1971).

Dawson, William H. Social Insurance in Germany, 1883–1911 (London: Scribner, 1912).

Doerfel, Hans-Juergen. *Moeglich-Keiten zur Schaetzung von Lebensein Kommenverlaeufen aus Queischnittsanalysen* (Darmstadt: dissertation, 1970).

Fisher, Paul. *Old-Age and Sickness Insurance in West Germany in 1965.* Research Report 13, U.S. Social Security Administration Office of Research and Statistics (Washington, D.C.: GPO, 1966).

Graefin von Bethusy-Huc, Viola. *Das Sozialleistungssystem der Bundesrepublik Deutschland* (Tübingen: 1965).

Horlick, Max, and Alfred M. Skolnik. *Private Pension Plans in West Germany and France,* Research Report 36, U.S. Social Security Administration Office of Research and Statistics (Washington, D.C.: GPO, 1971).

Mackenroth. "Die Reform der Sozialpolitik durch einen Deutschen Sozialplan," *Schriften des Vereins für Socialpolitik,* New Series, 4 (1952), 39–76.

Rimlinger, Gaston. *Welfare Policy and Industrialization in Europe, America, and Russia* (New York: Wiley, 1971).

Schewe, Dieter, Karlhugo Nordhorn, and Klaus Schenke. *Survey of Social Security in the Federal Republic of Germany.* 8th ed. (Bonn: Federal Ministry for Labour and Social Affairs, 1972).
———. *Übersicht über die Soziale Sicherung,* 8th ed. (Bonn: Minister für Arbeit und Sozialordnung, 1970).

Schreiber, Wilfred. "Existenzsicherheit in der Industriellen Gesellschaft," in Boettcher, E., ed., *Sozialpolitik und Sozialreform* (Tübingen: J. C. B. Mohr, 1957).

Sozialdemokratischen Partei Deutschlands. *Sozialplan für Deutschland,* Gutachten Erstattet auf Anregung des SPD—Vorstands Von Auerbach (Berlin: Dietz Verlag, 1957).

Wang, Gisela C. "Flexible Retirement Feature of German Pension Reform," *Social Security Bulletin,* 36 (1973), 36–41.

SWEDEN

Allmänna Pensionsfonden (The National Pensions Insurance Fund). *Report for the Year 1972* (1973).

————. *The Swedish National Pension Insurance Fund: A Survey* (undated).

Carlson, Valdemar. "Institutional Change in a Welfare State," *Journal of Risk and Insurance*, 33 (1966), 587–96.

Federation of Swedish Industries. *Modern Trends in Swedish Pension Systems* (Stockholm: The Federation, 1968).

Heckscher, Eli F. *An Economic History of Sweden* (Cambridge: Harvard University Press, 1963).

Heclo, H. Hugh. "Politics and Social Policy," Ph.D. dissertation, Yale University, New Haven (1970).

Holmquist, I. "Swedish Practice in Adjusting Pensions," paper presented at the International Social Security Association Conference on Social Security Research (mimeo., undated).

Lagerström, Lennart. *Social Insurance and Private Occupational Pensions in Sweden* (Stockholm: Svenska Personal-Pensionskassan, 1971).

Michanek, Ernst. *For and Against the Welfare State: the Swedish Experience* (Stockholm: The Swedish Institute, 1964).

Molin, Björn. *Tjänstepensionsfrogan: En Studie i Svensk Partipolitik* (Göteborg: Scandinavian University Books, 1965).

National Insurance Board. *The Swedish Social Insurance Scheme: Statistical Data covering 1968* (1960)–1972, 6th ed. (Stockholm: the Board, 1971).

Rosenthal, Albert H. *The Social Programs of Sweden: A Search for Security in a Free Society* (Minneapolis: University of Minnesota Press, 1967).

The Swedish Institute. *Social Benefits in Sweden* (Stockholm: Trygg Hansa, 1972).

Swedish Ministry of Health and Social Affairs. *National Insurance Act—May 25, 1962*, revised English translation (Stockholm: The Ministry, 1971).

Uhr, Carl G. *Sweden's Social Security System*, Research Report 14, U.S. Office of Research and Statistics Social Security Administration (Washington, D.C.: GPO, 1966).

UNITED STATES

Aaron, Henry J., John A. Brittain, Joseph A. Pechman, Alice Rivlin, Charles Schultze, and Nancy H. Teeters, letter to the *Washington Post* (October 4, 1972).

AAUP. "Statement of Principles on Academic Retirement and Insurance Plans," *AAUP Bulletin,* 55, No. 3 (September 1969), 386–89.

Advisory Council on Social Security, 1965. *The Status of the Social Security Program and Recommendations for Its Improvement* (Washington, D.C.: U.S. Social Security Administration, 1965).

Advisory Council on Social Security, 1971. *Reports of the 1971 Advisory Council on Social Security,* communication from the Secretary of Health, Education, and Welfare, 92nd Congress, 1st session (Washington, D.C.: GPO, 1971).

Ball, Robert M. Testimony in U.S. Senate Special Committee on Aging, *Economics of Aging: Toward a Full Share in Abundance,* Part I, Survey Hearing (Washington, D.C.: GPO, 1969).

————. HEW News Release dated December 29, 1972.

————. "Policy Issues in Social Security," *Social Security Bulletin,* 29 (1966), 7.

————. "Some Reflections on Selected Issues in Social Security," in U.S. Joint Economic Committee, *Old Age Income Assurance,* Part I: General Policy Guidelines, 90th Congress, 1st session (Washington, D.C.: GPO, 1967), 48–57.

Barfield, Richard. *The Automobile Worker and Retirement: A Second Look* (Ann Arbor, Michigan: Institute for Social Research, University of Michigan, 1970).

Barfield, Richard, and James Morgan. *Early Retirement: The Decision and the Experience* (Ann Arbor, Michigan: Braun-Brumfield, 1969).

Bixby, Lenore E. "Income of People Aged 65 and Older: Overview from 1968 Survey of the Aged," *Social Security Bulletin,* 33 (1970), 3–34.

Bixby, Lenore E., and Virginia Reno. "Second Pensions among Newly Entitled Workers: Survey of New Beneficiaries," *Social Security Bulletin,* 34 (1971), 3–7.

Bok, Derek C. "Emerging Issues in Social Legislation: Social Security," *Harvard Law Review,* 80 (1967), 717–64.

Brittain, John A. "The Real Rate of Interest on Lifetime Contributions toward Retirement under Social Security," in U.S. Joint Economic Committee, *Old-Age Income Assurance,* Part III, 90th Congress, 1st session (Washington, D.C.: GPO, 1967).

————. *The Payroll Tax for Social Security* (Washington: Brookings Institution, 1972).

Brown, J. Douglas. *An American Philosophy of Social Security* (Princeton: Princeton University Press, 1972).

Byrnes, John, Floor statement appearing in the *Congressional Record* (June 30, 1972), p. H6511.

Cagan, Phillip. *The Effect of Pension Plans on Aggregate Saving,*

Occasional Paper, 95 (New York: National Bureau of Economic Research, 1965).

Campbell, Colin D. "Social Insurance in the United States: A Program in Search of an Explanation," *Journal of Law and Economics,* 12 (1969), 249–65.

Ceccarelli, Jane M., and Alfred M. Skolnik. "Wage-Replacement Rates under the OASDHI Retirement Provisions," *Research and Statistic Note,* 18, Office of Research and Statistics U.S. Social Security Administration (Washington, D.C.: Dept. of HEW, December 3, 1973).

Chen, Yung-Ping. *Income,* background paper for the 1971 White House Conference on Aging (Washington, D.C.: GPO, 1971).

————. "Inflation and Productivity in Tax-Benefit Analysis for Social Security," in U.S. Joint Economic Committee, *Old-Age Income Assurance,* Part III, 90th Congress, 1st session (Washington, D.C.: GPO, 1967).

Cohen, Wilbur J. "Toward a National Policy on the Aging," Address given to the 25th Conference on Aging of the Institute of Gerontology at the University of Michigan—Wayne State University (September 1972).

Cohen, Wilbur J., and Milton Friedman. *Social Security: Universal or Selective,* Rational Debate Seminars (Washington: American Enterprise Institute, 1972).

Cruikshank, Nelson H. *The Stake of Today's Workers in Retirement Security,* U.S. Senate Special Committee on Aging, Committee Print, 91st Congress, 2nd session (Washington, D.C.: GPO, 1970).

Eckstein, Otto. "Financing the System of Social Insurance." in William R. Bowen, *The Princeton Symposium on the American System of Social Insurance* (New York: McGraw Hill, 1968).

Epstein, Lenore A. *Income Security Standards in Old-Age,* U.S. Research Report 3 (Washington: U.S. Social Security Administration, undated).

Epstein, Lenore A., and Janet H. Murray. *The Aged Population of the United States.* Research Report 19, U.S. Social Security Administration Office of Research and Statistics (Washington, D.C.: GPO, 1967).

Faulkner, E. J. "Social Security and Insurance—Some Relationships in Perspective," *Journal of Insurance,* 30 (1963), 197–218.

Gordon, Robert J. "Inflation in Recession and Recovery," *Brookings' Papers on Economic Activity,* 1 (1971), 105–66.

Greene, Mark R., Charles H. Pyron, Vincent Manion, and Howard Winklevoss. *Early Retirement: Company Policies and Retirees' Experiences* (Washington, D.C.: Administration on Aging, 1969).

Heidbreder, Elizabeth, W. W. Kolodrubetz, and Alfred Skolnik. "Old-Age Programs," in U.S. Joint Economic Committee, *Old-Age Income Assurance*, Pt. II (Washington, D.C.: GPO, 1966).

Henle, Peter. "Recent Trends in Retirement Benefits Related to Earnings," *Monthly Labor Review*, 95 (1972), 12–20.

Holland, Daniel M. "Building the Base to Support Retirement," in Tax Foundation, *Financing Retirement: Public and Private*, 23rd National Conference (New York: The Foundation, 1972), pp. 33–38.

Katona, George. *Private Pensions and Individual Saving*, Monograph 40 (Ann Arbor, Michigan: Survey Research Center, 1965).

Kolodrubetz, W. A *Methodological Study of Private Pensions*, Social Security Administration Staff Study (Washington, D.C.: Social Security Administration, 1972).

———. "Employer-Benefit Plans, 1971," *Social Security Bulletin*, 36 (1973a), 27–23.

———. "Private Retirement Benefits and Relationship to Earnings: Survey of New Beneficiaries," *Social Security Bulletin*, 36 (1973) 16–37.

———. "Two Decades of Employee-Benefit Plans, 1950–70: A Review," *Social Security Bulletin*, 35 (1972), 10–22.

Morris, Robert. "What Do You Do after the Doctor Leaves?" *Harper's Magazine* (January 1973), 89–90.

Murray, Janet. "Homeownership and Financial Assets: Findings from the 1968 Survey of the Aged," *Social Security Bulletin*, 35 (1972), 3–23.

Murray, Roger F. *Economic Aspects of Pensions: A Summary Report*, National Bureau of Economic Research (New York: Columbia University Press, 1968).

Musgrave, Richard. "The Role of Social Insurance in an Overall Program for Social Welfare," in Bowen et al., *The American System of Social Insurance* (New York: McGraw Hill, 1968).

Myers, Robert J. *Social Insurance and Allied Government Programs* (Homewood, Illinois: Irwin, 1965).

———. "Government and Pensions," in American Enterprise Institute for Public Policy Research, *Private Pensions and the Public Interest* (Washington, D.C.: The Institute, 1970), 29–49.

———. "Social Security's Hidden Hazards," *Wall Street Journal* (July 28, 1972).

Nader, Ralph and Kate Blackwell. *You and Your Pension* (New York: Grossman, 1973).

National Insurance Board. *The Swedish Social Insurance Scheme*, Statistical *Data Covering 1968* (1960)–1972, 6th ed. (Stockholm: The Board, 1971).

Nationale Actie voor Bestaanszekerheid. *De Derde Leeftijd . . . Een Avontuur* (Brussels: Nationale Actie, May 1969).

Naylor, Thomas H., ed., *The Design of Computer Simulation Experiments* (Durham, N.C.: Duke University Press, 1969).

Norwood, Janet L. "Cost-of-Living Escalation of Pensions," *Monthly Labor Review*, 95 (1972), 21–23.

Orcutt, Guy, Steven Caldwell, Harold Guthrie, Gary Hendricks, Gerald Peabody, James Smith, and Richard Wertheimer. *Microanalytic Simulation for Policy Exploration*, Working Paper 5095 (Washington, D.C.: Urban Institute, 1974).

Orshansky, Mollie. "Counting the Poor: Another Look at the Poverty Profile," *Social Security Bulletin*, 28 (1965), 3–29.

Pechman, Joseph A, Henry J. Aaron, and Michael K. Taussig. *Social Security: Perspectives for Reform* (Washington, D.C.: Brookings Institution, 1968).

Prest, A. R. "Some Redistributional Aspects of the National Superannuation Fund," *The Three Banks Review*, 32 (1970), 3–22.

Price, Daniel N. "OASDHI Benefits, Prices, and Wages: Effect of 1967 Benefit Increase," *Social Security Bulletin*, 31 (1968), 28–35.

Projector, Dorothy S. "Should the Payroll Tax Finance Higher Benefits Under OASDI? A Review of the Issues," *The Journal of Human Resources*, 4 (1969), 61–75.

Pryor, Frederic L. *Public Expenditures in Communist and Capitalist Nations* (Homewood, Illinois: Irwin, 1968).

Riley, Matilda White, and Anne Foner. *Aging and Society*, Vol. 1, *An Inventory of Research Findings* (New York: Russell Sage Foundation, 1968).

Rimlinger, Gaston. *Welfare Policy and Industrialization in Europe, America, and Russia* (New York: Wiley, 1971).

Rosenthal, Albert H. *The Social Programs of Sweden: A Search for Security in a Free Society* (Minneapolis: University of Minnesota Press, 1967).

Samuelson, Paul. "Social Security," *Newsweek* (February 13, 1967), 8.

Schewe, Dieter, Karlhugo Nordhorn, and Klaus Schenke. *Survey of Social Security in the Federal Republic of Germany*, 8th ed. (Bonn: Federal Ministry for Labour and Social Affairs, 1972).
——. *Ubersicht uber die Soziale Sicherung*, 8th ed. (Bonn: Minister für Arbeit und Sozialordnung, 1970).

Schoetter, P., and Spitaels, G. "Sociale Zekerheid en Openbare Onderstand," *Belgisch Tijdschrift voor Sociale Zekerheid* (May 1966), 499–599.

Schreiber, Wilfred. "Existenzsicherheit in der Industriellen Gesellschaft," in E. Boettcher, ed., *Sozialpolitik und Sozialreform* (Tübingen: J. C. B. Mohr, 1957).

Schultze, Charles, Edward R. Fried, Alice M. Rivlin, and Nancy H. Teeters. *Setting National Priorities: The 1972 Budget* (Washington, D.C.: Brookings Institution, 1971).

Thurow, Lester C. "The Optimum Lifetime Distribution of Consumption Expenditures," *American Economic Review,* 59 (1969), 324–30.

U.S. Bureau of the Census. "Poverty in the United States 1959 to 1966," *Current Population Reports,* Consumer Income, Series P-60, No. 68 (Washington, D.C.: GPO, December 1969).

————. "Characteristics of the Low-Income Population: 1971," *Current Population Reports,* Consumer Income, Series P-60, No. 82 (Washington, D.C.: GPO, July 1972a).

————. "Money Income in 1971 of Families and Persons in the United States," *Current Population Reports,* Consumer Income, Series P-60, No. 83 (Washington, D.C.: GPO, July 1972b).

————. "Illustrative Population Projections for the United States: The Demographic Effects of Alternative Paths to Zero Growth," *Current Population Reports,* Population Estimates and Projection, Series P-25, No. 82 (Washington, D.C.: GPO, 1972c).

————. "Money Income in 1972 of Families and Persons in the United States," *Current Population Reports,* Consumer Income, Series P-60, No. 87 (Washington, D.C.: GPO, June 1973a).

————. "Characteristics of the Low Income Population: 1972," *Current Population Reports,* Consumer Income, Series P-60, No. 88 (Washington, D.C.: GPO, June 1973b).

————. "One-in-a-Thousand Sample Description and Technical Documentation," *U.S. Census of Population and Housing: 1960* (Washington, undated).

United States Bureau of Labor Statistics. *Digest of 100 Selected Pension Plans under Collective Bargaining, Spring 1968,* BLS Bulletin 1597 (Washington, D.C.: GPO, 1969).

————. *Retired Couple's Budget for a Moderate Living Standard,* BLS Bulletin 1570–4 (Washington, D.C.: GPO, 1966).

————. *Revised Equivalence Scale,* BLS Bulletin 1570–2 (Washington, D.C.: GPO, 1968).

————. "Three Budgets for a Retired Couple, Autumn, 1972," news release (August 10, 1973).

United States Committee on Ways and Means. "President's Proposals for Revision in the Social Security System," *Hearings,* Part 1 (Washington, D.C.: GPO, 1967a).

————. *Social Security Amendments of 1967: Report of the Committee on Ways and Means.* House Report 544, 90th Congress, 1st session (Washington, D.C.: GPO, 1967b).

United States Department of Health, Education, and Welfare. *Social Security Programs in the United States* (Washington, D.C.: GPO, 1971).

United States Labor-Management Services Administration. *Union Status and Benefits of Retirees* (Washington, D.C.: GPO, 1973).

United States Senate Special Committee on Aging. *A Constant Purchasing Power Bond: A Proposal for Protecting Retirement Income*, 87th Congress, 1st session (Washington, D.C.: GPO, 1961).

————. *Economics of Aging: Toward a Full Share in Abundance— Task Force Working Paper*, 91st Congress, 1st session (Washington, D.C.: GPO, 1969).

————. *Economics of Aging: Toward a Full Share in Abundance*, Part 10B—*Pension Aspects* (Washington, D.C.: GPO, 1970a).

————. *Pension Aspects of the Economics of Aging: Present and Future Roles of Private Pensions*, Committee Print, 91st Congress, 2nd session (Washington, D.C.: GPO, 1970b).

U.S. Social Security Administration. *Reports of the 1971 Advisory Council on Social Security*, House Document 92-80. 92nd Congress, 1st session (Washington, D.C.: GPO, 1971a).

————. *The Research Program of the Social Security Administration*, Report of the 1967 SSA Advisory Committee on Research Development (Washington, D.C.: GPO, 1968).

————. *United States Projections for OASDI Cost Estimates, Actuarial Study 62* (Washington, D.C.: GPO, 1971b).

United States Subcommittee on Aging, Committee on Labor and Public Welfare. *History of the Provisions of Old-Age, Survivors, Disability, and Health Insurance 1935–1972*, DHEW Pub. (SSA) 73-11510 (Washington, D.C.: DHEW, 1973).

MISCELLANEOUS

Atkinson, A. B. "Income Maintenance and Income Taxation," *Journal of Social Policy*, 1 (1972), 135–48.

————. "National Superannuation: Redistribution and Value for Money," *Bulletin of the Oxford University Institute of Economics and Statistics*, 32 (1970), 171–85.

Becker, Gary S. *Human Capital* (New York: National Bureau of Economic Research and Columbia University Press, 1964).

Boulding, Kenneth. *Principles of Economic Policy* (Englewood Cliffs, N.J.: Prentice Hall, 1958).

Galbraith, John K. *The New Industrial State* (New York: New American Library, 1967).

Goldstein, Sidney. "Changing Income and Consumption Patterns of the Aged, 1950–1960," *Journal of Gerontlogy*, 20 (1965), 453–61.

Krupp, Hans-Juergen. "The Use of Simulation Methods in Urban Public Finance," paper presented at the Congress of the Institut International Finances Publiques (New York, 1972).

Marshall, T. H. "Value Problems of Welfare-Capitalism," *Journal of Social Policy*, 1 (1972), 15–32.

McClung, Nelson, John Moeller, and Eduardo Siguel. *Transfer Income Program Evaluation*, Urban Institute Paper (Washington: The Urban Institute, 1971).

Miller, S. M., and P. A. Roby. *The Future of Inequality* (New York: Basic Books, 1970).

Morgan, James, Martin H. David, W. J. Cohen, and H. E. Brazer. *Income and Welfare in the United States* (New York: McGraw Hill, 1962).

Morris, Robert. "What Do You Do after the Doctor Leaves?" *Harper's Magazine* (January 1973), 89–90.

Naylor, Thomas H., ed., *The Design of Computer Simulation Experiments* (Durham, N.C.: Duke University Press, 1969).

Orcutt, Guy, Steven Caldwell, Harold Guthrie, Gary Hendricks, Gerald Peabody, James Smith, and Richard Wertheimer. *Microanalytic Simulation for Policy Exploration*, Working Paper 5095 (Washington, D.C.: Urban Institute, 1974).

Orshansky, Mollie. "Counting the Poor: Another Look at the Poverty Profile," *Social Security Bulletin*, 28 (1965), 3–29.

Prest, A. R. "Some Redistributional Aspects of the National Superannuation Fund," *The Three Banks Review*, 32 (1970), 3–22.

Riley, Matilda White, and Anne Foner. *Aging and Society*, Vol. 1, *An Inventory of Research Findings* (New York: Russell Sage Foundation, 1968).

Schultze, Charles, Edward R. Fried, Alice M. Rivlin, and Nancy H. Teeters. *Setting National Priorities—the 1972 Budget* (Washington, D.C.: Brookings Institution, 1971).

Secretary of State, Department of Health and Social Security. *Strategy for Pensions—The Future Development of State and Occupational Provision* (London: Stationery Office, 1971).

United States Council of Economic Advisors. "Annual Report of the Council of Economic Advisors," in *Economic Report of the President* (Washington, D.C.: GPO, 1973).

United States Joint Economic Committee. *The Distribution of Personal Income*, 88th Congress, 2nd session (Washington, D.C.: GPO, 1964).

United States Subcommittee on Aging, Committee on Labor and Public Welfare. *Post–White House Conference on Aging Reports, 1973* (Washington, D.C.: GPO, 1973).

Weisbrod, Burton A., and W. Lee Hansen. "An Income–Net Worth

Approach to Measuring Economic Welfare," *American Economic Review*, 58 (1968), 1315–29.

White House Conference on Aging, 1971. *A Report to the Delegates from the Conference Sections and Special Concerns Sessions* (Washington, D.C.: the Conference Staff, 1971).

INDEX

INDEX

INDEX

126–127, 131–143; Socialist-Conservative coalition, 126; Workers System, 131

Bismarck, Otto von, 69n, 99, 108, 109, 111, 116

Bixby, L., vii, 14, 45, 271. *See also* Epstein, L.

Blackwell, K., 272n

Board of Management, 272n

Bok, D., 17, 39, 226

Boulding, K., 6, 69, 70, 259

Brittain, J., 65, 66n, 67n, 142

Broberg, R., 189

Brown, J. D., 69n, 232

Bryden, W., 155, 157–163

Budget for a retired couple, 16

Bundesminister für Arbeit und Sozialordnung, 108, 193

Bundestag, 100, 102, 218

Burns, E., vii

Byrnes, J., 64

Cagan, P., 43n

Campbell, C., 65

Canada: adequacy goals, 187, 194; adjustments, 59, 221, 233, 235; Annuities Program, 168–172; Canada Pension Plan, 152–154, 161, 168–169, 171, 173–181, 183–185, 221; Committee on Portable Pensions, 181; Congress of Labour, 170–172; Department of Finance, 160; Department of Insurance, 160, 170; Department of Labour, 158; financing social security, 184–185; flat pension benefit, 24; French Canadian nationalism, 174; Government Annuities Act, 156, 161n; government annuities program, 156–160; guaranteed income supplement, 153, 184; Indians, 164, 166n; Labour Minister, 160; Labour Party, 163, 176; Left, 163, 167; Liberal Party, 162, 163, 167, 168, 171–174; measures of preretirement earnings, 52; New Democratic Party, 172; objectives, 224n; Old Age Assistance Act of 1951, 174; Old Age

Pension Act of 1927, 163–164; Old Age Security Act of 1951, 152, 153, 166; Old Age Security Act of 1952, 168, 174, 184; Ontario Pension Benefits Act, 175, 181; Parliament, 157, 162, 163; pension reform, 230, 232; pension replacement rate, 209–212; Post Office, 158; Prime Minister of Ontario, 181; private pensions, 71, 175, 180–186, 266; proportion of aged in population, 61, 68; Quebec, 174–176, 178n, 182; Quebec Pension Plan, 152, 154, 169, 175–176, 178n, 183–185, 221n; Saskatchewan, 182; Senate Committee, special, 173, 174; simulation analysis, 236n; social security, 49, 152–186; Trades and Labour Congress of Canada, 162; Trades and Labour Council, 167

Canadian Manufacturers Association, 167

Canadian Provinces, 174, 175, 178n, 180–182

Carlson, V., 74, 76, 78, 81, 82

Carrin, G., 37, 38

Cartwright, R., 157, 158

Ceccarelli, J., 20n

Central Bank (Sweden), 91

Central Organization of Salaried Employees (Sweden), 79

Centre de Recherche et de l'Information Sociales et Politique (Belgium), 144–147

Centre Party (Sweden), 79–81, 83–85, 92, 96

Chamber of Commerce (Canada), 160, 172

Chen, Y., 13n, 65

Christian Democratic Party: Belgium, 126; West Germany, 112, 113, 115, 119

Christian Pensioners' Association (Belgium), 149

Clark, R., 156, 157, 171

Clark Amendment, 69n

Cohen, W., 65, 66n

Commissie van de Kamer can Volksvertegenwoordigers, 125